unforgettable
desserts

unforgettable
desserts

More than 140
Memorable Dessert Recipes
for All Year Round

Dede Wilson

Photography by Alexandra Grablewski

WILEY

John Wiley & Sons, Inc.

Food styling by Brian Preston-Campbell
Prop styling by Barb Fritz
Book design by Cassandra J. Pappas

Published by John Wiley & Sons, Inc., Hoboken, New Jersey
Published simultaneously in Canada

For general information on our other products and services or for technical support, please contact our Customer Care Department within the United States at (800) 762-2974, outside the United States at (317) 572-3993, or fax (317) 572-4002.

Wiley also publishes its books in a variety of electronic formats. Some content that appears in print may not be available in electronic books. For more information about Wiley products, visit our Web site at www.wiley.com.

Original versions of the following recipes published in *Bon Appétit*: Spiced Pear–White Chocolate Tiramisu Trifle (page 224) copyright © (2007) Condé Nast Publications; Amaretto-Almond Crunch Pumpkin Pie (page 201) copyright © (2006) Condé Nast Publications; Spiced Plum Pavlovas (page 95) copyright © (2002) Condé Nast Publications; Ginger Shortcakes with Caramelized Nectarines and Sour Cream (page 93), Pecan-Coconut Tart with Chocolate Crust (page 181), and Cranberry-Apricot Linzer Torte (page 179) copyright © (2001) Condé Nast Publications.

Library of Congress Cataloging-in-Publication Data
Wilson, Dede.
    Unforgettable desserts / Dede Wilson ; photography by Alexandra Grablewski.
       p. cm.
    Includes index.
    ISBN 978-0-470-18649-7 (cloth)
1. Desserts. I. Title.
    TX773.W6976 2009
    641.8'6--dc22   2008049896

Printed in China
10 9 8 7 6 5 4 3 2 1

contents

For Ravenna, TNG

preface

Desserts are something that we want, not something that we need, so when we do indulge, we want the experience to be memorable. The flavors should unfold in our mouths, arousing interest and giving deep satisfaction. This can happen with the most modest looking of desserts— devouring a simple square of brownie can become a most sensual experience. Other times a dessert is so visually enticing, so spectacular, that you cannot wait to dig in. *Unforgettable Desserts* presents the kind of delectable desserts that will make your mouth water in anticipation, ones you will swoon over as you indulge and will remember for years to come. These are no ordinary desserts; these are unforgettable dessert experiences.

The desserts in this book will all follow through on this promise: that you have never tasted anything like them before, that they will be the kind of dessert experiences that leave a lasting impression. Some will immediately hit your eyes with that wow factor, even before the first taste. Others will have a more modest appearance, but all will be desserts that linger in your memory as unforgettable.

acknowledgments

A huge Thank You to my favorite team: agents Maureen and Eric Lasher and editor Justin Schwartz. I am thrilled that we are together again. Much love to my emotional support system of Juanita Plimpton and Mary McNamara. And to Holly Leonard and Patty Rene at BeFit (Hadley, MA) who have helped me fit back into my jeans, yet who respect my chocolate fixation.

To David: XOXO and thank you for putting up with dogs, dozens of cakes, hundreds of cookies and brownies, and more dogs. . . .

basics

THESE ARE BUILDING-BLOCK recipes, most of which are used more than once in the book—and that I think you will find handy to have in your repertoire. Familiarize yourself with the recipes in this chapter, from pie and tart crusts to pastry creams, Italian Meringue Buttercream, and a basic chocolate cake. You will think of many new uses for them—and begin to create recipes of your own.

butter piecrust

MAKES TWO 9-INCH OR ONE 9-INCH PIECRUST

> After years of making piecrust in a variety of ways I have come to prefer an all-butter crust made in the food processor with ice water. The flavor is exceptional, and since the metal blade is so sharp and fast, it cuts the chilled butter in quickly, yielding a flaky textured crust. The proportions are quite typical, and if you do not have a food processor, feel free to make it by hand. In either case take care not to overwork it.

DOUBLE BUTTER PIECRUST

2½ cups all-purpose flour

½ teaspoon salt

1 cup (2 sticks) chilled unsalted butter, cut into small pieces

4 to 6 tablespoons ice-cold water

SINGLE BUTTER PIECRUST

1¼ cups all-purpose flour

¼ teaspoon salt

½ cup (1 stick) chilled unsalted butter, cut into small pieces

2 to 3 tablespoons ice-cold water

TIPS Ideally, the butter pieces should be frozen for 15 minutes before proceeding. To make the ice-cold water, pour a generous amount of water in a measuring cup, add some ice cubes, and let it sit for a few minutes. Remove any remaining cubes, re-measure the water, and proceed. If it's really hot in your kitchen, it helps to freeze the flour for 15 minutes, too.

to make with a food processor Put the flour and salt in the bowl of a food processor fitted with the metal blade attachment and pulse to combine. Add the butter and pulse on and off until it forms a very coarse meal; there might be pockets of butter that are larger, which is fine. Drizzle in the smaller amount of water through the feed tube and pulse until the dough is moistened and just holds together if squeezed. Add additional water only if necessary.

to make by hand Whisk together the flour and salt in a medium bowl to blend. Add the butter and cut in, using a pastry blender or two knives, until the fat is cut into approximately ⅛-inch pieces. Sprinkle the smaller amount of water over the flour mixture and toss with fingers or a fork until evenly moistened and the dough just holds together if squeezed. Add additional water only if necessary.

to continue for either technique Gather the dough into one or two balls and flatten into a disk or disks. Wrap the dough in plastic wrap and refrigerate for at least 2 hours or up to 2 days. It may also be frozen for 1 month, in which case, protect it further by placing in a zipper-top bag; defrost in the refrigerator overnight. Let the dough soften slightly at room temperature before rolling out.

(2) UNFORGETTABLE DESSERTS

sugar tart crust

MAKES ONE 10-INCH TART CRUST

This is my favorite sweet tart dough due to its crispness, sweetness, and ease of preparation. The key is the cake flour, which because of its low protein content makes the dough particularly crisp and prevents it from shrinking. You do not even need to line it while blind-baking; just make sure to chill it well.

1) Coat a 10-inch loose-bottomed fluted tart pan with nonstick spray; set aside.

2) In the bowl of a stand mixer, beat the butter with the flat paddle attachment on medium-high speed until creamy, about 1 minute. Add the sugar gradually and continue to beat on medium-high speed until lightened and creamy, about 2 minutes. Beat in the egg yolk until well combined. Add the flour and pulse the mixer on and off until it begins to combine, and then run the mixer on medium-low speed just until the dough begins to form. Scrape out onto plastic wrap and use the wrap to help press the dough into a flat disk shape. Wrap the dough thoroughly. Refrigerate for at least 2 hours or overnight.

3) Roll out on a lightly floured surface to a 13-inch round and fit into the pan, pressing into corners and trimming the top. Refrigerate for at least 2 hours or freeze for 15 minutes while the oven preheats. At this point, you can double-wrap the tart shell very well in plastic wrap and then aluminum foil and refrigerate for up to 2 days before baking, or freeze for up to 1 week.

4) Position a rack in the middle of the oven. Preheat the oven to 350°F. For a partially baked tart shell, bake directly on the oven rack for 8 to 12 minutes, or until dry to the touch and beginning to color around the edges. For a fully baked tart shell, bake for 15 to 20 minutes, just until it is very light golden brown. If crust puffs up during baking, gently press back down with the back of a fork. Cool the tart pan set on a rack. Fill and proceed as directed in recipes.

½ cup (1 stick) unsalted butter, at cool room temperature, cut into small pieces

5 tablespoons sugar

1 large egg yolk

1¼ cups sifted cake flour

TIP If you are in a hurry, you can pat the freshly made dough right into the prepared pan using floured fingers before the first chilling period. The final look will not be as refined, but it will still taste great. Chill and proceed as described. Baking directly on the oven rack ensures a crisper bottom crust.

blitz puff pastry

MAKES ABOUT 1 POUND

P uff pastry is known for its incomparable flakiness—literally hundreds of crisp, buttery, flaky layers are the hallmarks of this classic pastry. It is also labor intensive and not a recipe that most home bakers want to tackle, especially if there is an easier option. This is a shortcut version and forms the basis for recipes such as my Thousand Leaves with Blackberry Pastry Cream (page 103). You will have two 30-minute resting periods and about 10 minutes of actual hands-on work, so this is a very doable recipe.

2½ cups all-purpose flour
1 teaspoon salt
1¼ cups (2½ sticks) chilled unsalted butter, cut into pieces
¾ cup ice-cold water

1) Put the flour and salt in the bowl of a stand mixer fitted with the flat paddle attachment. Turn on low speed briefly to combine. Add the butter and mix on medium-low speed until butter forms large pieces, about the size of flattened grapes. With the mixer running, drizzle in the water and mix only just until the dough begins to come together; it will look ragged and shaggy.

2) For the following patting and rolling techniques, you will need to keep your surface and palms very lightly dusted with flour. Scrape the dough out onto the work surface. It will be a fairly crumbly pile. Use a bench scraper to bring the pile together and use your palms to pat it into a ½-inch-thick rectangle, with long sides on the top and bottom. Use the bench scraper to fold the dough into thirds, like a business letter, beginning with a short end. Turn the dough 90 degrees. Use the bench scraper to square off the edges, and roll it out with a rolling pin to about a ½-inch-thick rectangle again. Fold into thirds again; by now the dough should be holding together nicely, folding more easily and not too sticky for the rolling pin. Make a total of 4 turns, rolling and folding at every stage.

3) Roll out the dough into a ½-inch-thick rectangle, long sides on the top and bottom, one last time. Bring the end of the short right

side to the middle. Do the same with the short left side. The two short ends should meet in the middle. Now fold one half over the other, using this center meeting point as the center fold. Wrap well with plastic wrap and refrigerate for 30 minutes, to allow the dough to rest. Roll out again to $1/2$ inch thick and fold again as you did for the last fold. Turn the dough 90 degrees, roll out, and fold the same way again. Wrap and refrigerate for 30 minutes. The dough is now ready to use or may be refrigerated for up to 2 days or frozen for up to 1 month. If freezing, double-wrap in plastic wrap and place in a zipper-top bag; defrost in the refrigerator overnight. Directions for use are in individual recipes.

dark and moist
chocolate cake MAKES TWO 9 X 2-INCH ROUND LAYERS

This cake comes together in a flash and works well as a building block for cakes such as The Voluptuous Chocolate-Covered Strawberry Ganache Cake (page 159) but feel free to use it anytime you need a moist, chocolaty cake. Due to the oil content, this cake also happens to freeze very well. Make sure to use natural, as opposed to Dutch-processed, cocoa. They have different levels of acidity, which react differently in recipes. Always use what is suggested.

3 cups all-purpose flour

2 cups sugar

⅔ cup sifted natural cocoa, such as Scharffen Berger

2 teaspoons baking soda

1 teaspoon salt

2 cups room-temperature water

⅔ cup flavorless vegetable oil, such as canola or sunflower

2 tablespoons apple cider or distilled white vinegar

1 tablespoon vanilla extract

1) Position a rack in the middle of the oven. Preheat the oven to 350°F.

2) Coat two 9 x 2-inch round cake pans with nonstick spray, line the bottoms with parchment rounds, and then spray the parchment.

3) Whisk together the flour, sugar, cocoa, baking soda, and salt in a large bowl to aerate and combine. Whisk together the water, oil, vinegar, and vanilla in a medium bowl. Pour the wet ingredients over the dry mixture and whisk vigorously until combined and very smooth. Divide the batter evenly between the 2 pans. Firmly tap the bottoms of the pans on the work surface to dislodge any bubbles.

4) Bake for 30 to 35 minutes, or until a toothpick inserted in the center shows a few moist crumbs when removed. Cool in the cake pans set on a rack for about 10 minutes. Unmold, peel off the parchment, and place directly on the racks to cool completely. Trim layers to be level, if necessary. The layers are ready to use. Alternatively, place the layers on cardboard rounds of the same size and double-wrap in plastic wrap; store at room temperature if assembling or serving within 24 hours. Otherwise, place in large zipper-top bags and freeze for up to 1 month; defrost in the refrigerator overnight.

dark chocolate
ganache MAKES ABOUT 2½ CUPS

> Ganache, at its simplest, is a blend of chocolate and cream. While fluid, it can be poured and used as a glaze or sauce. When chilled or allowed to sit until thick, it can be spread or piped. The flavor and ultimate texture of the ganache will greatly depend on which semisweet or bittersweet chocolate you use. I don't think of any as "better" than any other—use a chocolate whose flavor you enjoy and you will like the ganache made with it.

1) Put the cream in a medium saucepan and bring to a boil over medium heat. Remove from the heat and immediately sprinkle the chocolate into the cream. Cover and allow to sit for 5 minutes; the heat of the cream should melt the chocolate. Gently stir the ganache until smooth. If the chocolate is not completely melted, place over very low heat, stirring often, until melted, taking care not to scorch the chocolate.

2) The ganache is ready to use. You may pour it over cakes as a glaze, or you may allow the ganache to firm up overnight at room temperature until it is a spreadable consistency (between mayonnaise and peanut butter). Refrigerate for up to 1 week in an airtight container or freeze for up to 1 month. You may rewarm ganache to its fluid state on low power in a microwave or over very low heat in a saucepan.

1¼ cups heavy cream

12 ounces semisweet or bittersweet chocolate, finely chopped, such as Valrhona Equitoriale (55%) or Caraque (56%), Ghirardelli (45%), Callebaut (52%), or Bissingers (60%)

TIP I cannot overemphasize the fact that your choice of chocolate will literally make or break this recipe; often when using higher cacao percentage chocolates the ganache will "break" and refuse to come together into a smooth mass. It might look curdled and the cocoa butter will separate, float to the top, and create a grease slick. In this case, whisk in some extra-cold cream and/or buzz it with an immersion blender (if you have one) and it should come together. It is simply a matter of chocolate/cream proportions, so do not give up.

italian meringue
buttercream MAKES ABOUT 6 CUPS

This is an ultra-smooth, not-too-sweet buttercream and my frosting of choice—not only because of its exceptionally silky texture and subtle flavor, but also because it can be varied endlessly. You can add chocolate, liqueurs, pureed fruits, juices, or even coffee. A stand mixer is best for this recipe, as the meringue will have to whip for quite a while to cool; a candy thermometer is also helpful. It is vitally important that any cake frosted with this buttercream be served at room temperature, or the texture and flavor will suffer; there is so much butter in it that it will be stiff and unpleasant on the tongue if cold. Once brought to room temperature, however, it is silky, light, and luscious. This recipe makes a very generous amount—plenty to fill and frost a 3- or 4-layer cake plus add lots of swirls and decorations on the outside. It freezes very well, so any extra can be stored for later.

1¼ cups sugar, divided

⅓ cup water

6 large egg whites, at room temperature

¾ teaspoon cream of tartar

2¼ cups (4½ sticks) very soft unsalted butter, cut into pieces

1) Put 1 cup of the sugar and the water in a small saucepan. Stir to wet the sugar. Bring to a boil over medium-high heat, swirling the pan occasionally. Dip a pastry brush in cold water and wash down the sugar crystals from the sides of the pot once or twice. Allow the sugar mixture to simmer gently as you proceed with the egg whites.

2) Meanwhile, in the clean, grease-free bowl of a stand mixer, whip the egg whites on low speed using the balloon whip attachment until frothy. Add the cream of tartar and turn the speed to medium-high. When soft peaks form, add the remaining ¼ cup sugar gradually. Continue whipping until stiff, glossy peaks form.

3) Bring the sugar-water mixture to a rapid boil and cook until it reaches 248° to 250°F. As the syrup cooks, check visual clues to assess the temperature: It starts out thin, with many small bubbles over the entire surface. As the water evaporates the mixture will become visibly thicker. The bubbles become larger and pop open more slowly. At this point the syrup definitely looks thickened, but it has not begun to color; this is the firm ball stage. If you drop a bit of the syrup into a

glass of cold water it will form into a ball. When you squeeze the ball between your fingertips it will feel firm; at this point the syrup is ready.

4) With mixer on medium speed, pour the syrup in a thin, steady stream directly over the meringue, taking care not pour any on the whip attachment or the sides of the bowl. Whip the meringue on high speed until cool to the touch; this could take several minutes. Add the butter a couple tablespoons at a time and keep beating until the buttercream is completely smooth. The buttercream is ready to use. Any flavorings may be added at this point; vanilla variation is given below. Refrigerate for up to 1 week in an airtight container or freeze for up to 1 month. If frozen, defrost in the refrigerator overnight and bring to warm room temperature before rebeating. Always rebeat before using.

variation

VANILLA BUTTERCREAM
Add 1 tablespoon of vanilla extract toward the end of beating.

TIPS Temperature is crucial with this buttercream. If the meringue is warm when the butter is added, it will become soupy. If the butter is too cold, the buttercream will be lumpy and too firm. If your buttercream is too loose, place the bottom of the bowl in a larger bowl filled with ice water. Check every few minutes until the texture firms up, then whip until smooth. If the mixture is too stiff, just keep whipping; it might smooth out. Alternatively, you can also aim a hot hair dryer at the outside of the bowl to warm up the buttercream quickly. Or, put a cup of buttercream in the microwave for a few seconds until it begins to melt, and then add it back to the larger amount to smooth out the texture. The ultimate texture should be soft and spreadable, with no lumps, somewhere between mayonnaise and peanut butter.

If you have refrigerated or defrosted frozen buttercream and need to bring it back to its original texture, follow the suggestions above as well. If you have a good feel for baking, you can also place the mixer bowl directly over very low heat on the stove top, folding the buttercream over itself all the while, and warm it up until it is just beginning to melt around the edges; then beat until smooth. When "reconstituting" buttercream in this way, I prefer to use the flat paddle attachment.

pastry cream

EACH MAKES ABOUT 2 CUPS

This creamy, smooth, rich pastry cream is a classic feature in many European desserts. Variations abound: those using whole eggs, some with just yolks, and some with a combination thereof. The dairy component can also range from milk to cream to a middle ground of half-and-half. None is "better" than another; they are just different. The texture can also range from stiff enough to slice to a creamy texture that barely holds its shape. I have provided you with a Light Pastry Cream, which I like to use in tarts, cakes, and mille-feuille-type desserts and a Rich Pastry Cream, which I prefer in pastries such as éclairs, where the shape and texture of the pâte à choux holds in the extra-creamy filling. You will find uses for both in your dessert repertoire. If you have a saucier pan, which has a very rounded bottom, you will be best able to whisk the custard without any scorching.

LIGHT PASTRY CREAM

2 cups whole milk

½ vanilla bean, split lengthwise

2 large eggs

½ cup sugar

3 tablespoons cornstarch

Pinch of salt

1 tablespoon soft unsalted butter, cut into tiny pieces

½ teaspoon vanilla extract

RICH PASTRY CREAM

1 cup whole milk

1 cup heavy cream

½ vanilla bean, split lengthwise

3 large egg yolks

½ cup sugar

3 tablespoons cornstarch

1) Put the milk (or milk and cream) in a medium saucepan and scrape in the vanilla bean seeds. Add the vanilla bean pod to the pot as well. Bring to a boil, remove from the heat, and allow to steep for 15 minutes. Discard the bean pod.

2) Meanwhile, whisk together the eggs (or yolks), sugar, cornstarch, and salt in a heatproof bowl until very smooth. For Rich Pastry Cream, the mixture will be very thick and will need extra whisking; set aside. Reheat the milk if it has become tepid.

3) Drizzle about one-quarter of the warm milk (or milk-cream mixture) over the egg mixture, whisking gently. Add the remaining warm milk (or milk-cream) and whisk to combine. Immediately pour the mixture back into the saucepan, and cook over medium-low heat until it begins to simmer and bubbles appear. Cook, whisking constantly to prevent scorching, for about 1 minute. The pastry cream should be thick enough to mound when dropped from a spoon, but still satiny. Remove from the heat and whisk in the butter and vanilla extract.

4) Allow the pastry cream to cool, stirring occasionally to release the heat. When almost at room temperature, scrape into an airtight container, press plastic wrap directly onto the surface, snap on the cover, and refrigerate for at least 4 hours or until thoroughly chilled. Refrigerate for up to 3 days.

Pinch of salt

1 tablespoon soft unsalted butter, cut into tiny pieces

½ teaspoon vanilla extract

LIQUEUR VARIATION

For either Pastry Cream, 2 tablespoons of liqueur, such as Cointreau, rum, eau de vie, Kahlúa, or the liqueur of your choice may be gently stirred into the pastry cream during the cooling phase at the end of the recipe.

TIP   All pastry creams are very perishable. By stirring occasionally while cooling to release the heat, you will cool it down most effectively, and you will be able to get it into the refrigerator more quickly. However, the firmness of the pastry cream is setting up during cooling as well, so stir very gently. My approach is to make one gentle rotation of a wooden spoon a couple of times during cooling, nothing more.

lemon cream

This tart, creamy lemon filling, often called lemon curd, is easy to make and adds a puckery addition to tarts, cakes, and more. Lemon cream is all about the bright, clean, lemon flavor; please use freshly squeezed juice. Also, while you can make this in the top of a double boiler, I have found that with constant supervision—do not walk away from the stove top—you can make this more quickly and easily over low to medium direct heat. Just use a pan with a heavy bottom and watch it carefully. If you have a saucier pan with a rounded bottom, you will be able to whisk the lemon cream most easily without any scorching.

2 large eggs

1 large egg yolk

¾ cup sugar

¼ cup freshly squeezed lemon juice

6 tablespoons (¾ stick) unsalted butter, at room temperature, cut into pieces

½ teaspoon finely grated lemon zest, optional

1) Put the eggs, yolk, sugar, and lemon juice in a medium heavy-bottomed saucepan and whisk together to break up the eggs. Add the butter and cook over medium-low heat, whisking frequently. When the mixture begins to bubble around the edges, lower the heat and whisk constantly until the mixture thickens and reaches 180°F. (The temperature is more important than the time it takes, and the cream itself should not boil.) The lemon cream will thicken and form a soft shape when dropped from a spoon. It will also begin to look a bit translucent. If desired, stir in the zest after removing from the heat. Let cool to room temperature, stirring occasionally to release the heat. Refrigerate for at least 6 hours or up to 1 week in an airtight container.

TIP   There are four ways to approach the "zest" issue. Citrus zest holds a lot of flavor, but cooking with it or adding it raw results in different levels of intensity. If cooked, it can lose its bright, fresh quality, and of course, if left in the cream, it adds texture. It all depends on what qualities you want. In terms of strength, from least to most intense flavor: Leave it out completely, add it after cooking, add it before cooking and strain it out, or add it before cooking and leave it in. Try each to see which you prefer. (In the Lemon Meringue Tart on page 185, which has its own version of lemon curd as a filling, I add it before cooking and leave it in for maximum lemon flavor.)

whipped cream

MAKES ABOUT 4 CUPS

Always use cream labeled *heavy*, *whipping*, or *heavy whipping* cream for best results, and begin with the bowl and beater well chilled, along with cold cream itself. Confectioners' sugar actually has a bit of cornstarch added to it to help prevent clumping. Used here, the cornstarch helps stabilize the finished whipped cream.

1) In the chilled bowl of a stand mixer, beat the cream, sugar, and vanilla on medium-high speed with the wire whip attachment until very soft peaks form. The whipped cream is best used immediately.

2½ cups chilled heavy cream

5 tablespoons sifted confectioners' sugar

½ teaspoon vanilla extract

TIP When whipping cream for serving as an accompaniment or for incorporating into a recipe, it should almost always be whipped softly. Surely sometimes it is whipped a little more stiffly than other times, but it will lose its textural appeal if it is ever whipped to the point of being stiff, and it should never look lumpy or have a granular texture. If this happens, stir in some liquid cream to smooth it out, but the best bet is to take care initially.

marzipan

MAKES ABOUT 1¼ POUNDS

A lmond paste, which is a combination of very finely ground almonds and sugar, is used as an ingredient in several recipes in the book. I consider it a "raw ingredient" even though I use professionally created brands, such as American Almond Products (see Resources, page 287). While it can be made at home, the ultra-fine texture that can be achieved commercially is superior, plus there is standardization, which makes a difference when trying to replicate recipes. Marzipan is made with almond paste and used in this book as a covering for a cake—see Chocolate-Glazed Marzipan Cake with Cognac-Soaked Apricots (page 116). You can also roll it into balls and dip in chocolate, for a simple candy.

10½ ounces almond paste, such as American Almond

¾ to 2 cups sifted confectioners' sugar

3 tablespoons light corn syrup

Extra confectioners' sugar for kneading

1) Put the almond paste in the bowl of a stand mixer. Using the flat paddle attachment, turn the machine on and off to break up the paste. Turn the machine off, add the sugar, and pulse on and off briefly on low speed. Once the sugar has begun to incorporate, run the machine on medium speed until the mixture looks like finely ground nuts; it will not come together in the bowl. Add the corn syrup to the mixture and beat on medium speed until it comes together. Do not process for too long, or the oils from the almonds will begin to rise to the surface and create a greasy layer. Remove from the machine and knead briefly by hand, dusting your hands and the surface with confectioners' sugar. Form into a ball and cover well with plastic wrap. Let sit overnight at room temperature. The resting time allows the oils to distribute evenly and will make the marzipan easier to work with.

2) Keep the marzipan very well wrapped in plastic and in an airtight container for up to 1 month. It should be kneaded again before using to ensure smoothness.

marzipan roses, leaves, and tendrils

MAKES AT LEAST 12 ROSES WITH LEAVES AND TENDRILS

Using the recipe for marzipan above, or using purchased marzipan, you can make exquisite roses, leaves, and tendrils to decorate your desserts, such as the Chocolate-Glazed Marzipan Cake with Cognac-Soaked Apricots (page 116). The petal cutters and leaf cutters can be purchased from Beryl's (see Resources, page 287). They typically come in sets of various sizes.

1 pound Marzipan
(see above recipe)

Confectioners' sugar for rolling

Petal cutters ranging from
1½ inches to 2½ inches

1-inch rose leaf cutter

2-inch rose leaf cutter

for the roses Knead a golf ball–sized piece of marzipan until soft. If it is very hard, hold it in your palms for a minute or two to warm it up.

1) Roll out to a ⅛-inch thickness on a surface dusted with confectioners' sugar. Cut out 4 petals with the same size rose petal cutter for every "closed" rose. Cut out 7 to 10 petals for "open, full-bloom" roses. Use a small offset spatula to remove petals from the surface. Use your fingers or a rolling pin to smooth out the broad edge of each petal; the thinner the better.

2) Form the rose's center: Take one petal and hold the center top of the petal between your index finger and thumb. Now take your right hand and gently but tightly roll the upper right hand part of the petal diagonally toward the middle. The top will be the tip and should be tighter and narrower. When you get to the middle, remove your thumb and finger and continue folding. (Reverse these directions if you are a lefty.) You should have a cone shaped "center."

3) Begin attaching petals: Take one of the petals and gently pinch the bottom, which will make the petal more of a curved, cup shape. The petal's top edge should be thinned out. Gently bend this top edge toward the back, forming a tight outward furl. Asymmetry is desirable and realistic. Repeat with the remaining petals.

4) Place 1 petal against the cone base with the pinched end down. Flatten 1 side against the cone, leaving the other side open and away from the cone. Place 1 edge of the second petal in the middle of the first petal and flatten it against the center. Your third petal will start in the center of the second petal and then be tucked under the first. These 3 petals, formed over the center, create a small rosebud. You may add additional petals, each beginning in the middle of the one before. The more you add, the larger the rose will become in diameter.

5) If the base of the rose is thick, trim any excess marzipan from the base with a sharp paring knife. You want to coax the base into a reverse cone shape. This end will be nestled into buttercream or frosting and under marzipan leaves, so it doesn't have to be perfect. You can also roll the bottom back and forth between your fingers to create this narrow shape. You may bend the petals inward or outward and mold them into any shape that you want. Brush off any excess confectioners' sugar with a soft brush. Place the roses in an airtight container in a single layer. They may be used immediately or stored for up to 1 month in a cool, dry place.

for the leaves Roll out the marzipan as described above. Cut out small and large leaf shapes. Use the edge of a sharp knife to imprint "veins." Curve into realistic shapes immediately while marzipan is still malleable. Store as above.

for the tendrils Simply roll marzipan into long, thin ropes with tapered ends. Store as above.

ingredients, equipment, and techniques

Y OU AND A friend both agree to make the same recipe and compare, so you go home to your own kitchens, follow the same written instructions, whip it up, and then get together for a tasting. The desserts don't look the same, and they don't taste the same. What happened? Sure, both are recognizable as whatever they are, such as a pear tart or a chocolate brownie, but there the similarity ends. What is the explanation?

We recipe writers face this dilemma every time someone follows one of our recipes, because the majority of readers don't follow them precisely, and/or the recipe isn't written well enough, with specific enough information, for the person to achieve success in the first place. Certainly we don't all have the same oven as one another, and this can affect the outcome too. But I think the two largest factors are choice of ingredients and preparation technique.

For instance, not all eggs are the same. If a recipe is written for large-size eggs, substituting extra-large simply won't do, but I would hope this would be rather obvious when it comes to baking, which demands such precision and accuracy. Some other things are more subtle. Different unsalted butters can have different amounts of moisture; cane and beet sugar, both of which are often packaged as "granulated sugar," perform differently. All flours certainly are not created equal. Even multiple brands labeled as "all-purpose" can have various types of wheat as their source and have varying protein content and milled texture. I know this is enough to drive any baker batty! What is one to do?

The best we can do, as bakers who are interested in making the best possible desserts, is to follow good recipes as closely as possible. I have written every recipe in this book very carefully, and every part of the recipe is there to guide you not only to ultimate success, but also to un-forgettable results. If you deviate from the recipe, you will probably get edible, tasty results, but the finished product will not be at its pinnacle of deliciousness. So for the very best possible results, please try to find all of the suggested ingredients and follow instructions to the letter.

how to bake unforgettable desserts

* Read the Basics chapter and this chapter at least once, to acquaint you with the approaches used in this book.

* Read each recipe through before beginning.

* Use the ingredients called for (for instance, do not substitute extra-large eggs for large).

* Use the equipment called for (for instance, do not substitute a 9-inch pan for an 8-inch pan).

* Refer to the Resources section (page 287) for hard-to-find ingredients or equipment.

* Take time to measure accurately with the proper tools.

* Use an oven thermometer to make sure that your oven is calibrated properly.

* Use the proper size pots: Use a smaller than suggested saucepan and a boilover might result; use a larger pot and a mixture might reduce too quickly.

* Baking and cooking times are approximate. Read and use the visual cues as well. Always begin checking toward the beginning of the suggested time range.

* Remember that there will almost always be residual heat in saucepans and in jelly-roll pans, cake pans, and other baking pans. My advice is to err on the side of caution.

* When I suggest using a toothpick to assess doneness, I am being literal. I think crumbs will adhere to a wooden toothpick more readily than to a metal "cake tester." I prefer wooden toothpicks, or the longer bamboo skewers when necessary.

* Cooling baked goods is an essential part of the process to ensure the best texture. Follow the cooling techniques in each recipe.

* Storage suggestions should be followed closely for optimal results.

~~~~~~

INGREDIENTS ~

The ingredients listed below are the most important as well as the most un-usual, as opposed to a complete list of every ingredient used in baking or these recipes.

all-purpose and cake flour ~ Using the right flour makes the difference be-tween an elegant, well-textured dessert and one that can end up being dry, coarse, and truly not up to par. Please make sure to use the correct flour, mea-sured accurately. For all-purpose, I use King Arthur unbleached all-purpose flour. For cake flour, I use Pillsbury's Softasilk cake flour, which is packaged in boxes and can be found in the supermarket baking aisle.
    TECHNIQUE: Store in an airtight container. Before measuring, whisk to lightly aerate, and then use the dip-and-sweep method. This entails using the proper-size dry measuring cup, dipping it into the flour so that it is mounded over the top of the cup, and then using the edge of a butter

knife or icing spatula to scrape any excess back into the container. Do not shake or tap down, as it will compact the flour and skew your measurement. Cake flour often has lumps. Sift it or shake and press it through a strainer into a bowl before measuring.

granulated sugar — This is simply referred to as "sugar" throughout the book. Use sugar labeled as cane sugar, as opposed to beet sugar, as they can act differently, particularly when melting for caramel. Some bakers think cane sugar blends more easily as well during creaming with butter, which ultimately gives cakes a better texture.

confectioners' sugar — Also referred to as powdered sugar, this is sugar that has a small percentage of cornstarch added to it to prevent clumping. It is sometimes labeled as 10X, which refers to that fact that it is 10 times finer than granulated sugar. I tested these recipes with Domino confectioners' sugar.

TECHNIQUE: Store in an airtight container. Before measuring, whisk to lightly aerate, then use the dip-and-sweep method. This entails using the proper-size dry measuring cup, dipping it into the sugar so that it is mounded over the top of the cup, and then using the edge of a butter knife or icing spatula to scrape any excess back into the container. Do not shake or tap down, as it will compact the sugar and skew your measurement. Oftentimes whisking will not get rid of clumps in confectioners' sugar; if this occurs, you need to sift it or shake and press it through a strainer into a bowl before measuring.

superfine sugar — This is a granulated sugar with a very fine grain. It dissolves more readily in certain recipes where its finer texture is appreciated.

butter — I only use sweet, unsalted butter. Refrigerate what you need and freeze the rest; it will keep frozen for months. Always keep it well wrapped, or it will pick up strong flavors and odors from other foods. I tested these recipes with Land O'Lakes unsalted butter.

TECHNIQUE: Please take note of the temperature of the butter called for in individual recipes, as it is vitally important to success. For instance, if you cream too-cold butter and sugar together for a cake, it will never truly "cream." On the other hand, if the butter is too warm, it will partially melt and become oily. With creaming you are trying to create air bubbles within the butter, which will give a proper texture to your baked goods. This is accomplished when the rough sugar crystals cut into the butter and create tiny air pockets, which the butter then holds in place. If the butter is too cold, air pockets will not form. If the butter is too warm, it can border on greasy, melt, and release any air bubbles that could have been. All of this means that your end result will never reach its full potential of texture or even flavor. When I call for room-temperature butter, it should be about 65°F. If you have forgotten to remove butter from the refrigerator early enough, a great technique is to grate it on the largest holes of a box grater, allow it to sit for a few minutes, and proceed. The small shreds will warm up quickly. Instructions will often say to cream butter and sugar until light and fluffy. In this case the mixture should have lightened in color and increased in volume (from those air bubbles), and while the texture will indeed be "light and fluffy," if the butter was at the proper temperature, it should still have what is described in baking parlance as a "plastic" quality. This means when you pick up the beater, the mixture should hold its shape. If you rub a dab between your fingers, you will still feel the grittiness of the sugar and the mixture should feel thick and never oily. Note that in some recipes there is a high proportion of sugar and you will never achieve the light and fluffy stage—in this case the mixture is creamy and "sandy" in texture.

eggs — All of the eggs used in these recipes are graded size large, grade AA, and you should use this size in the recipes when you are baking. The size of egg does make a difference. Two large eggs equals three medium eggs, and obviously the difference between small and jumbo is even greater.

TECHNIQUE: Many recipes call for room-temperature eggs. A fast and easy way to accomplish this is to place eggs into a bowl of warm water for a few minutes; it warms them up quite quickly. If you need to separate eggs, do so while they are cold, as the whites will be firmer, making the process easier. Health and sanitation

egg safety

The miraculous egg brings its many features to a variety of baked goods and desserts. It provides structure, texture, creaminess, and volume, depending on its use, and many dishes would simply be impossible without them. Most of the recipes featuring eggs in this book are cooked or baked, but some feature egg whites that are either raw or lightly cooked. The standard approach should be that you use grade AA eggs purchased from a reliable source, and they should be kept refrigerated at all times. Keeping them in their cardboard carton protects them from refrigerator odors, which they are apt to absorb. Eggs with any cracks, no matter how small, should be discarded. Hands should be clean when handling eggs to prevent cross-contamination of any kind. Recipes featuring raw or lightly cooked egg white should not be served to the elderly, pregnant women, or very young children. Alternatively, you can purchase pasteurized egg whites and use those instead. They are readily available in most supermarkets, either in the refrigerator section or, occasionally, in the freezer section.

The chocolates listed below are ones that I enjoy working with and that are similar to the most frequently called-for percentages in the recipes:

unsweetened chocolates

Callebaut:
Unsweetened (100%)

Scharffen Berger:
Unsweetened (99%)

Michel Cluizel:
Noir Infini (99%)

Valrhona:
Cacao Pâte Extra (100%)

bittersweet chocolates

Amedei:
"9" (75%)
Chuao (70%)
Porcelana (70%)
Toscano Black Extra (63%)

Bissinger's:
Bittersweet (75%)

Callebaut:
Extra Bittersweet (71%)

Felchlin:
Cru Savage Couverture (68%)
Maracaibo Clasificado Grand
Cru Couverture (65%)

Ghirardelli:
Extra Bittersweet Baking Bar
(70%)
Bittersweet Baking Bar (60%)

Guittard:
Sur del Lago (65%)

Lindt:
Excellence Dark (85%)
Excellence Dark (70%)

Excellence Origins Ecuador
(65%)
Excellence Origins
Madagascar (65%)

Michel Cluizel:
Hacienda Concepcion
Couverture (66%)

Scharffen Berger:
Extra Dark Bittersweet (82%)
Bittersweet (70%)

Valrhona:
Araguani (72%)
Guanaja (70%)
Caraïbe (66%)
Manjari (64%)
Tainori (64%)
Extra Bitter (61%)
La Noir Gastronomie (61%)

semisweet chocolates

Bissinger's:
Semisweet (60%)

Callebaut:
Semisweet (54%)
Semisweet (52%)

Ghirardelli:
Semisweet Chocolate Baking
Bar (45%)

Guittard:
Tsaratana (61%)

Scharffen Berger:
Semisweet (62%)

Valrhona:
Caraque (56%)
Equitoriale Noir (55%)

milk chocolates

Amedei:
Brown Cioccolato al Latte
(32%)

Callebaut:
Milk (31.7%)

Felchlin:
Maracaibo Criolait Grand
Cru Couverture (38%)

Ghirardelli:
Milk (31%)

Guittard:
Orinoco Milk (41%)

Michel Cluizel:
Mangaro Milk (50%)
Grand Lait Milk (45%)

Valrhona:
Guanaja Lactée Milk (41%)
Jivara Lactée (40%)
Equitoriale Lactée Milk (35%)
Tanariva Lactée (33%)

white chocolates

Callebaut:
White Callets (pieces)
White Bloc

El Rey:
Icoa (34% nondeodorized
cocoa butter)

Felchlin:
Edelweiss Couverture (36%
cocoa butter)

Ghirardelli:
White (26% cocoa butter)

Guittard:
Crème Francais White (31%
cocoa butter)

Valrhona:
Ivoire (40.5% cocoa butter)

cocoa powders

Bensdorp:
Bensdorp Dutch Process (22
to 24% cocoa butter)

Cacao Barry:
Extra Brute Dutch Processed
(22 to 24% cocoa butter)

Ghirardelli:
Ghirardelli Natural Cocoa
(22 to 24% cocoa butter)

Michel Cluizel:
Dark Cocoa Powder (20 to
22% cocoa butter)

Scharffen Berger:
Scharffen Berger Natural
Cocoa

Valrhona:
Cocoa Powder Dutch
Processed (21% cocoa
butter)

codes suggest not letting eggs stay at room temperature for more than 1 hour, so plan accordingly.

nuts — Many of the recipes feature nuts, which must always be very fresh. They should smell like the nut that they are. Any musty or rancid smell means they are stale and will transmit those off flavors to your baked goods. Note that when the recipe says "1 cup walnut halves, chopped," it means that you measure out the walnut halves first, then chop after measuring. This will give the proper amount.

cacao nibs — These are the tiny seeds found inside the cacao pod's beans. They are a relatively new ingredient available to home cooks and they have opened up a world of possibilities for creative recipe development. All chocolate begins with the cacao pod. Pods are harvested when ripe. Beans are scooped out, then fermented, dried, and roasted. Then the shells of the beans are removed, leaving the cacao nib. These are crushed until smooth, and the resulting paste is then formed into blocks of unsweetened chocolate. Bittersweet and semi-sweet chocolates are made from this crushed paste with the addition of sugar, emulsifiers, vanilla, and so on. But the cacao nibs themselves can be used in recipes in a similar way as chocolate morsels or chopped nuts. They are small and very crunchy and add an elusive chocolate flavor and aroma whenever they are included.

vanilla beans — Several recipes suggest using vanilla beans, as opposed to extract. I recommend using Bourbon-Madagascar beans, which are long and slender and, when fresh, have a thick, moist, almost oily skin. They should be plump and moist upon purchase and they should be stored airtight to preserve those qualities. If your beans have dried out and become brittle, try rehydrating them in a bit of warm water.

gold and silver — Gold and silver, if used in certain forms and purity levels, are indeed edible. Gold leaf for food decoration should be at least 22 karat (or "kt"). Silver should be pure and not high in aluminum. Both gold and silver edible products can be found in many

toasting nuts

Nuts add texture and flavor to many desserts, from simple cookies to elegant cakes. In some recipes I do not call for the nuts to be toasted before incorporating them into the recipe, because they "toast" enough within the actual recipe, or the recipe doesn't require the step. However, where I do call for toasted nuts, it is because the extra step is necessary for the nuances of the dish. Some nuts, when raw, are actually exceedingly subtle, whereas a gentle toasting will bring out flavors in such a way as to more than double the taste experience. Preheat your oven to 350°F and spread the nuts in a single layer on a jelly-roll pan. Toast them, shaking the pan occasionally for even toasting, just until they begin to give off fragrance and begin to color. Cool them completely before proceeding. If you try to chop the nuts while they are warm, the mixture will be oily and greasy. As with so many baking techniques, it is the nuances that will make a big difference.

forms. Books of "leaves" (thin square sheets) are typical, and you can also find flakes and powders. Individual recipes will give specific suggestions.

EQUIPMENT ~

ovens and oven thermometers — Actual oven temperatures often vary from the dial temperatures by as much as 25 to 50 degrees. Because of this I strongly suggest using an oven thermometer, adjusting your oven accordingly, and keeping an eye on your baking times, or else your dessert's final texture will suffer.

ice-cream scoops or food dishers — Homemade cookies often vary in size and shape within the same batch, and yet, at the bakery, they are uniform and consistent. One of the reasons for this is that professional kitchens have a

oven rack positioning and oven hot spots

The recipes in this book that require the oven will indicate oven rack placement. I have done this hesitantly because ovens vary tremendously from one to another. Even if we both have the same brand oven, mine might have a hot spot in the upper right area, while yours might have one in the lower left. Hot spots are areas of the oven that seem to accumulate and reflect more heat. Perhaps you have noticed when baking a tray of cookies that one quadrant or half of the cookies on a baking pan always seems to brown more quickly. This indicates the location of your hot spot. Knowing your individual oven's quirks will help you plan. Rotating pans front to back and from an upper to lower rack halfway through baking is a good way to encourage even baking. Many of these recipes call for either a middle oven rack positioning, when only one rack is required, or one rack positioned in the upper third and one in the lower third, when two racks are required. This is an attempt to provide proper air circulation for your baked goods, which is very important for even baking. I will admit that when I have been in a hurry, I have baked three racks of cookies at a time, and it really does not give optimal results. Stick with one or two racks at a time. If your oven has an even number of rack positions, place the rack in the "lower" middle position whenever I call for a "middle" position.

reliable way to form cookies so that they are exactly the same size and shape every time. This is not just for a polished look; evenly formed cookies bake more evenly and also give a proper yield. The easiest way to do this at home is to use small spring-like scoops—they look like diminutive ice-cream scoops. Cookie recipes often call for a cookie to be formed in a "rounded teaspoon" or "rounded tablespoon" size. I use Zeroll brand scoops available online through The Baker's Catalogue (see page 288). Their #100 scoop (which holds about $1^{3}/_{4}$ teaspoons liquid) is perfect for truffles and "rounded teaspoon"–size cookies. The #40 scoop (which holds $1^{1}/_{2}$ tablespoons liquid) is larger and should be used where I call for "rounded tablespoon"–size cookies.

TECHNIQUE: To take advantage of a scoop's round shape and exact size, dip it into the cookie batter (truffle ganache, etc.) and generously overfill the scoop. Then scrape the edge of the scoop against your mixing bowl so that the scoop is full but leveled off. Then use the spring-like action of the tool to drop the cookie right onto your prepared pan. All your cookies will be perfectly formed.

scales   While most of the ingredients in this book are measured with cups and spoons, some are best weighed. I prefer electronic scales for their precision. A tare feature is usually standard and a necessary feature. This allows you to place a bowl on the scale and reset it to zero so that the bowl is not being weighed. Then put your ingredient, such as chopped chocolate, in the bowl, to be weighed quickly and cleanly.

baking pans for cakes, bars, pies, tarts, and cookies — To bake beautiful, even cake layers, well-formed muffins, and properly browned pies and cookies, you need the right pans. You can bake the same cake batter side by side in the same oven but in different pans, and get completely different results. A heavy, sturdy pan that conducts heat well will yield an evenly baked cake with a relatively flat top. A thin, flimsy pan produces a cake with a high peak, over-cooked edges, and a tough, uneven texture. For cakes, brownies, and bars, I use heavy aluminum cake pans with straight sides and a 2-inch depth.

For pies, I prefer Pyrex pie plates for their even browning ability and also because you can actually see the level of browning as it progresses. I use two different sizes, and the recipes will specify. If you do not use the correct size, the recipe will not work as desired. The smaller 9 × $1^{1}/_{4}$-inch and the larger

storing your desserts

Proper storage is critical for maximum dessert enjoyment. This might sound like an overstatement, but trust me—it is not. My aim is to get you to consider storage as carefully as your preparation. It should not be an afterthought. A tart filled with pastry cream and covered with fresh fruit left out at room temperature will become soggy and potentially dangerous to eat. A simple pound cake left out and exposed to the air will stale very quickly. Very specific instructions are given in individual recipes, and if followed, your desserts will be the best they can be and last as long as possible.

With regard to cookies, at the very least, crisp should be stored with crisp and soft with soft, or they will all end up soft. The soft cookies lend moisture to crisp cookies if stored together. That said, I think the optimum situation is to store individual cookies by themselves following individual instructions. This way chocolate cookies will remain tasting like chocolate, pure butter cookies will retain that purity, spiced cookies will not lend their flavor and aroma to others, etc. Also, believe me when I say that some must be stored in single layers separated by parchment; it is because I learned the hard way that this extra step is helpful.

$9\frac{1}{2} \times 1\frac{1}{2}$-inch sizes are both readily found in supermarkets and housewares stores.

Tarts and individual tartlets in this book are formed in either straight-edge tart rings or fluted-edge loose-bottomed tart pans. Diameter is measured across the bottom of the pan. Make sure that you use the exact size called for.

For cookies, I rely on standard-size aluminum jelly-roll pans, also known as half sheet pans. These are my holy grail of cookie sheets and will bake your cookies the most evenly; in addition, they will last a lifetime if properly cared for. Thinner pans warp and burn cookies and insulated pans do not encourage proper browning.

pastry brushes — My favorite new kitchen gadget is the silicone pastry brush. Buy one with soft, fine "bristles." Old-style brushes will often shed bristles on your creations, and they also hold flavors. Silicone brushes never lose their bristles, and they can be cleaned thoroughly so that you can use them for barbecue sauce one day and for a delicate pastry glaze the next.

zesters — I use two kinds of tools to remove citrus zests from my fruit. My go-to tool is the Microplane zester, which is really a very sharp rasp-like instrument. If you do not own one already, it should be on your list to purchase. These tools effortlessly remove zest without any of the bitter white pith. They make zesting a breeze, and because they are so easy to use, you will most likely save your knuckles as well. If the recipe does not specify, assume I have used a Microplane zester where citrus zest is called for. This is important because the zest created by these tools is so light and fluffy that it measures quite differently than zest made in any other way. I do call for a classic citrus zester in the Double-Decker "Key" Lime Pie (page 208) when making the candied zest. This is a small tool usually with a row of five small, round, sharp holes that are dragged over the fruit to create very thin, thread-like pieces of zest. Oxo makes a good one.

icing spatulas and decorator's turntables — These are two tools that are not typically found in the basic kitchen, but if you are serious about making cakes and decorating them as professionally as possible, you should consider purchasing them. The proper icing spatula is paramount for frosting your cakes smoothly. It is made up of a flat metal blade with a rounded tip, which is affixed to a plastic or wood handle. Spatulas come in a variety of sizes from about 5 inches to over 14 inches for the blade length alone. They can also be perfectly straight or they can be offset, and trying different ones will tell you which works best for you.

For turntables, I like the heavy ones made by Ateco, although you can use an inexpensive plastic lazy Susan. Once you have both of these tools, you will see that they make frosting and decorating even a simple 9-inch layer cake much easier and your results so much better. If you have never had much success decorating cakes, maybe it is that you haven't had the proper tools!

thermometers — Oven thermometers play an important role in any baking project. Your baked goods can only come out their best if they are baked at the proper temperature, and an oven thermometer will tell you if your oven is calibrated properly or not.

A chocolate thermometer is used during tempering. This type of thermometer has 1-degree increments (usually ranging from 30° to 140°F), that allow you to accurately judge the temperature of the chocolate, which is crucial during this procedure.

parchment paper — Parchment is available in rolls, like aluminum foil, from kitchenware stores, mail-order sources, and now, thankfully, in many supermarkets. Cut out shapes to fit pan bottoms, and use it to line jelly-roll pans. Parchment can also be cut into triangles to make paper cones.

pastry bags — I like the polyester bags made by Wilton called Featherweight Decorating Bags. They come in sizes ranging from 8 inches to 18 inches, in 2-inch increments. The openings need to be trimmed to allow a large decorating tip to fit, or to fit a coupler, which allows you to change small tips easily. I use the 14-inch size most often. To clean, they may be boiled, or simply washed well with hot, soapy water. Do not store in a drawer with loose tips or other sharp objects, which can pierce the bags and ruin them for future use.

decorating tips — Decorating tips are inexpensive and an easy way to add beauty to your cake. Ateco and Wilton make great tips, which are numbered for convenience. Note that while many companies number their tips, one company's numbers are not necessarily the same as another's. I give you specific brand numbering information in individual recipes.

cake cardboards — As a leftover from my bakery days, I would never attempt to decorate a cake without using a cardboard as a base. The boards are used as guides for your icing spatula, to help give a smooth, clean look to your buttercream. You must buy precut shapes for the edges to be smooth enough for the job. For example, for a 9-inch round cake, you use a 9-inch round cardboard. They come in a variety of shapes and sizes, so you will be able to find what you need.

gum paste cutters — You have probably used cookie cutters to shape cookies, but there are other cutters—specifically gum paste cutters—that come into use for cake decorations. For instance, after rolling out marzipan for making marzipan roses, you will use petal-shaped cutters for the flowers and leaf-shaped cutters for, well, the leaves. For the marzipan roses in this book I used cutters manufactured by a company called FMM, and they are available through Beryl's Cake Decorating & Pastry Supplies (see Resources, page 287). They make a set of rose petal cutters in various sizes and a set for rose leaves. Beryl herself is marvelously informative and helpful and can guide you to the proper purchase.

how to make a recipe your own

I've made the point that recipes should be followed faithfully in order to achieve the best results. I am now going to suggest something that at first might seem contrary. We have all had that culinary experience where we taste something and think to ourselves, "I might prefer raspberries standing in for the strawberries," or "I wonder what would happen if I halve the sugar," or "Raisins would add something to this batter." These are the seeds of a unique dessert creation. I have taken pains to develop and write recipes for you that work, and, I think, work well, if the recipe is followed. However, each and every one of us has a unique palate and personal preferences, and I am a huge proponent of individual creativity. Here is my potentially confusing statement: Yes, I still strongly suggest you make these recipes as written, at least once. Follow the recipes as described, but take detailed notes. I will go as far as to suggest you have a notebook devoted just to this process, which you can use very time you cook or bake. Write down your impressions of the recipe as you go along (e.g., "batter is nice and thick," "needs more chocolate chips") and again once you are finished. With your oven and equipment, did the cake bake in 25 minutes instead of 30? Would you like to try using dark brown sugar instead of light brown next time? How about the chocolate chunks; maybe milk chocolate could substitute in for the dark chocolate. Would a dose of lemon zest add to the flavor of this recipe? Perhaps you would prefer nutmeg instead of cinnamon. Then go one step further and make notes for yourself as to how you want to approach the recipe next time. In this way you can begin to experiment and make the recipe your own. When you make the recipe the second time, try your own suggestions, and then make notes again. If the recipe seems off balance, always know you can go back to the original and veer off again from there. I absolutely encourage you to create your own versions. It is not only an engaging and stimulating creative process, but you also get something delicious to eat in the end that is all your own.

breakfast, brunch, and snack cakes

THE WORD "UNFORGETTABLE," in terms of desserts, might conjure up images of sweets with multiple components, or with crowns of spun sugar, but the definition is much more nuanced than that. Turn to this chapter for great brunch and breakfast treats, sweets for coffee breaks, and simple snacks. These are the sleeper recipes of the book. Breakfast baked goods and cakes good for snacking, such as scones and coffee cakes, might not have the kind of high visual "wow" factor found in desserts served at an elegant restaurant, but their flavor and texture combinations can be just as impressive, delicious, and satisfying.

lemon-ginger scones

MAKES 6 SCONES

Scones are my favorite treat to have with my breakfast tea, and I never tire of coming up with new variations. This flavor combo was a favorite at my bakery, as it provided a different take than those featuring fresh or dried fruit or nuts. I like the balance of lemon zest and crystallized ginger as listed, but you can vary these amounts depending on which flavor you would like to highlight. Scones must be eaten as freshly baked as possible. The coarse sanding sugar can be found at Beryl's (see Resources, page 287).

1) Position a rack in the middle of the oven. Preheat the oven to 400°F. Line a jelly-roll pan with parchment paper; set aside.

2) In the bowl of a stand mixer, put the flour, ginger, sugar, baking powder, lemon zest, and salt and combine on low speed using the flat paddle attachment. Add the butter and pulse on and off until it forms a very coarse meal; there might be pockets of butter that are larger, which is fine. Drizzle in ¾ cup cream with the mixer running on low speed and mix just until combined.

3) Turn the mixture out onto the prepared pan in one large clump and pat down into a large round about 1 inch thick and about 7½ inches across. Brush the top with the remaining 1 tablespoon cream and sprinkle with the coarse sugar. Cut into 6 even wedges, and barely separate the wedges by wiggling your knife back and forth. There should be ⅛ inch to ¼ inch between each scone.

4) Bake for 17 to 22 minutes, or until very light golden brown and a toothpick inserted in the center just tests clean. Cool on the jelly-roll pan set on a rack for about 5 minutes. These are best served warm from the oven or the same day they are baked. Store in an airtight container at room temperature for up to 1 day. Reheat in a toaster oven, if desired.

2¼ cups all-purpose flour

⅓ cup minced crystallized ginger

⅓ cup sugar

1 tablespoon baking powder

1½ teaspoons finely grated lemon zest

Pinch of salt

12 tablespoons (1½ sticks) cold unsalted butter, cut into pieces

¾ cup plus 1 tablespoon heavy cream

2 teaspoons coarse sanding sugar (or substitute regular granulated)

TIP By baking in a hot oven they become browned top and bottom, developing a slightly crisp exterior texture while the interior and sides remain soft. The sides stay soft because they are baked so close together, so do not separate too much. It is this contrast, and the inherent richness of the dough, that make these scones so special.

brown sugar–buttermilk snack cake
with blackberries and caramel-walnut drizzle SERVES 9 TO 12

Recipes can develop in many ways. In this instance, I had the idea of combining buttermilk, brown sugar, and blackberries—the combo "tasted" good in my head, so I set about putting them together in the kitchen. It worked. This is a simple, velvety crumbed cake made with buttermilk and dark brown sugar for a pronounced caramel flavor. Fresh blackberries offer pockets of deep purple, juicy fruitness, and their distinct flavor stands up to the brown sugar. To further enhance the caramel notes, a brown sugar caramel icing is drizzled on top. This cake is perfect to bring into the office for a special day—perhaps a birthday coffee break for a friend.

for the cake Position a rack in the middle of the oven. Preheat the oven to 350°F. Coat an 8-inch square pan with nonstick spray.

1) Whisk together the flour, baking soda, and salt in a medium bowl to aerate and combine; set aside.

2) In the bowl of a stand mixer, beat the butter with the flat paddle attachment on medium-high speed until creamy, about 1 minute. Add the brown sugar and beat until light and fluffy, about 3 minutes, scraping down the bowl once or twice. Beat in the egg until well combined. Add the flour mixture in two additions, alternately with the buttermilk. Begin and end with the flour mixture and beat briefly until smooth. Scrape the batter evenly into the pan and smooth the top with an offset spatula. It will be a fairly shallow layer. Scatter the blackberries evenly on top, reserving about 5 of them; do not press into the batter, as they will sink during baking.

3) Bake for 15 to 25 minutes, or until a toothpick inserted in the center shows a few moist crumbs when removed. The cake will just have begun to come away from the sides of the pan. Cool in the pan on a rack before decorating.

CAKE

1½ cups sifted cake flour

Heaping ½ teaspoon baking soda

⅛ teaspoon salt

6 tablespoons (¾ stick) unsalted butter, at room temperature, cut into pieces

⅓ cup firmly packed dark brown sugar

1 large egg, at room temperature

½ cup plus 1 tablespoon low-fat buttermilk, at room temperature

1 cup fresh blackberries

ICING

⅓ cup firmly packed dark brown sugar

3 tablespoons unsalted butter, at room temperature

2½ tablespoons heavy cream

¾ cup sifted confectioners' sugar

½ teaspoon vanilla extract

⅓ cup walnut halves, toasted (see page 23) and chopped

for the icing Combine the brown sugar, butter, and cream in a small saucepan and bring to a simmer over medium-high heat. Simmer for 1 minute, whisking frequently. Remove from the heat and whisk in the confectioners' sugar and vanilla until smooth and fluid. It will firm up very quickly, and if you whisk or cool it for too long, it will become too firm and sugary. Use a spoon to immediately drizzle about half the icing all over the top of the cake, then quickly sprinkle the walnuts and reserved berries evenly over the top while the icing is still wet. Drizzle with the remaining icing, which will set up almost immediately, and serve. Store at room temperature, well wrapped in plastic wrap for up to 1 day.

TIPS You might be tempted to add extra berries to the batter, but they add too much moisture and will throw off the balance of the cake. Also, when making the icing, make sure you stop combining the ingredients the moment the mixture becomes smooth. If it becomes grainy and sandy, you have stirred too long and must start again.

butter and cream
sugar crunch cake serves 12

This is a great example of a very simple buttery, velvety, vanilla-scented cake. It contains very basic ingredients, but the specific techniques yield an unusually smooth cake and contrasting crackly topping. We begin by liberally buttering the inside of the pan and then dusting with coarse sanding sugar, which you can find at specialty resources such as Beryl's (see Resources, page 287). The batter includes a whole cup of heavy cream, which lends richness and a velvety quality. Finally, the technique of baking in a very low oven bakes the cake very gently, which also helps the texture remain moist and smooth. Cake flour is a must, as all-purpose flour will yield a coarse crumb.

for the pan coating Position a rack in the middle of the oven. Preheat the oven to 300°F. Coat a 10-inch tube pan with a removable bottom with the butter. Make sure to coat the bottom, sides, and center tube. Coat the sides and bottom with the coarse sugar, then coat just the bottom with the flour.

for the cake Whisk together the flour and salt in a medium bowl to aerate and combine; set aside.

1) In the bowl of a stand mixer, beat the butter with the flat paddle attachment on medium-high speed until creamy, about 2 minutes. Add the sugar gradually and continue to beat, about 3 minutes at medium-high speed, until creamy and sandy. Split the vanilla bean, scrape in the vanilla seeds, and add the vanilla extract; beat to incorporate. Add the eggs one at a time, beating well after each addition. Add the flour mixture in three additions, alternately with the heavy cream. Begin and end with the flour mixture and beat briefly until smooth. Scrape the batter into the pan and smooth the top with an offset spatula.

for the topping Sprinkle 1 tablespoon of the coarse sugar evenly over the top of the cake.

PAN COATING

1 tablespoon unsalted butter

2 tablespoons coarse sanding sugar

1 tablespoon cake flour

CAKE

3 cups sifted cake flour

½ teaspoon salt

1 cup (2 sticks) unsalted butter, at room temperature, cut into pieces

3 cups sugar

1 moist and plump vanilla bean

2 teaspoons vanilla extract

6 large eggs, at room temperature

1 cup heavy cream

TOPPING

2 tablespoons coarse sanding sugar, divided

1) Bake for 1 hour and 20 minutes to 1 hour and 30 minutes, or until a long bamboo skewer inserted in the center shows a few moist crumbs when removed. Halfway through the baking time, sprinkle the remaining tablespoon of coarse sugar evenly over the top of the cake. When done, the top of the cake will be light golden brown and will look crackly and uneven, which is the way it should be. Cool in the pan set on a rack until barely warm, about 20 minutes. Run a knife or icing spatula between the cake and pan's sides and remove the cake, with the bottom and center tube still attached; place the cake on a rack to cool completely. Run a knife or icing spatula between the cake and pan bottom; twist the center tube to loosen it from the cake. Use two broad, stiff metal spatulas beneath the cake to help lift it up and away from the center tube and pan bottom and place on a display plate. The cake is ready to serve. Store at room temperature, well wrapped in plastic wrap, for up to 4 days.

marble streusel pound cake
with pecans, lemon, and orange   SERVES 10

For this recipe, I wanted to combine all of the wonderful qualities of a marble cake with those of a streusel coffee cake. The chocolate part of the cake is very dark and chocolaty, and there is a generous amount of streusel filled with brown sugar, pecans, cinnamon, cardamom, and lemon and orange zest—all the necessities for a very special breakfast and snack cake. It is fancy as far as these sorts of cakes go. The pan will also go a long way toward creating a visually beautiful cake. I use the Kaisercast Classic Bundform, a 12-cup ring-style pan that has a classic design dating back to the fourteenth century. Its deep swirl design is perfect. A standard-size (½-cup) ice-cream scoop is the perfect tool for placing the alternating different colored batters in the pan. In its place, you could use a ½-cup measuring cup and use a small rubber spatula to scrape the batter out.

for the streusel Position a rack in the middle of the oven. Preheat the oven to 350°F. Thoroughly coat a 12-cup Bundt pan with butter, taking care to coat the center tube as well. Toss together the pecans, brown sugar, lemon and orange zests, cinnamon, and cardamom in a small bowl; set aside.

for the cake Stir together the hot water and espresso powder until dissolved. Combine with the chocolate and melt in the top of a double boiler or a microwave; stir until smooth and set aside.

1) Whisk together the flour, baking powder, baking soda, and salt in a medium bowl to aerate and combine; set aside.

2) Beat the butter with the flat paddle attachment on medium-high speed until creamy, about 2 minutes. Add the sugar gradually and continue to beat for about 3 minutes at medium-high speed, until very light and fluffy. Beat in the vanilla and almond extract. Add the eggs one at a time, beating well after each addition. Add the flour mixture in three additions, alternately with the sour cream.

STREUSEL

⅔ cup pecan halves, toasted (see page 23) and chopped

⅓ cup firmly packed light brown sugar

2 teaspoons finely grated lemon zest

2 teaspoons finely grated orange zest

1½ teaspoons ground cinnamon

½ teaspoon ground cardamom

CAKE

1½ tablespoons hot water

1 teaspoon instant espresso powder, such as Medaglia D'Oro

3 ounces unsweetened chocolate, finely chopped, such as Scharffen Berger (99%)

2¼ cups sifted cake flour

1 tablespoon baking powder

½ teaspoon baking soda

¼ teaspoon salt

½ cup (1 stick) unsalted butter, at room temperature, cut into pieces

1¼ cups sugar

1 teaspoon vanilla extract

¼ teaspoon almond extract

2 large eggs, at room temperature

1 cup full-fat sour cream

Begin and end with the flour mixture and beat briefly until smooth.

3) Remove and put about $1^{1}/_{2}$ cups of batter in a small bowl and thoroughly stir in the melted chocolate mixture.

4) The look of the cake depends on how carefully you fill the baking pan using the following technique, which is best accomplished with a $^{1}/_{2}$-cup ice-cream scoop. The scoop will create equal portions of batter. Scoop alternating portions of chocolate and white batter in the bottom of the pan, creating a full and even layer. This first layer will only be as thick as the ice-cream scoop–size portions. Sprinkle the streusel evenly over the batter. Use a butter knife to very gently and superficially swirl the streusel into the batter; go only about $^{1}/_{4}$ inch down into the batter. Scoop the remaining batter into the pan, again using the ice-cream scoop and alternating batters. With the pan on the counter, firmly rotate back and forth once (left and right). This will help all the layers settle into one another.

5) Bake for 25 to 35 minutes, or until a long bamboo skewer inserted in the center shows a few moist crumbs when removed. The cake will look dry and perhaps a bit crusty on top. Cool in the pan set on a rack until just barely warm. Unmold and place directly on the rack to cool completely. The cake is ready to serve. Store at room temperature in an airtight container for up to 3 days.

almond mounds of joy
cake SERVES 14 TO 18

I f you are a candy bar fan, then the name of this cake will give you a good idea as to what's in store—loads of dark chocolate and flaked coconut. This rich sour cream chocolate Bundt-style cake has a thick tunnel of sweet, moist coconut in the center, just like a Mounds candy bar. And, like its other namesake candy bar, Almond Joy, it has whole almonds on top drenched in a satiny chocolate ganache glaze. This cake is moist and a good keeper; make it on Friday for Saturday or a Sunday brunch.

for the filling Put all the ingredients in a medium bowl and stir with a wooden spoon until combined; set aside.

for the cake Position a rack in the middle of the oven. Preheat the oven to 350°F. Thoroughly coat a 12-cup Bundt pan with nonstick spray, taking care to coat the center tube as well.

1) Whisk together the flour, cocoa, baking powder, baking soda, and salt in a medium bowl to aerate and combine; set aside.

2) In the bowl of a stand mixer, beat the butter with the flat paddle attachment on medium-high speed until creamy, about 2 minutes. Add the sugar and brown sugar gradually and continue to beat for about 3 minutes at medium-high speed, until very light and fluffy. Beat in the vanilla. Add the eggs one at a time, beating well after each addition. Add the flour mixture in three additions, alternately with the sour cream. Begin and end with the flour mixture and beat briefly until smooth. Spoon a little less than half of the batter (do this by eye) evenly into the pan and smooth the top with an offset spatula. Very carefully spoon the filling in a ring all the way around the pan, making sure that it is centered over the batter. You want to create a tunnel of coconut filling, so make sure that the filling does not touch the center or the outer edge of the pan. Carefully spoon the remaining batter on top; it will come almost to the top of the pan.

FILLING

2 cups lightly packed sweetened flaked coconut

½ cup plus 2 tablespoons sweetened condensed milk

¼ teaspoon vanilla extract

⅛ teaspoon almond extract

CAKE

3 cups all-purpose flour

¾ cup sifted Dutch-processed cocoa

1 teaspoon baking powder

½ teaspoon baking soda

½ teaspoon salt

2 cups (4 sticks) unsalted butter, at room temperature, cut into pieces

1¼ cups sugar

1 cup firmly packed light brown sugar

1 tablespoon vanilla extract

5 large eggs, at room temperature

2 cups full-fat sour cream

GLAZE

½ cup heavy cream

5 ounces semisweet chocolate, finely chopped, such as Valrhona Equitoriale (55%) or Ghirardelli (45%)

24 whole almonds, natural or blanched

3) Bake for 1 hour and 10 minutes to 1 hour and 15 minutes, or until a long bamboo skewer inserted in the center shows a few moist crumbs when removed. (Make sure you test the cake; do not insert the skewer into the filling). The cake will rise gently just over the top of the pan and develop a crust.

4) Cool in the pan set on a rack until just barely warm; this will take over an hour. Unmold and place directly on the rack to cool completely. The cake is ready to glaze.

for the glaze Put the cream in a large saucepan and bring to a boil over medium heat. Remove from the heat and immediately sprinkle the chocolate into the cream. Cover and allow to sit for 2 minutes to melt the chocolate. Gently stir the ganache until smooth. Allow to cool until slightly thickened. Use a pastry brush to brush some glaze all over the curved top of the cake; this will provide a sticky surface for the almonds. Arrange the almonds, broad side down, evenly around the top of the cake, nestling them among the ribs formed by the pan shape. Pour the rest of the glaze over the top of the cake, covering the almonds and allowing it to drip down the inside and outside of the cake. Chill briefly, or allow to sit at room temperature, to set the glaze. The cake is ready to serve. Store at room temperature in an airtight container for up to 3 days; after that, refrigerate for up to 2 days longer. Bring to room temperature before serving.

poppy seed–honey-apricot
pastries MAKES 20 PASTRIES

The idea for this recipe grew from my love of moist poppy seed fillings often found in Danish, hamantaschen, and similar pastries. Getting the right texture does involve grinding the poppy seeds, and while some Hungarian bakers might have a poppy seed grinder handy, most of us do not. You could crush them with a mortar and pestle, but I have had the best luck with blade-style coffee grinders. A food processor does not work; the seeds are too small. Once ground, the poppy seeds are combined and cooked with honey, milk, raisins, and apricot spread, and the mixture becomes rich, thick, and almost chewy. Poppy seeds are most economical when bought in bulk from a natural foods store or from a purveyor such as Penzeys (see Resources, page 287; order the blue poppy seeds). The apricot spread can be found near the jams and jellies and is simply a 100 percent fruit "jam." It allows for maximum fruit flavor without added sugar. The pastry is rich and flaky and you will not believe how easy it is. It rivals classic Danish dough in flakiness and buttery satisfaction yet is as easy to make as cookie batter. These freeze very well.

for the pastry Whisk together the flour and salt; set aside.

1) In the bowl of a stand mixer, beat the butter and cream cheese with the flat paddle attachment on medium-high speed until smooth, about 2 minutes. Beat in the sugar gradually and continue beating until creamy. Gently beat in the sour cream and vanilla by pulsing the machine on and off a few times. Add the flour and salt in two to three batches, beating briefly between each addition, scraping down the bowl once or twice. Beat until just combined.

2) Scrape the dough onto a large sheet of plastic wrap, wrap it up completely, and shape it into a flat, round disk. Refrigerate for at least 2 hours, or overnight. The dough may be frozen for up to 1 month; defrost in the refrigerator overnight.

for the filling Grind the poppy seeds in a clean coffee grinder in two or three batches. Scrape into a medium saucepan as each batch is

PASTRY

2 cups all-purpose flour

⅛ teaspoon salt

1 cup (2 sticks) unsalted butter, at room temperature, cut into pieces

4 ounces whole-milk cream cheese, at room temperature

¼ cup sugar

¼ cup full-fat sour cream

1 teaspoon vanilla extract

FILLING

1¼ cups poppy seeds

⅔ cup whole milk

Generous ½ teaspoon finely grated lemon zest

½ cup raisins, chopped
5 tablespoons apricot spread
5 tablespoons honey

EGG WASH AND GLAZE
1 large egg
3 tablespoons apricot spread
2 tablespoons water

finished. Add the remaining filling ingredients and stir to combine. Bring to a simmer over medium heat, stirring frequently, and cook for 3 to 5 minutes, until very thick. Cool completely. The filling is ready to use or may be refrigerated in an airtight container for up to 3 days.

1) Line 2 jelly-roll pans with parchment paper; set aside. Roll out the dough on a lightly floured work surface into a 24 X 12-inch rectangle; it will be about ⅛ inch thick. Spread the filling evenly over the dough, leaving a ½-inch border on one long side. Starting with the opposite long side, roll up tightly like a jelly roll and use your hands to compress the roll and form it into an even cylindrical shape. That bare ½-inch border you left will help create a seal. Cut crosswise into 20 even pieces (which will be a little over 1 inch wide) and place on the prepared pans, leaving the pieces upright. Compress the pieces gently, if necessary, to keep them from falling over. Refrigerate while the oven preheats.

2) Position racks in the upper and lower third of the oven. Preheat the oven to 350°F.

for the egg wash Whisk the egg well in a small bowl. Brush over the tops of the pastries.

1) Bake for 30 to 35 minutes, or until the pastries are light golden brown. Cool completely on the jelly-roll pans set on racks.

for the glaze Whisk together the apricot spread and water in a small bowl until combined. Brush the glaze all over the cooled pastries.

1) The pastries may be served right away or stored at room temperature in an airtight container in single layers separated by parchment paper for up to 3 days. The pastries may also be frozen in an airtight container for up to 1 month. Defrost overnight in the refrigerator and bring to room temperature before serving.

passion fruit–citrus pound cake

with tropical fruit SERVES 12

Here is a rich, buttery pound cake brightened with lemon, lime, and orange zest, served with a mélange of tropical fruit and a tart and tangy passion fruit curd. Read the Tip on the next page for more information on buying fresh passion fruit. To extract the pulp, simply slice in half crosswise over a bowl to catch any juices, and scoop the pulp and seeds into the bowl with a teaspoon.

for the curd Put the yolks, eggs, pulp, and sugar in a heavy-bottomed medium saucepan. Whisk together to break up the eggs. Add the butter and cook over medium-low heat, whisking frequently. When the mixture begins to bubble around the edges, lower the heat and whisk constantly until it thickens and reaches 170°F. (The temperature is more important than the time it takes, and the curd itself should not boil.) The curd will thicken and should form a soft shape when dropped from a spoon. Strain into a clean bowl and discard the seeds and any stringy pulp. Let cool to room temperature, stirring occasionally to release the heat. Scrape into an airtight container and refrigerate for at least 6 hours or up to 3 days.

for the cake Position a rack in the middle of the oven. Preheat the oven to 325°F. Thoroughly coat a 12-cup Bundt pan with nonstick spray, taking care to coat the center tube as well.

1) Whisk the flour, baking powder, and salt together in a small bowl to aerate and combine; set aside.

2) In the bowl of a stand mixer, beat the butter on medium-high speed with the flat paddle attachment until creamy, about 3 minutes. Add the sugar gradually, beating until light and fluffy, about 3 minutes, scraping down the bowl once or twice. Beat in the zests and lemon juice. Beat in the eggs one at a time, scraping down after each addition, allowing each egg to be absorbed before continuing. Add the

PASSION FRUIT CURD

6 large egg yolks

2 large eggs

¾ cup passion fruit pulp, with seeds (from 7 or 8 passion fruit, see headnote)

¼ cup sugar

¼ cup (½ stick) unsalted butter, at room temperature, cut into pieces

CITRUS POUND CAKE

3 cups sifted cake flour

1¼ teaspoons baking powder

⅓ teaspoon salt

2 cups (4 sticks) unsalted butter, at room temperature, cut into small pieces

2¼ cups sugar

2 tablespoons plus 2 teaspoons finely grated lemon zest

1½ tablespoons finely grated lime zest

1½ tablespoons finely grated orange zest

1½ tablespoons freshly squeezed lemon juice

8 large eggs, at room temperature

TROPICAL FRUIT

2 medium ripe mangoes

1 medium (6- to 8-inch) ripe papaya

2 ripe green kiwi

1 ripe carambola (star fruit)

½ cup red raspberries

½ cup blackberries

DECORATION

2 ripe passion fruit

Small orchids, optional, such as *Oncidium* orchids in complementary colors

flour mixture in three additions, beating until smooth on low-medium speed after each addition. Scrape the batter into the prepared pan.

3) Bake for 50 to 55 minutes, or until a long bamboo skewer inserted in the center shows a few moist crumbs when removed.

4) Cool in the pan set on a rack until barely warm, then unmold onto a cooling rack to cool completely. The cake is ready to serve or store at room temperature in an airtight container for up to 3 days. It may also be wrapped in plastic wrap and placed in a zipper-top bag and frozen for up to 1 month.

for the fruit Dice the mangoes and papaya. Peel and slice the kiwi in half lengthwise, then cut crosswise in ¼-inch-thick slices. Cut the star fruit into ¼-inch-thick slices and toss the fruit together gently in a bowl. Toss in the berries. The fruit is ready to serve or may be refrigerated in an airtight container for up to 6 hours.

for the decoration and assembly Place the cake on a decorative platter. Cut open the passion fruit and scrape the pulp and seeds along the top of the cake and fill the center with the fruit mixture (any extra fruit can be placed around the cake or served in a bowl on the side). If desired, further decorate with a few orchids here and there; remove before serving.

1) Serve the passion fruit curd on the side and serve some with each slice.

TIPS Passion fruit are about the size of a small lemon; I prefer the rusty purple-brown variety. When ripe they will be extremely wrinkled; if you buy them when they are still smooth, it might take a week or more for them to ripen at room temperature. The pulp will vary from greenish yellow to bright orange. For the pan, I use the Kaiser La Forme Charlotte Bundform pan for its great decorative shape. Just make sure you use a 12-cup ring pan. When testing doneness, use a long bamboo skewer so that you can get all the way down to the bottom of the pan. The other technique to follow is to allow the cake to cool until barely warm, which might take 30 minutes or more. If you unmold it too early, the cake will break. The orchids can be found at or ordered from a florist.

gianduja banana baby cakes

with hazelnut streusel MAKES 48 MINI MUFFIN–SIZE BABY CAKES OR

ABOUT 16 STANDARD MUFFINS

> G ianduja (jahn-DOO-ya) is an Italian chocolate-hazelnut blend, in this case milk chocolate. It looks like bar chocolate, but is a tad softer due to the nut content, and there is no coarse texture; it is ultra-smooth. These baby cakes are big on flavor and texture: a moist banana cake, studded with chunks of gianduja, topped with a crunchy hazelnut streusel. For best banana flavor, make sure the bananas have no trace of green and have begun to take on black speckles.

STREUSEL

⅔ cup all-purpose flour

⅔ cup firmly packed light brown sugar

½ cup hazelnuts, toasted (see page 23), skinned, and roughly chopped

5 tablespoons unsalted butter, melted

¼ teaspoon salt

BATTER

2 cups all-purpose flour

2 teaspoons baking powder

1 teaspoon baking soda

1 teaspoon salt

4 ounces gianduja, cut into ¼-inch chunks, such as Callebaut (26%)

⅔ cup firmly packed light brown sugar

6 tablespoons (¾ stick) unsalted butter, melted

for the streusel Stir together all of the ingredients in a small bowl, using a wooden spoon, until well blended. Use your fingers to clump the streusel together into small ¼- to ½-inch pieces; set aside.

for the batter and assembly Position a rack in the middle of the oven. Preheat the oven to 400°F. Line four 12-cup miniature muffin tins with miniature paper liners. Coat the tops of the pans with nonstick spray; some batter might overflow and this will prevent sticking.

1) Whisk the flour, baking powder, baking soda, and salt together in a small bowl to aerate and combine. Toss in the gianduja chunks; set aside.

2) Whisk together the brown sugar and butter in a medium bowl until well blended. Whisk in the egg and vanilla until combined, then fold in the banana. Gently fold in the dry mixture just until combined. Divide the batter evenly in the pans. Top evenly with the streusel, pressing gently into the batter to help it adhere.

3) Bake for 12 to 15 minutes, or until a toothpick inserted in the centershows a few moist crumbs when removed. Cool in the pans

set on racks for 5 minutes, and then remove the cakes to a cooling rack to cool completely. Store at room temperature in an airtight container for up to 3 days.

1 large egg, at room temperature

1½ teaspoons vanilla extract

3 medium ripe bananas, roughly smashed with a potato masher

TIP You may bake these in standard-size muffin tins, in which case the yield will be about 16 and they will bake for 18 to 20 minutes.

baking unforgettable muffins and baby cakes

Call them what you will, what these have in common is that they are all individual cakes baked in cupcake/muffins tins, either of standard size or miniature. There is something special about getting a whole cake to oneself, even if it's diminutive in nature. To make them even more distinctive, you can choose from a large selection of paper liners; there is so much more out there than the expected pastel-colored ones from the supermarket. They instantly give the cakes a more polished look, and you can easily find ones simple, whimsical, or elegant in both standard and miniature size. See the Resources section (page 287) for my favorite suppliers.

These tiny cakes require very careful baking, as even 1 minute too long or too little, especially for the mini size, can make the difference between a moist result and one that is very dry. Follow the time cues suggested in the recipes, but also pay careful attention to the visual cues. Also, pans will make a huge difference. Flimsy cupcake/muffin pans that do not conduct heat evenly are a recipe for disaster from the get-go. I use heavyweight nonstick pans such as Wilton's Excelle nonstick muffin pans. I like them because of their even heating capabilities, and also because they have a broad area on either end that makes it easy to grab them while wearing an oven mitt. Believe it or not, whether or not you use paper liners—and what liners you choose—will also affect baking times. If you use paper liners, the cupcakes or muffins, in general, will take a tad longer to bake than if the batter is baked directly in the pans. This is because the paper actually insulates the batter a little bit. However, if you use aluminum or other foil-type liners, they will conduct heat and the cupcakes or muffins will be done sooner.

browned butter–almond brunch cake

with blueberry sauce SERVES 8

This single-layer cake, covered with toasted almonds, boasts the rich flavor of browned butter. Ground almonds also add to the texture. It is a simple cake, perfect for brunch or afternoon coffee or tea, with or without its blueberry sauce. The sauce can be made up to 3 days ahead, so take advantage of this do-ahead component.

SAUCE

1½ cups fresh or defrosted frozen blueberries

¼ cup sugar

¼ cup water, divided

½ teaspoon cornstarch

½ teaspoon freshly squeezed lemon juice

CAKE

½ cup (1 stick) unsalted butter, at room temperature, cut into pieces

1½ teaspoons vanilla extract

1½ cups blanched sliced almonds, divided

½ cup all-purpose flour

1 cup sugar, divided

¼ teaspoon salt

6 large egg whites

¼ teaspoon cream of tartar

for the sauce Put the blueberries, sugar, and 3 tablespoons of the water in a medium saucepan and bring to a boil over medium heat. Stir until the sugar dissolves. Stir the remaining 1 tablespoon water and the cornstarch together in a small bowl and add to the sauce. Simmer the sauce for 1 to 2 minutes, until thickened. Stir in the lemon juice. Cool to room temperature. Refrigerate in an airtight container for up to 3 days. Bring the sauce to room temperature before serving.

for the cake Position a rack in the middle of the oven. Preheat the oven to 350°F. Coat a 9-inch round loose-bottom or springform pan with nonstick spray, line the bottom with a parchment round, then spray the parchment.

1) Melt the butter in a small saucepan over medium heat. Continue cooking until the surface looks foamy and the butter begins to brown. The aroma will smell nutty and there will be brown specks sinking to the bottom of the pan. Remove from the heat and cool to warm. Stir in the vanilla.

2) In a food processor fitted with the metal blade attachment, combine 1¼ cups of the almonds, the flour, ½ cup of the sugar, and the salt. Process until the mixture is very finely ground and powdery.

3) In the clean, grease-free bowl of a stand mixer, add the egg whites and whip until frothy on low speed using the wire whip attachment.

Add the cream of tartar and turn the speed to medium-high. When soft peaks form, add the remaining ½ cup sugar gradually. Continue whipping until stiff, but not dry, peaks form. Fold the dry mixture into the egg whites, taking care not to deflate the mixture. Drizzle the butter over the batter and fold in thoroughly, again taking care to preserve as much volume as possible. Scrape the batter into the pan and smooth the top with an offset spatula. Sprinkle the remaining ¼ cup almonds evenly over the top.

4) Bake for 35 to 40 minutes, or until a toothpick inserted in the center shows a few moist crumbs when removed. The cake will be tinged light golden brown and will have begun to come away from the sides of the pan. Cool the cake in the pan set on a rack for 5 minutes. Unmold, peel off the parchment, and place top side up directly on the rack to cool completely. The cake is ready to serve. Alternatively, place the layer on cardboard and double-wrap in plastic wrap; store at room temperature if serving within 24 hours. Simply cut the cake into wedges and serve with some sauce poured on top and alongside.

fresh red currant scones

with currant cream   MAKES 6 SCONES

The currant scones you are most likely familiar with are made with dried currants. These feature fresh tart red currants, which retain their jewel-like color even after baking. You will be rewarded with a rich, tender, slightly crumbly scone flecked with bright red pockets of fruit. The same fruit, made into a spreadable cream, turns deep pink. These obviously can only be made when fresh currants are available, so keep an eye out at the market and take advantage when you see them, which will typically be in late summer. The cream can be made several days ahead; the scones are best eaten within a day.

CURRANT CREAM

1¾ cups stemmed fresh red currants (about two 5.6-ounce packages)

1 tablespoon water

¼ cup sugar

2 large eggs, at room temperature

1 tablespoon unsalted butter, cut into pieces

SCONES

½ cup plus 1 tablespoon heavy cream

1 large egg

2¼ cups all-purpose flour

¼ cup plus 2 tablespoons sugar

1 tablespoon baking powder

½ teaspoon salt

6 tablespoons (¾ stick) unsalted butter, chilled

Scant 1 cup stemmed fresh red currants (about one 5.6-ounce package)

1 tablespoon coarse sanding sugar

for the cream Put the currants and water in a small saucepan and cook over medium heat for about 2 minutes. Crush with a potato masher and simmer for about 3 minutes more. Scrape into a strainer set over a deep bowl. Press the fruit very firmly so as to extract as much pulp and liquid as possible. Discard the solids, which will be mostly seeds. You should have about ¾ cup of thin puree; it will be very liquidy. Return the liquid to the saucepan and whisk in the sugar. Whisk in the eggs to blend well, then add the butter. Cook over medium heat, whisking often. When the mixture begins to bubble around the edges, lower the heat and whisk constantly until the mixture thickens and reaches 170°F. Let cool to room temperature, stirring occasionally to release the heat. Refrigerate in an airtight container for at least 6 hours or up to 1 week.

for the scones Position a rack in the middle of the oven. Preheat the oven to 425°F. Line a jelly-roll pan with parchment paper; set aside.

1) Whisk the cream and egg together in a small bowl; set aside. In the bowl of a stand mixer, put the flour, sugar, baking powder, and salt and combine on low speed using the flat paddle attachment. Add the butter and pulse on and off until it forms a very coarse meal; there might be pockets of butter that are larger, which is fine. Drizzle

in the cream-egg mixture with the mixer running on low speed and mix just until beginning to combine.

2) When it is about halfway mixed, add the currants and continue mixing just until combined.

3) Turn the mixture out onto the prepared pan in one large clump and pat down into a large patty about 1 inch thick and about 8 inches across. Sprinkle the top with coarse sugar. Cut into 6 even wedges; separate the wedges by wiggling your knife back and forth, and then scoop up with a spatula and arrange evenly spaced on the pan.

4) Bake for 15 to 20 minutes, or until very light golden brown and a toothpick inserted in the center just tests clean. Cool on the pan set on a rack for about 5 minutes. These are best served warm from the oven or at least the same day they are baked. They can be stored loosely wrapped in aluminum foil for up to 1 day and reheated in a toaster oven. Serve with the Currant Cream.

french crullers

with rose-amaretto glaze MAKES 8 CRULLERS

Starting with a choux paste, these are piped with a pastry bag, and then deep-fried. They are simply the lightest and most elegant of doughnuts. The glaze is scented with both a touch of amaretto liqueur and rose water, and while the glaze is still sticky, edible rose petals are strewn on top. Needless to say, these are showstoppers. The batter and glaze come together very quickly, and these are best eaten ultra-fresh, so plan accordingly. The rose water can be found in specialty stores or some supermarket international aisles. The petals should be unsprayed; the color or colors are up to you.

ROSE-AMARETTO GLAZE

1 cup sifted confectioners' sugar

2 tablespoons whole milk

1 teaspoon Disaronno Amaretto

½ teaspoon rose water, such as Al Wadi

Edible rose petals (from about 5 large roses)

PÂTE À CHOUX

Flavorless vegetable oil, such as canola or sunflower

1 cup water

6 tablespoons (¾ stick) unsalted butter, cut into pieces

¼ teaspoon salt

1 cup all-purpose flour

3 large eggs, at room temperature

Pastry bag

Large star decorating tip, such as Ateco #827

for the glaze Whisk together the sugar, milk, amaretto, and rose water in a small bowl until smooth. Cover the bowl with plastic wrap and set aside. Put the loose rose petals in a small bowl.

for the pâte à choux Pour the oil into a heavy, straight-sided pan (such as a 4¼ quart about 11 inches across) to a depth of 3 inches. Clip a deep-fry thermometer to the side of the pan with the tip immersed in the oil but not touching the bottom of the pan. Alternatively, use a deep-fat fryer as directed by the manufacturer. Line a jelly-roll pan with several layers of paper towels and place near the fryer. Cut eight 5-inch squares of parchment paper, arrange them on another jelly-roll pan, and coat them thoroughly with nonstick spray; set aside.

1) Combine the water, butter, and salt in a medium saucepan. Bring to a rolling boil over medium-high heat, make sure the butter has melted, and immediately remove from the heat.

2) Quickly stir in the flour all at once. Keep stirring with a wooden spoon until the batter comes together. Place over very low heat and keep stirring. You want the dough to dry out. This will take 1 minute or less; the pâte à choux should come cleanly away from the sides of the saucepan. Scrape the dough into the bowl of a stand mixer fitted with the flat paddle attachment.

3) Turn on low-medium speed and add the eggs one at a time, allowing each egg to be absorbed before continuing. The batter should be smooth, golden yellow, and firm enough to hold a shape when mounded with a spoon.

4) Scrape the dough into a pastry bag fitted with the tip. Pipe out 8 rings, 2½ to 3 inches across, each one on a prepared parchment square. It is fine if the ends of the rings overlap a bit. If the end of the ring sticks to the pastry tip, use kitchen scissors to snip it free.

5) Heat the oil over high heat to 350°F (and adjust the heat to maintain the temperature). Pick up one parchment square and carefully but swiftly invert it so that the cruller slides into the oil (take care and do not let your fingers touch the hot oil). Fry 3 or 4 crullers at a time; do not crowd them in the pan. Fry until golden brown on the first side, about 2 minutes, then turn over using a slotted spoon and fry until the second side is golden brown. Drain on the paper towel–lined pan.

6) Immediately apply the glaze all over the top surfaces of each cruller with a pastry brush. Sprinkle with the rose petals while the glaze is wet. Serve as soon as possible, preferably within 2 hours.

cookies and bars

COOKIES AND THEIR brethren, bar cookies, range from simple, buttery shortbread with four ingredients to the elegant, and admittedly persnickety, French macaroon that requires a pastry bag to form. The simpler ones are a great place to begin one's exploration of baking. When I ask home bakers what the first recipe is that they ever made, they all say "chocolate chip cookies," which makes sense, as they are easy to make with readily available ingredients and universally loved. Whether they are simple or more involved, cookies still require attention to detail. This is because, especially with a recipe such as shortbread with so few ingredients, the choice and measurement of ingredients and the care with which one approaches the remaining techniques will greatly affect the outcome. This chapter might be for "just cookies," but you absolutely can create exceptional, unforgettable ones with attention to detail.

I believe the one major mistake that bakers make with cookies is to overbake them. Baking pans hold residual heat and cookies will continue to bake after they are removed from the oven. Thirty seconds to a minute more of heat can mean the difference between a chewy cookie turning crispy and a crispy cookie over browning taking on burnt flavors, and drying out. The recipes give suggested baking times as well as visual cues for doneness, and when used together, they will give you great results.

how to bake unforgettable cookies and bars

* Always measure out cookie batter accurately.

* For best uniformity, use a sized scoop when suggested in recipes.

* Always use the exact size brownie/bar pan called for.

* Use the time cues and the visual cues when mixing and baking for best results.

* Rotate pans front to back halfway through the baking time for even baking.

* Do not overbake—I believe the number-one problem with baking cookies is overbaking.

* Baking cookies even 1 minute extra can be the difference between chewy and crispy.

* Cool cookies properly. There is a lot of residual heat on baking pans, so if the recipe calls for transferring to a cooling rack at a particular time, please follow the directions.

* If your cookies cannot afford to take on any residual heat while cooling, slide the parchment paper onto a cooling rack immediately.

* Make sure cookies are cooled completely before placing in a storage container or else the heat might create condensation.

* Store cookies according to individual instructions. In general, store crisp cookies separately from soft, chewy cookies. Soft cookies will lend moisture to crisp cookies, making them soggy. I store each and every recipe in separate containers so there is no flavor transfer either (in other words, chocolate cookies separate from simple shortbread).

* To keep cookies crisp, there is a product called Blue Magic. It is a device the size of a Ping-Pong ball with a hollow clear glass bottom and metal perforated top. Inside the glass cup is a dry chemical that absorbs moisture. It is inexpensive and can be mail-ordered (See Resources, page 288). Just place in the storage container along with your crisp cookies—it's great for meringues and dacquois too.

baking cookies on jelly-roll pans and using parchment paper

After baking literally thousands of cookies at home, in my bakery, and while researching my books on cookies, I have found the best tools and techniques for the task. Commercial-style aluminum jelly-roll pans, also referred to as half sheet pans, have repeatedly given me the best results. They do not warp, they are inexpensive and sturdy, and because they conduct heat so evenly, burned cookie bottoms become a thing of the past. The fact that they have a lip is no detriment, in my opinion, and in fact, since they can also be used for thin layers of cake batter or rounds of meringue and dacquoise, they are more versatile. I am not partial to air-cushioned pans, as they sometimes prevent browning so efficiently that hardly any browning takes place at all; some is necessary to bring out the best flavor in many cookies.

Parchment paper is used for several reasons. It provides a nonstick surface for your cookies and makes cleanup easier. But my favorite reason is one you might not have thought of. When baking cookies we must always take into consideration that the pans will hold residual heat, and the cookies will continue to bake even after they come out of the oven. If you have miscalculated your baking time, and your cookies are done but bordering on being overdone, you can remove the pan from the oven, grasp the edge of the parchment paper, and in one swift motion transfer the cookies, still on the paper, onto a cooling rack. In this way, you have removed them from the hot pan and effectively ceased any further baking. It is a great technique that has saved many a batch for me.

dark brown sugar–chocolate chunk bars
with chocolate-molasses glaze MAKES 25 BARS

These bars are based on a blondie-style recipe, but the dark brown sugar brings a deeper, richer level of molasses flavor; it is indeed molasses that is added to sugar to make it brown. The molasses is echoed in the glaze; if you have never tasted dark chocolate and molasses together, you are in for a treat. The combination is sophisticated, with a bitter edge. They would make a surprising addition to an upscale bake sale or an office party.

BARS

1¼ cups all-purpose flour

Heaping ½ teaspoon baking powder

⅛ teaspoon salt

4 ounces bittersweet chocolate, cut into shards, such as Valrhona Caraïbe (66%) or Scharffen Berger (70%)

½ cup (1 stick) unsalted butter, melted

1 cup firmly packed dark brown sugar

1 teaspoon vanilla extract

1 large egg

CHOCOLATE-MOLASSES GLAZE

⅓ cup heavy cream

7 ounces bittersweet chocolate, finely chopped, such as Valrhona Caraïbe (66%) or Scharffen Berger (70%)

2 tablespoons unsulphured molasses

for the bars Position a rack in the middle of the oven. Preheat the oven to 350°F. Coat an 8-inch square pan with nonstick spray.

1) Whisk the flour, baking powder, and salt together in a small bowl to aerate and combine; toss in the chocolate shards and set aside.

2) Whisk together the melted butter and brown sugar. Whisk in the vanilla and then the egg, blending well. Allow the mixture to cool slightly, then stir in the flour mixture, mixing just until blended. Spread evenly into the prepared pan.

3) Bake for 20 to 25 minutes, or until a toothpick inserted in the center shows a few moist crumbs when removed. The bars should be light golden brown, slightly puffed, and the edges will have begun to come away from the sides of the pan. Cool in the pan set on a rack.

for the glaze Heat the cream in a medium-size saucepan over medium heat just until it comes to a boil. Remove from the heat and immediately sprinkle the chocolate into the cream. Cover and let sit for 5 minutes; the heat will melt the chocolate. Stir gently until smooth; then stir in the molasses. Allow to cool at room temperature until thick enough to spread, about the consistency of soft mayonnaise. Spread evenly over the cooled bars still in the pan using a small offset spatula. Chill briefly to set the glaze. Cut into 25 bars (5 x 5). Store at room temperature for up to 3 days in an airtight container in single layers separated by parchment paper.

TIP Start with a large hunk of bulk chocolate and use a large chef's knife to shave off shards. They will vary from very tiny rice-size pieces to ones more closely approaching pecan size. These textures are more sophisticated than morsels or chips, although you may substitute about ¾ cup morsels, if desired.

cacao percentages and substituting chocolates

When chocolate is called for in a recipe, I have given you the cacao percentage, when available from the manufacturer. The total cacao percentage is made up of cacao solids and cocoa butter. We do not know the individual percentages of the cacao solids and the cocoa butter within any brand. This is just one of the reasons why one 60 percent dark chocolate can taste so different from another 60 percent chocolate—and why tasting individual chocolates is so important. Generally, the higher the cacao mass number, the darker the chocolate, but because the rest of the chocolate is typically made up of sugar, additional cocoa butter, lecithin, and vanilla, and each chocolate is unique in its blend, you really do need to taste and make your own flavor comparisons. With milk chocolates you will see dairy products such as milk added to the list. White chocolate does not contain any cacao mass, but the better brands will have cocoa butter as their only fat and it is from this ingredient that they will derive whatever "chocolate" flavor that they do possess. Steer clear of any chocolates that list artificial flavors, preservatives, or any fat other than cocoa butter (such as palm oil, cottonseed oil, vegetable oil). If you want to successfully substitute one for another in a recipe, the place to start is with similar cacao percentages. The chocolates on page 22 are ones that I enjoy working with.

matcha tea leaf
shortbreads MAKES EIGHTY 2-INCH COOKIES

Classic shortbread cookies will never go out of style. The rich, buttery flavor and irresistible crumbly texture are incomparable. They are also very simple to make and lend themselves easily to variations. Matcha is Japanese green tea that is finely ground into a powder and used in the traditional Japanese tea ceremony. It is very concentrated in flavor and color, and you will probably have to mail-order it unless you have a well-stocked tea purveyor near you. As with all teas, there is a huge range of quality and prices. Ito En is a Japanese tea company that offers many matchas from which to choose. For baking I like their Kiri No Ne matcha, which not only has a lovely color and flavor profile, but also happens to be less expensive than many (see Resources, page 287). I suggest a range for the amount of the matcha; it has a distinct flavor that some might prefer on the nuanced side, in which case use the lesser amount. If you are a matcha fan, use the more generous proportion. The optional coarse sanding sugar can be sprinkled on half of the cookies; after baking, when both the sugared and plain cookies are arranged on a platter, it creates a nice contrast between sparkly and matte. The sugar can be ordered from Beryl's (again, see Resources). The leaf-shaped cookie cutter is a playful nod to that fact that these contain leaves—tea leaves.

1) Line 2 jelly-roll pans with parchment paper; set aside.

2) Whisk the flour and salt together in a small bowl to aerate and combine; set aside.

3) In the bowl of a stand mixer, beat the butter on medium-high speed with the flat paddle attachment until creamy, about 3 minutes. Add the matcha and beat until the mixture is a uniform green color and very creamy. Add the sugar gradually and continue beating on high speed until very light and fluffy. Turn the machine off, add about one third of the flour, then turn the machine on to low speed. Gradually add the remaining flour, mixing just until blended, scraping down the bowl once or twice. The mixture will look crumbly; if

2¼ cups all-purpose flour

¼ teaspoon salt

1 cup (2 sticks) unsalted butter, at room temperature, cut into pieces

1 to 2 tablespoons matcha (powdered green tea), to taste

½ cup sugar

1 tablespoon coarse sanding sugar, optional

you squeeze it between your fingers, it will come together. Gather it together into a ball with your hands while it is still in the bowl.

4) Roll out the dough to a ¼-inch thickness between two pieces of lightly floured parchment. Peel off the top parchment and cut the dough in half. Sprinkle the sanding sugar evenly over one half of the cookie dough and gently, with hardly any pressure, roll over it with a rolling pin to help it adhere. Using a 2 X 1-inch leaf-shaped cookie cutter, cut out as many cookies as possible from both doughs and place on the prepared pans 1 inch apart. Use the back of a sharp paring knife to make vein patterns on each cookie (see photo). Refrigerate for 1 hour or up to overnight, if desired.

5) Position racks in the upper and lower third of the oven. Preheat the oven to 325°F. Bake for 17 to 22 minutes, or until the cookies are dry and firm to the touch; their color will not change. They should retain their shape if you try to pick one up and there should also be a fragrant butter and matcha scent emanating from the oven. Cool on the pans set on racks for a couple of minutes, and then carefully transfer the cookies to racks to cool completely. Store at room temperature for up to 2 weeks in an airtight container.

TIP I used a "rose leaf" cookie cutter that is just shy of 2 inches long and 1 inch wide, which you can find at Beryl's (see Resources, page 287). You can certainly use a larger cookie cutter, or even a different shape, but the yield and baking times might change.

extreme milk chocolate
brownies

Milk chocolate contains milk solids, of course, and typically more sugar than dark chocolate, but there is a relatively new class of milk chocolate referred to as "dark" milk chocolate or "extreme" milk chocolate. These often have less sugar and they all have a higher cacao content. Whereas classic milk chocolate might have 11 percent or less cacao solids, now you can find milk chocolates with cacao contents of 30 percent, 40 percent, and more. They are darker in color and deeper and richer in flavor, and they add a whole new dimension to the baker's pantry. This thin, moist brownie features classic milk chocolate for the batter with darker milk chocolate bits scattered throughout. One caveat: This is a fairly plain-looking brownie, but if you like milk chocolate, its "plain brown wrapper" won't stop you.

1) Position a rack in the middle of the oven. Preheat the oven to 350°F. Coat a 9-inch square pan with nonstick spray.

2) Whisk the flour and salt together in a small bowl to aerate and combine. Add the dark milk chocolate and toss to coat; set aside.

3) Melt the butter and Callebaut or Ghirardelli chocolate together in the top of a double boiler or a microwave. Stir until smooth and let cool slightly.

4) In the bowl of a stand mixer, add the sugar, eggs, and vanilla and beat on high speed using the wire whip attachment until light and fluffy, 2 to 5 minutes. Gently fold in the chocolate-butter mixture until no chocolate streaks remain. Fold the flour-chocolate mixture into the batter until just combined. Spread evenly into the prepared pan.

5) Bake for 20 to 25 minutes, or until a toothpick inserted in the center shows a few moist crumbs when removed. The bars do not really change color. They will be slightly puffed and the edges will have begun to come away from the sides of the pan. Cool in the pan set on a rack. Cut into 16 bars (4 x 4). Store at room temperature for up to 4 days in an airtight container in single layers separated by parchment paper.

1 cup all-purpose flour

Pinch of salt

4 ounces dark milk chocolate, such as Valrhona Guanaja Lactée (41%), Michel Cluizel Mangaro Milk (50%), or Michel Cluizel Grand Lait Milk (45%), finely chopped

½ cup (1 stick) unsalted butter, at room temperature, cut into tablespoon-size pieces

4 ounces milk chocolate, such as Callebaut (31.7%) or Ghirardelli (31%), finely chopped

½ cup sugar

2 large eggs

1 teaspoon vanilla extract

cacao nib and caramelized
almond biscotti makes 36 biscotti

This is a fairly tender biscotti, due to the addition of butter in the dough, which is speckled with sliced almonds and cacao nibs. The finished biscotti are partially dipped in semisweet chocolate and sprinkled with caramelized almonds. These are an elaborate cookie, fancy enough to give as a gift.

CARAMELIZED ALMONDS

¾ cup blanched sliced almonds

¼ cup sugar

BISCOTTI

2 cups all-purpose flour

1½ teaspoons baking powder

¼ teaspoon salt

½ cup (1 stick) unsalted butter, at room temperature, cut into pieces

¾ cup sugar

2 large eggs

½ cup blanched sliced almonds

½ cup cacao nibs, such as Scharffen Berger

TOPPING

8 ounces semisweet chocolate, melted, such as Ghirardelli (45%), Callebaut (52%), Scharffen Berger (62%), or Bissinger's (60%)

for the almonds Line a jelly-roll pan with aluminum foil; set aside. Toss the almonds and sugar together in a 10-inch nonstick skillet. Heat over medium heat, watching carefully and stirring often, until the sugar begins to melt and caramelize. The mixture will not change for several minutes and will continue to look sandy, and then all of a sudden the sugar will begin to melt and darken in color very quickly. Stir continuously at this point; you are trying to evenly coat the almonds with a golden brown liquefied caramelized sugar, at which point immediately scrape them out onto the prepared pan, separating the nuts as well as you can. Allow to sit at room temperature to harden for about 10 minutes. The nuts are ready to use. They may be made 1 week ahead and stored at room temperature in an airtight container.

for the biscotti Position racks in the upper and lower third of the oven. Preheat the oven to 350°F. Line 2 jelly-roll pans with parchment paper; set aside.

1) Whisk the flour, baking powder, and salt together in a small bowl to combine and aerate; set aside.

2) In the bowl of a stand mixer, beat the butter on medium-high speed with the flat paddle attachment until creamy, about 3 minutes. Add the sugar gradually and continue beating on high speed until very light and fluffy. Add the eggs one at a time, beating well after each addition. Turn the machine off, add about one-third of

the flour, then turn the machine on to low speed. Gradually add the remaining flour, mixing just until blended, scraping down the bowl once or twice. Fold in the almonds and cacao nibs.

3) Form the dough into two 10-inch-long logs directly on one of the prepared pans, spaced evenly apart. Bake for 25 to 35 minutes, or until just turning light golden brown. The logs will be dry to the touch but still have some spring to them. Cool in the pan on a rack for 20 minutes, then carefully transfer the logs to a cutting board. Use a serrated knife and cut the biscotti on a diagonal into pieces $^1\!/_2$ to $^3\!/_4$ inch wide. You will have many biscotti and will now need both pans. Use a wide, flat spatula to carefully transfer the biscotti to the pans, spacing at least $^1\!/_4$ inch apart. Place flat side down and bake for 12 to 15 minutes, flipping them over halfway through baking. They should be very dry and light golden brown. Cool completely on the pans set on racks.

for the topping Have the caramelized almonds at hand. Have the melted chocolate in a deep, narrow bowl. Dip one end of each cookie into the melted chocolate to cover about one-quarter of the cookie on both sides. Gently shake excess chocolate back into the bowl. Place the cookie back on the pan and immediately sprinkle the wet chocolate with some of the caramelized almonds. Repeat with the remaining biscotti and chill briefly in the refrigerator to set the chocolate. Store at room temperature for up to 5 days in an airtight container in single layers separated by parchment, or refrigerate for up to 2 weeks. Bring to room temperature before serving.

TIPS Natural, skin-on almonds can be used, but they will make the biscotti look a little less elegant and the texture will be a bit drier; but I understand that in some markets that is all you can find. When caramelizing the almonds, it is all about the color. You want the caramel to be dark enough to give that rich caramel flavor, but not so dark that it is burnt. This fine line can literally be a 10-second window, so watch the caramelization process carefully.

florentine bars

with candied orange and cherries MAKES 40 SQUARES

F lorentine cookies are my very favorite, owing to the combination of caramelized sugar, chocolate, nuts, and sweet/tart fruit. However, their classic round shape is often hard to accomplish, due to their lacy, freeform nature. Here, the traditional cookie is a topping for a thin shortbread, all of which is formed in a pan—easier to make and to serve but with all of the classic ingredients and flavors. These cookies are so fabulous, by the way, that it was rumored that fellow rivals thought I had bribed a dog show judge with them during a very high-level competition. "What an insult to the judge," I exclaimed to a friend. "And," she said, "what a compliment to your cookies!"

SHORTBREAD

2¼ cups all-purpose flour

¼ teaspoon salt

1 cup (2 sticks) unsalted butter, at room temperature, cut into pieces

½ cup sugar

½ teaspoon vanilla extract

FLORENTINE FILLING

6 tablespoons (¾ stick) unsalted butter, at room temperature, cut into pieces

⅔ cup sugar

⅓ cup heavy cream

3 tablespoons honey

1 cup blanched sliced almonds

½ cup dried cherries, chopped

½ cup diced candied orange peel

¼ cup all-purpose flour

1) Position a rack in the middle of the oven. Preheat the oven to 350°F. Coat a 13 x 9-inch pan with nonstick spray, line the bottom with parchment cut to fit, then spray the parchment.

for the shortbread Whisk the flour and salt together in a small bowl to aerate and combine; set aside.

1) In the bowl of a stand mixer, beat the butter with the flat paddle attachment on medium-high speed until creamy, about 2 minutes. Add the sugar and continue to beat until very light and fluffy, about 3 minutes more. Beat in the vanilla. Gradually add the flour, mixing just until blended, scraping down the bowl once or twice. Pat the crust into an even layer in the prepared pan.

2) Bake the crust for 20 to 25 minutes, or until just beginning to turn very light golden brown along the edges; it should be dry to the touch. Prepare the filling while the crust is baking.

for the filling Put the butter, sugar, cream, and honey in a medium saucepan, attach a candy thermometer, and cook over medium heat, stirring occasionally, until the butter melts. Turn the heat to medium-high, bring to a boil, and cook to 235°F. The mixture will have thickened and the surface will be covered with large bubbles. Remove from the heat and stir in the nuts, fruit, and flour until well combined.

TOPPING

2 ounces semisweet chocolate, melted, such as Scharffen Berger (62%) or Bissinger's (60%)

1) Pour the filling over the partially baked crust and bake for another 20 to 25 minutes, or until the filling is bubbling and has turned light golden brown all over. The color might be darker around the edges. Cool completely in the pan set on a rack.

for the topping Put the melted chocolate in a parchment cone and make a freeform zigzag pattern all over the bars. Chill to set the chocolate; cut into 40 bars (5 × 8). Refrigerate for up to 1 week in an airtight container in single layers separated by parchment paper. Bring to room temperature before serving. Do not serve to judges of any sort, ever.

cutting bar cookies

To cut bar cookies cleanly and evenly, my preferred approach uses a metal bench scraper. Grab the tool firmly by the handle and press the long, straight, sharp edge straight down into the bars; repeat to make a complete cut either across or down the length of the pan by lifting and pressing, lifting and pressing. If the bars are sticky, wipe the blade clean between cuts with a warm, damp cloth. Cutting in this fashion eliminates the drag created by pulling a knife through a pan of bars; the edges will be cleaner and you will get prettier results. Also, since you can look down upon the bars and press and cut, it is easier to keep the lines straight. After you have cut your grid (8 x 5, 6 x 6, etc.), you can also use the bench scraper as a lever to pop the first one out and help get the subsequent ones out as well, although at this point, switching to a small offset spatula is usually best.

classic shortbread

MAKES ABOUT FORTY 1-INCH SHORTBREADS

I have been making shortbread for years and thought I had arrived at a formula that was "best." It was rich and buttery and very pale—all the qualities I thought I desired. And then one day, while eating a Walker's shortbread that was part of an airline snack (Is this ironic or what?), I reveled in its butteryness but also its richness, and perhaps for the first time also noticed that there was a pronounced hit of salt. I had always liked their version, and all of a sudden I realized that they were also actually quite golden. It was a light-bulb moment. It made so much sense that further baking, which allows for browning of the cookie and caramelization of the sugar, would produce a richer taste. Back to the drawing board for me. After much research, and arriving at the fact that the classic Scottish recipe was one part sugar, two parts butter, and three parts flour, I followed this lead, making sure there was a sufficient amount of salt. Then, baking at 350°F instead of 325°F, as I used to do, and baking them enough so that there was some coloration, I arrived at my current favorite shortbread. It is crisp, very buttery, and flavorful, with a balance of sweet and salt that makes it a perfect partner for fruit-based or custard desserts or any cookie tray. It also keeps very well and is sturdy enough to mail, making it a great cookie for gift giving.

¾ cup all-purpose flour

⅛ teaspoon salt

½ cup (1 stick) unsalted butter, at room temperature, cut into pieces

¼ cup sugar

1) Line two jelly-roll pans with parchment paper; set aside.

2) Whisk the flour and salt together in a small bowl to combine and aerate; set aside.

3) In the bowl of a stand mixer, beat the butter on medium-high speed with the flat paddle attachment until creamy, about 3 minutes. Add the sugar gradually and continue beating on high speed until very light and fluffy. Turn the machine off, add about one-third of the flour, then turn the machine on to low speed. Gradually add the remaining flour, mixing just until blended, scraping down the bowl once or twice. The mixture might look crumbly; if you squeeze it between your fingers, it will come together. Gather it together into a ball with your hands while it is still in the bowl.

4) Lightly flour your work surface. Roll the dough out to a ¼-inch thickness and cut out cookies with a 1-inch round cookie cutter, fluted or plain. Transfer the cookies to the pan, spacing them 1 inch apart. Gently gather together the extra dough and cut out as many cookies as possible. Refrigerate until firm, about 1 hour or up to overnight, if desired.

5) Position racks in the upper and lower third of the oven. Preheat the oven to 350°F. Bake for 15 to 20 minutes, or until the cookies are golden brown around the edges and a light golden brown all over. Cool on the pans set on racks for 5 minutes, then carefully transfer the cookies to racks to cool completely. Store at room temperature for up to 2 weeks in an airtight container.

TIP Although I have made these bite-size, they can of course be made larger. A 2-inch round cookie cutter will yield approximately 20 cookies; they should be baked a few minutes longer. Just bake until beginning to turn light golden brown in whatever shape you choose. Hearts are lovely for Valentine's Day; these also make great winter holiday cutout cookies. Just make sure you bake similar-size cookies on each pan.

cranberry gingerbread
cookies MAKES ABOUT TWENTY-TWO 3-INCH SANDWICH-STYLE COOKIES

The spicy aroma of these cookies wafting from the oven seems to herald the holiday season in one whiff. This is a classic gingerbread cookie filled with cinnamon, ginger, nutmeg, and cloves, along with molasses and brown sugar. You assemble them sandwich-style, the top with a peekaboo cutout allowing the cranberry jam to show through. The jam is very quickly and simply made from cranberries and sugar; the berries have enough natural pectin to gel. You will need a 3-inch cookie cutter and a 1-inch cookie cutter, but you can pick and choose shapes as you like, even mixing and matching, such as a 3-inch round cookie cutter and a 1-inch star.

FILLING

¾ cup sugar

⅓ cup water

One 12-ounce bag fresh or frozen cranberries, washed and picked over

COOKIES

3¼ cup all-purpose flour

1 teaspoon baking soda

¼ teaspoon salt

1 cup (2 sticks) unsalted butter, at room temperature, cut into pieces

¾ cup firmly packed light brown sugar

2 teaspoons ground ginger

1 teaspoon ground cinnamon

¼ teaspoon ground nutmeg

¼ teaspoon ground cloves

½ cup unsulphured molasses

1 large egg, at room temperature

for the filling Stir the sugar and water together in a medium saucepan until the sugar dissolves. Add the cranberries and bring to a boil over medium-high heat. Turn the heat down and simmer until most of the berries pop, about 3 minutes. Allow to cool, stirring occasionally to release the heat. Scrape into the bowl of a food processor fitted with the metal blade attachment and process until smooth, about 10 seconds. The filling is ready to use. It may be refrigerated in an airtight container for up to 3 days.

for the cookies Whisk together the flour, baking soda, and salt in a small bowl to aerate and combine; set aside.

1) In the bowl of a stand mixer, beat the butter with the flat paddle attachment on medium-high speed until creamy, about 2 minutes. Add the brown sugar gradually and continue to beat until very light and fluffy, about 3 minutes more. Beat in the spices, molasses, and egg, beating well until combined, scraping down the bowl once or twice. Turn the machine off, add about one-third of the flour, then turn the machine on to low speed. Gradually add the remaining flour, mixing just until blended, scraping down the bowl once or twice. Scrape the dough onto a large piece of plastic wrap. Use the wrap to help shape a large, flat disk, and then cover it with plastic

wrap. Refrigerate for at least 2 hours or until firm enough to roll. The dough may be refrigerated overnight. You may freeze the dough for up to 1 month, double-wrapped in plastic wrap; defrost in the refrigerator overnight before proceeding.

2) Position racks in the upper and lower third of the oven. Preheat the oven to 350°F. Line 2 jelly-roll pans with parchment paper; set aside.

3) Remove about one-quarter of the dough from the refrigerator. Keep the remaining dough refrigerated while you proceed. Roll out the dough to a ¼-inch thickness on a lightly floured surface. Cut out 3-inch cookies in the shape of your choice. Place on the prepared sheets 2 inches apart. Cut out 1-inch cookies from the center of half the cookies. If you like, you can bake the 1-inch cookies together on a third pan, as their baking time will be less. They will not be used in the 3-inch cookie assembly, but can be served as is, or sandwiched together with one another. Repeat with the remaining dough. You will need to reuse the pans a few times. Take care to make sure you have the same number of solid cookie bottoms and cutout cookie tops.

4) Bake for 10 to 12 minutes, depending on size. They should just begin to color, which is hard to see because they are naturally tawny. They should feel dry to the touch, but still give a little toward the centers. It is very important to bake them just until this point and to still be able to feel some softness. They firm up upon cooling, and you actually want them to remain a bit soft and chewy. Cool on the pans set on racks for a few minutes, and then transfer the cookies to racks to cool completely.

for the assembly One at a time, take a solid cookie and spread about 1 tablespoon of the cranberry filling on the flat bottom side of the cookie. Top with another cookie, with cutout top, placing the flat bottom side against the filling. Gently press together. Repeat with the remaining cookies. Store at room temperature in an airtight container in single layers separated by parchment for up to 2 days, or refrigerate for up to 4 days. Bring to room temperature before serving.

TIP You will use the jelly-roll pans a few times, but these cookies bake best if there are only two pans in the oven at a time. Cool the pans in between batches.

mallowmores

In the northeastern United States, you can find Nabisco Mallomars in the cookie aisle on a seasonal basis, but they are so much more than a cookie. This nostalgic favorite is comprised of a circular graham cracker–like cookie topped with a thick marshmallow filling and covered with a crisp, dark chocolate shell. They are sort of a commercial s'more and have been produced since 1913. They have fierce devotees and similar confections can be found worldwide, sometimes with more of a shortbread base, sometimes differing in shape from the domed, squat American classic. They are called Whippets in Canada, Krembos in Israel, Flodebolle in Denmark, Tunnock's teacakes in the United Kingdom, Zefir in Russian-speaking countries, Schokokuss in Germany, and Mallowpuffs in New Zealand. Now you can make them in your own kitchen. The graham cookie can be made a day or two ahead, as can the marshmallow, so take advantage of these do-ahead steps to make the whole recipe easier. I went with a square shape to eliminate waste—and as an homage to our campfire s'mores.

for the marshmallows Coat a 13 x 9-inch pan with nonstick spray, line the bottom with parchment cut to fit, and then spray the parchment.

1) Pour $^1/_2$ cup of the water into a small bowl. Sprinkle the gelatin over the water and set aside for 5 minutes to soften the gelatin.

2) Put the sugar, corn syrup, the remaining $^1/_3$ cup water, and the salt in a medium saucepan and stir to combine. Attach a candy thermometer and cook over medium heat until it reaches 240°F. Remove from the heat and whisk in the softened gelatin until dissolved. Cover the pot and leave on the stove with the burner turned off, to keep warm.

3) In the clean, grease-free bowl of a stand mixer, whip the egg whites on low speed using the wire whip attachment until frothy. Add the cream of tartar, turn the speed to medium-high, and whip until soft

MARSHMALLOWS

½ cup plus ⅓ cup room temperature water

2 tablespoons plus ½ teaspoon unflavored powdered gelatin

2 cups sugar

½ cup light corn syrup

⅛ teaspoon salt

2 large egg whites, at room temperature

⅛ teaspoon cream of tartar

¾ teaspoon vanilla extract

Cornstarch, sifted

GRAHAM CRACKERS

1 cup plus 1 tablespoon all-purpose flour

½ teaspoon baking soda

¼ teaspoon salt

¼ cup (½ stick) unsalted butter, at room temperature, cut into pieces

¼ cup plus 1 tablespoon firmly packed dark brown sugar

1 tablespoon honey

½ teaspoon vanilla extract

2 tablespoons whole milk

TOPPING

24 ounces semisweet chocolate, finely chopped, such as Ghirardelli (45%) or Valrhona Equitoriale (55%)

peaks form. Pour a thin, steady stream of the sugar syrup directly over the meringue with the mixer running. Do not pour any on the whip or the sides of the bowl. Whip the meringue until cool to the touch; this could take 5 minutes or more. Beat in the vanilla. The marshmallow should be thick and glossy and form medium-firm peaks.

4) Immediately spread the marshmallow in the prepared pan with an offset spatula, pressing down into the corners and smoothing the top. Lightly dust the top with a thin veneer of cornstarch. Let sit at room temperature for 6 hours or overnight. Sprinkle a piece of parchment with cornstarch, run an icing spatula around the edges of the marshmallow, and invert it on top of the parchment. Peel the parchment off of the marshmallow if it comes loose from the pan. Use a long, sharp, thin-bladed knife to cut into about forty $1\frac{1}{2}$-inch squares (8 X 5). The marshmallows may be used immediately, or they may be stored, in which case toss with some cornstarch to prevent them sticking to one another. Store at room temperature in an airtight container for up to 3 days before assembling the cookies.

for the grahams Line 2 jelly-roll pans with parchment paper; set aside.

1) Whisk together the flour, baking soda, and salt in a small bowl to aerate and combine; set aside.

2) In the bowl of a stand mixer, beat the butter with the flat paddle attachment on medium-high speed until creamy, about 2 minutes. Add the sugar and honey and continue to beat until creamy, about 3 minutes more. Beat in the vanilla. Add the flour mixture in two additions, alternately with the milk. Begin and end with the flour mixture and beat until combined. Lightly flour your work surface. Roll the dough out to a $\frac{1}{4}$-inch thickness and cut out cookies in $1\frac{1}{2}$-inch squares. Transfer the cookies to the prepared pans, spacing them 1 inch apart. Gently gather together the extra dough and cut out as many cookies as possible. Refrigerate while the oven preheats. Position racks in the upper and lower third of the oven. Preheat the oven

to 350°F. While the oven preheats, make sure the marshmallows are ready to use. If they have been coated with cornstarch, shake them gently to remove any excess.

3) Bake the grahams for 12 to 14 minutes, or until the cookies are dry to the touch but still have a tiny bit of spring to them. Do not bake until crisp. Their color will barely change. Place the pans on racks and immediately, while the cookies are still warm, place a marshmallow on top of each. The heat of the cookie will seal the marshmallow to the cookie, which is very important for the following chocolate dipping step. Cool completely on the pans set on racks.

for the assembly Melt the chocolate in the top of a double boiler or in a microwave. Put in a narrow, deep bowl. Pick up one cookie at a time and plunge it, marshmallow side down, into the chocolate. The chocolate should cover the marshmallow completely as well as the sides of the cookie. Lift out of the chocolate and shake gently back and forth to encourage excess chocolate to drip off. Place cookie side down back on the pan and repeat with the remaining cookies. Refrigerate briefly to set the chocolate. Store at room temperature for up to 3 days in an airtight container in single layers separated by parchment paper. Alternatively, they may be refrigerated for up to 1 week. Bring to room temperature before serving.

TIPS The physical beauty of these cookies will depend on how cleanly and neatly you cut the cookies and the marshmallows, so take care during those steps. Also, dipping the cookies can be tricky. If you do not place the marshmallows on the cookies immediately after they come out of the oven, the heat from the cookies will have dissipated and not be enough to semi-melt the bottoms of the marshmallows. There won't be enough heat to affix them to the cookie. You will know whether this step worked or not when you try to dip the cookies because the marshmallows will fall off. An alternate method for dipping would be to place the marshmallow-topped cookies on a clean cooling rack set over a clean jelly-roll pan lined with aluminum foil. The melted chocolate can be poured over the cookies, and you can help it stick to the sides with a few swipes of a small offset spatula. Any excess chocolate that drips down onto the pan can be reused.

giant meringue pillows
with almonds   MAKES 8 LARGE MERINGUES

Meringues are naturally fat-free, so they make a great treat for those watching their fat intake. They are also very sweet, because by their very nature they proportionally have a large quantity of sugar. They are often baked until dry and crisp but still white in color. By allowing them to lightly brown, the sugar caramelizes, and the flavors deepen and become more complex. They are still sweet, but somewhat less so with the deepened color and flavor, and they will hit the spot if you are looking for a sugary, low-fat treat. Try these crumbled in a bowl with dead-ripe strawberries, crème fraîche, and perhaps a drizzle of honey

8 large egg whites
1 teaspoon cream of tartar
2 cups sugar
1 teaspoon vanilla extract
1½ cups sifted confectioners' sugar
¼ cup blanched sliced almonds

1) Position racks in the upper and lower third of the oven. Preheat the oven to 250°F. Line 2 jelly-roll pans with parchment paper.

2) In the clean, grease-free bowl of a stand mixer, beat the egg whites with the wire whip attachment on medium speed until foamy. Add the cream of tartar and whip until soft peaks begin to form, increasing the speed to medium-high. Add the sugar gradually and whip on high speed until stiff, glossy, but not dry, peaks form. Beat in the vanilla. Sift the confectioners' sugar over the meringue and fold in using a large rubber spatula. Use two large spoons to create 4 large oval mounds (about 5 X 4 inches) equally spaced apart on each pan. The tops do not have to be smooth and, in fact, a few peaks here and there will add texture. Scatter the almonds on top, dividing equally.

3) Bake for 1 hour and 25 minutes to 1 hour and 35 minutes, or until the exterior is dry; at this point they will still be white. Turn the oven up to 275°F. Continue to bake for 45 to 55 minutes more, or until they are an even pale beige overall. Cool completely on the pans set on racks. Store at room temperature for up to 2 weeks in an airtight container.

giant ginger chews

These are big, gingery, and spicy, with a crackled appearance on top. They are on the soft side and have a great chew, which will be obliterated if overbaked, so take care. To add an interesting option, try the chopped chocolate-covered crystallized ginger.

1) Position racks in the upper and lower third of the oven. Preheat the oven to 350°F. Line 2 jelly-roll pans with parchment paper; set aside.

2) Whisk together the flour, chocolate-covered crystallized ginger, if using, minced crystallized ginger, baking soda, and salt in a medium bowl to aerate and combine; set aside.

3) In the bowl of a stand mixer, beat the butter with the flat paddle attachment on medium-high speed until creamy, about 2 minutes. Add the sugars gradually and continue to beat until creamy, about 3 minutes more. Add the spices, egg, and molasses and beat until smooth. Add the flour mixture in two additions and beat briefly on low speed until combined. Put the sugar into a small bowl. Use a $\frac{1}{4}$-cup ice-cream scoop (such as a Zeroll #16) or a $\frac{1}{4}$-cup dry measure to form cookies. Drop the cookies, one at a time, into the sugar and roll around to coat. Place the cookies on the prepared pans.

4) Bake for 12 to 15 minutes, or just until the cookies are firm around the edges and cracked on the surface, but still soft across most of the cookie when pressed lightly with a fingertip.

5) Cool completely on the pans set on racks. Store at room temperature for up to 4 days in an airtight container in single layers separated by parchment paper.

TIPS The flavor of these cookies depends on the freshness of your ground spices.

2¼ cups all-purpose flour

½ cup chopped chocolate-covered crystallized ginger, optional

¼ cup minced crystallized ginger

2 teaspoons baking soda

¼ teaspoon salt

3/4 cup (1½ sticks) unsalted butter, at room temperature, cut into pieces

½ cup firmly packed dark brown sugar

½ cup firmly packed light brown sugar

1 teaspoon ground cinnamon

1 teaspoon ground ginger

1 teaspoon finely grated fresh ginger

½ teaspoon ground cloves

1 large egg, at room temperature

¼ cup unsulphured molasses

⅓ cup sugar

pistachio macaroons

MAKES 20 SANDWICH-STYLE COOKIES

French-style macaroons have a bit of a reputation. Not only for being delectable—they are chewy, delicate, and melt-in-your-mouth wonderful all at the same time—but also for being problematic to make. They are among those recipes that seem to come out different every time. I do not want this to make you shy away from trying them, for they are simply one of the most impressive and tasty cookies that you will ever make. Just take care to read through the recipe thoroughly and follow my tips; the grinding and sifting of the nuts to a powder is most important. You will be rewarded with delicate pale green pâtisserie-worthy cookies filled with pistachio flavor, from the ground nuts in the batter as well as the filling.

MACAROONS

¾ cup shelled unsalted raw green pistachios, rubbed clean of papery skin

1¼ cups sifted confectioners' sugar

3 large egg whites

Pinch of salt

¼ cup sugar

Pastry bag and ½-inch plain round decorating tip, such as Ateco #806, Wilton #1A, or a standard coupler

FILLING

1 cup sifted confectioners' sugar

¼ cup shelled unsalted raw green pistachios, rubbed clean of papery skin

6 tablespoons (¾ stick) unsalted butter, at room temperature, cut into pieces

¼ teaspoon almond extract

¼ teaspoon vanilla extract

for the macaroons Line 2 jelly-roll pans with parchment paper; set aside. Put the nuts in a food processor fitted with the metal blade attachment and pulse on and off several times to begin the grinding process. Add the confectioners' sugar and process until they are as finely ground as possible. Scrape into a fine-mesh strainer set over a bowl and shake and press as much of the fine powder as possible through the strainer. Return what is left in the strainer to the food processor and grind again. Repeat the straining and processing one or two more times. You should be able to grind almost all of it into a fine powder; there might be a scant tablespoon of coarse nut-sugar mixture left in the strainer, which you should discard. Set the fine powder aside. Do not bother to wash the food processor; it will be used for the filling, and any leftover nut particles are fine.

1) In the clean, grease-free bowl of a stand mixer, whip the egg whites on low speed using the wire whip attachment until frothy. Increase the speed to medium-high and add the salt. When soft peaks form, add the sugar gradually. Continue whipping until stiff peaks form. Remove 2 tablespoons of the pistachio powder and set aside. Fold the remaining pistachio powder into the meringue in two

batches until evenly combined. Dollop about a tablespoon of batter onto a prepared pan. It should not completely hold its shape, nor should it puddle out into a flat disk, but rather should be somewhere in between. It should relax and soften slightly, losing any pointed "kiss"-like peak on top. Add the reserved pistachio powder if necessary to achieve the proper texture.

2) Scrape the batter into a pastry bag fitted with the tip and pipe mounds, about $1\frac{1}{4}$ inches across, at least 2 inches apart on the pans. Rap the pans firmly (and flatly) on the counter to release any air bubbles. Allow to sit at room temperature for 1 hour.

3) Position racks in the upper and lower third of the oven. Preheat the oven to 325°F. Bake for 10 to 12 minutes, or until the cookies are dry on the top. They should be smooth and gently domed; the insides will still be a little soft and moist and they should have developed a ruffled ring, or "foot," around the bottom of each cookie. Cool completely on the pans set on racks.

for the filling Grind the confectioners' sugar and nuts together in a food processor fitted with the metal blade attachment until as fine and powdery as possible (no need to sift). Add the butter with the machine running until creamy and combined. Pulse in the extracts.

for the assembly Make sure the macaroons are completely cooled. Use a small offset spatula to spread a small amount of filling on one cookie bottom, then sandwich together with another cookie (matching the cookies by size, if there is some variation). Macaroons may be served immediately, but I like to let them sit overnight at room temperature in an airtight container. Their flavor and texture seem to improve. Store at room temperature for up to 4 days in an airtight container. You may also experiment with freezing them. Many bakers do, but I think they suffer a little.

TIP Here is what can go wrong: The tops will crack; the cookies will not spread out into a nice domed circle; no foot will develop; they will look flat. However, these "problems" will still leave you with a very tasty cookie. So give it a go. Very experienced chefs have admitted to having issues with French-style macaroons, so you won't be alone in your plight or efforts. But it is still quite worthwhile to try.

almond macaroons

with raspberry–rose filling MAKES 20 SANDWICH-STYLE COOKIES

Review the Pistachio Macaroon headnote and Tip (pages 78 and 79) for some general information on French-style macaroons. These pale pink creations have a whimsical color as well as a delicate raspberry-rose flavor. You will need a tiny bit of fresh raspberry puree (jam will not do). I suggest buying frozen raspberries (no sugar added), defrosting ½ cup, and proceeding from there. The rose water can often be found at specialty markets, especially those featuring Indian foods. I use Al Wadi brand; it happens to be inexpensive, too.

MACAROONS

1⅓ cups blanched sliced almonds

1¼ cups sifted confectioners' sugar

3 large egg whites

Pinch of salt

¼ cup sugar

Pink gel or paste food coloring, such as Wilton Pink, optional

Pastry bag and ½-inch plain round decorating tip, such as Ateco #806, Wilton #1A, or a standard coupler

FILLING

½ cup raspberries, either fresh or defrosted frozen

1 cup sifted confectioners' sugar

6 tablespoons (¾ stick) unsalted butter, at room temperature, cut into pieces

¾ teaspoon rose water

for the macaroons Line 2 jelly-roll pans with parchment paper; set aside. Put the nuts in a food processor fitted with the metal blade attachment and pulse on and off several times to begin the grinding process. Add the confectioners' sugar and process until they are as finely ground as possible. Scrape into a fine-mesh strainer set over a bowl and shake and press as much of the fine powder as possible through the strainer. Return what is left in the strainer to the food processor and grind again. Repeat the straining and processing one or two more times. You should be able to grind almost all of it into a fine powder; there might be a scant tablespoon of coarse nut-sugar mixture left in the strainer, which you should discard. Set the fine powder aside. Do not bother to wash the food processor; it will be used for the filling, and any leftover almond particles are fine.

1) In the clean, grease-free bowl of a stand mixer, whip the egg whites on low speed using the wire whip attachment until frothy. Increase the speed to medium-high and add the salt. When soft peaks form, add the sugar gradually. Continue whipping until stiff peaks form. Remove 2 tablespoons of the almond powder and set aside. Fold half of the remaining almond powder into the meringue. Add the second half as well as a tiny bit of pink coloring, if desired. Fold until combined. Dollop about a tablespoon of batter onto a prepared

pan. It should not completely hold its shape, nor should it puddle out into a flat disk, but rather should be somewhere in between. It should relax and soften slightly, losing any pointed "kiss"-like peak on top. Add the reserved almond powder if necessary to achieve the proper texture.

2) Scrape the batter into a pastry bag fitted with the tip and pipe mounds, about 1¼ inches across, at least 2 inches apart on the pans. Rap the pans firmly (and flatly) on the counter to release any air bubbles. Allow to sit at room temperature for 1 hour.

3) Position racks in the upper and lower third of the oven. Preheat the oven to 325°F. Bake for 10 to 12 minutes, or until the cookies are dry on the top. They should be smooth and gently domed; the insides will still be a little soft and moist and they should have developed a ruffled ring, or "foot," around the bottom of each cookie. Cool completely on the pans set on racks.

for the filling Process the raspberries until smooth in the food processor fitted with the metal blade attachment. Scrape the raspberry mixture into a fine-mesh strainer set over a bowl and push through as much puree as possible. Measure out 1 tablespoon plus 1 teaspoon puree; set aside. (There should be just about this amount, with little waste). Discard the seeds. Replace the metal blade attachment in the processor. Put the confectioners' sugar and butter in the food processor and process until combined and creamy. Add the reserved puree and rose water and pulse on and off until combined.

for the assembly Make sure the macaroons are completely cooled. Use a small offset spatula to spread a small amount of filling on one cookie bottom, then sandwich together with another cookie (matching the cookies by size, if there is some variation). Macaroons may be served immediately, but I like to let them sit overnight at room temperature in an airtight container. Their flavor and texture seem to improve. Store at room temperature for up to 4 days in an airtight container. You may also experiment with freezing them. Many bakers do, but I think they suffer a little.

nutella linzer cookies

MAKES ABOUT 28 COOKIES

Ground hazelnuts make this a very rich cookie; the chocolate-hazelnut Nutella filling completes the picture and the resulting sandwich-style cookie is fancy, elegant, and, as a boon, keeps quite well. After chilling the dough, it becomes very hard. You might think it is too crumbly to roll out, but if you allow it to soften and knead it a bit, it will actually roll out very easily, especially if done between two pieces of parchment paper as suggested. While I do love the Nutella, I often fill some of the cookies with raspberry jam and some with apricot as well—three cookies in one! If you take this approach, I suggest using 100 percent fruit spread for maximum fruit-flavor impact. You will need two sizes of cookie cutters in the shape of your choice, although I particularly like hearts or stars. The larger should be about 2½ inches at its largest dimension and the smaller should be about 1¼ inches.

for the cookies Put the flour, nuts, sugar, and salt in the bowl of a food processor fitted with the metal blade attachment and process until the nuts are finely ground. Turn the machine on, add the butter a few pieces at a time through the feed tube, and process until evenly combined. Pulse in the almond extract and run the machine until the mixture begins to form large, moist clumps. Form into two very flat disks, wrap in plastic wrap, and refrigerate for at least 2 hours or until firm enough to roll. The dough may be refrigerated overnight or frozen for up to 1 month; defrost in the refrigerator overnight before proceeding.

1) Position racks in the upper and lower third of the oven. Preheat the oven to 325°F. Line two jelly-roll pans with parchment paper; set aside.

2) Remove one disk from the refrigerator and roll out to a ¼-inch thickness between two very lightly floured pieces of parchment. Cut out large cookies and place on the prepared cookie sheet at least 1 inch apart. Cut out a small cookie from the center of half the

COOKIES
2½ cups all-purpose flour

1 cup skinned whole hazelnuts

⅔ cup sugar

¼ teaspoon salt

1 cup (2 sticks) unsalted butter, at room temperature, cut into pieces

¼ teaspoon almond extract

TOPPING AND ASSEMBLY
½ cup confectioners' sugar

4 ounces semisweet chocolate, melted, such as Ghirardelli (45%), Callebaut (52%), or Bissinger's (60%)

¾ cup Nutella chocolate-hazelnut spread, at room temperature

cookies. If you like, you can bake these smaller cookies together on a third pan, as their baking time will be less. They will not be used in the large cookie assembly, but can be served as is, or sandwiched together with one another. Repeat with the remaining dough. You will need to reuse the pans a few times. Take care to make sure you have the same number of solid cookie bottoms and cutout cookie tops.

3) Bake for 10 to 12 minutes for the small cookies and 20 to 25 minutes for the larger cookies, or just until the cookies turn light golden brown around the edges. Cool completely on the pans set on racks.

for the topping and assembly To decorate the cookies, you have an option. Some of the cookies can be topped with a dusting of confectioners' sugar, while others can get a zebra-stripe of melted chocolate. Have all the large cutout "tops" on a jelly-roll pan. If you want a confectioners' sugar dusting, simply put that sugar in a fine-mesh strainer and dust the tops of the cookies. Alternatively, fill a parchment cone with the melted chocolate, snip a small opening, and make zigzags back and forth over the cookies. Allow the chocolate to firm up.

1) Use a small offset spatula to spread a thin layer of Nutella on the flat bottoms of the large solid cookies. Carefully sandwich the decorative cutout cookie tops with the cookie bottoms. The small cookies can be served as is, or sandwich them with filling as well. Refrigerate for up to 2 weeks in an airtight container in single layers separated by parchment paper. Bring to room temperature before serving.

butterscotch-pecan brownies
with boozy raisins   MAKES 36 BARS

This began life as a classic brownie, but that is where all similarity ends. These have the addition of semisweet chocolate, pecans as well as raisins, and a ribbon of a spirited, chewy whisky-enhanced caramel. Save these for the adults

1) Position a rack in the middle of the oven. Preheat the oven to 325°F. Coat a 9-inch square pan with nonstick spray.

2) Whisk the flour and salt together in a small bowl to aerate and combine. Toss in the raisins; set aside.

3) Melt 5½ ounces of the semisweet chocolate and the unsweetened chocolate in the top of a double boiler or a microwave. Stir until combined and smooth, then cool until just warm.

4) In the bowl of a stand mixer, beat the butter with the flat paddle attachment on medium-high speed until creamy, about 2 minutes. Add the sugars and continue to beat until light and creamy, about 3 minutes more. Beat in the vanilla. Add wwthe eggs one at a time, beating well after each addition. Beat in the melted chocolates until well combined. Add the flour mixture and beat briefly until smooth. Spread evenly into the prepared pan. Dollop the ButterScotch Sauce here and there over the brownies; use a butter knife to swirl it through the batter. Evenly scatter the remaining semisweet chocolate chunks and the pecan halves on top.

5) Bake for 25 to 30 minutes, or until a toothpick inserted into the brownie part shows a few moist crumbs when removed. Place the pan on a rack, brush the top with the whisky, and allow to cool completely. Cut into 36 bars (6 × 6). Store at room temperature for up to 3 days in an airtight container in single layers separated by parchment paper. They may be frozen for up to a month, in which case I double-wrap in plastic, then foil, and then slip into a zipper-top bag.

1¾ cups all-purpose flour

⅛ teaspoon salt

2 tablespoons raisins

8 ounces semisweet chocolate, cut into chunks, such as Ghirardelli (45%) or Callebaut (52%), divided

1 ounce unsweetened chocolate, finely chopped, such as Scharffen Berger (99%)

5 tablespoons unsalted butter, at room temperature, cut into pieces

⅓ cup sugar

⅓ cup firmly packed light brown sugar

1 teaspoon vanilla extract

2 large eggs, at room temperature

½ cup Boozy Raisin-Pecan ButterScotch Sauce (page 267; make sure to stir well to include the nuts and raisins)

¼ cup pecan halves, toasted (see page 23)

1 tablespoon Scotch whisky

almond–apricot brownies
with tart cherry ganache

Tart cherries and apricots both blend so harmoniously with almond paste that I can never decide which to use, so I have used both in this sophisticated, multilayered bar. A crisp almond shortbread forms the base; next comes a layer of 100 percent fruit (no sugar) apricot spread topped with a layer of almond paste. A fudgy brownie is baked right on top, and after cooling, the entire creation is spread with a bittersweet chocolate ganache bursting with moist pockets of tart cherries.

for the shortbread Position a rack in the middle of the oven. Preheat the oven to 325°F. Coat a 13 x 9-inch pan with nonstick spray.

1) In the bowl of a stand mixer, beat the butter with the flat paddle attachment on medium-high speed until creamy, about 2 minutes. Add the sugar gradually and continue to beat until very light and fluffy, about 3 minutes more. Beat in the almond extract. Add the flour and beat just until combined. Press the dough evenly into the pan.

2) Bake for 10 to 12 minutes, or until dry and just starting to color. Cool in the pan on a rack while preparing the subsequent layers. Increase the oven temperature to 350°F.

for the middle layer Heat the apricot spread in a small pan over medium-low heat. Brush or spoon an even layer over the shortbread, which will still be warm.

3) Roll out the almond paste on a lightly floured surface to the same size and shape as the pan and about ¼ inch thick. Place on top of the apricot layer. If it breaks into pieces, that's fine; just patch it together into an even layer, covering the apricot completely.

for the brownie Melt the chocolate and butter together in the top of a double boiler or a microwave. Cool briefly. Whisk in the sugar,

SHORTBREAD
½ cup (1 stick) unsalted butter, at room temperature, cut into pieces

¼ cup sugar

¼ teaspoon almond extract

1¼ cups all-purpose flour

MIDDLE LAYER
½ cup apricot spread

10 ounces almond paste (not marzipan)

BROWNIE
5 ounces bittersweet chocolate, finely chopped, such as Ghirardelli (60%), Callebaut (71%), or Scharffen Berger (70%)

6 tablespoons (¾ stick) unsalted butter, cut into large pieces

¾ cup sugar

2 large eggs, at room temperature

1¼ cups all-purpose flour

¼ teaspoon baking powder

¼ teaspoon salt

GANACHE

2 cups tart cherries, drained water-packed or defrosted frozen

3 tablespoons Disaronno Amaretto

⅔ cup heavy cream

14 ounces bittersweet chocolate, finely chopped, such as Ghirardelli (60%), Callebaut (71%), or Scharffen Berger (70%)

then whisk in the eggs one at a time, beating well after each addition. Stir in the flour, baking powder, and salt just until no white streaks remain. Pour the batter over the almond paste layer and smooth into an even layer using a small offset spatula.

1) Bake for 15 to 20 minutes, until a toothpick inserted in the brownie layer shows a few moist crumbs when removed. The brownie layer will look dull and a bit puffed, and the edges will have begun to come away from the sides of the pan. Cool completely in the pan set on a rack.

for the ganache Roughly chop the cherries so that most of them are halved, and some are still whole, but do not chop finely. Stir together with the liqueur in a small bowl and allow to macerate while you make the ganache. Put the cream in a medium saucepan over medium heat just until it comes to a boil. Remove from the heat and immediately sprinkle the chocolate into the cream. Cover and let sit for 5 minutes; the heat will melt the chocolate. Stir gently until smooth, then stir in the cherries and any of the macerating liquid. Allow to cool at room temperature until thick enough to spread, about the consistency of soft mayonnaise. Spread evenly over the brownies using a small offset spatula. Chill briefly to set the glaze. Cut into 32 bars (8 x 4). Refrigerate for up to 3 days in an airtight container in single layers separated by parchment paper, or freeze for up to 1 month.

pistachio butterballs

MAKES ABOUT 40 COOKIES

The pale green color of pistachios shows through the hefty coating of confectioners' sugar that envelops these cookies. They are rich and elegant and keep quite well. I love giving these as host/hostess gifts, since they are as pretty as they are unusual.

1) Put the pistachios, ½ cup of the confectioners' sugar, and the salt in the bowl of a food processor fitted with the metal blade attachment. Pulse on and off to break up the nuts, then process until the nuts are finely ground. Add the butter a few pieces at a time, pulsing on and off to incorporate, then run the machine until the mixture is smooth. Pulse in the almond extract. Add the flour and pulse the machine on and off until incorporated, scraping the dough down once or twice. Process until the dough begins to form a ball. Remove the dough from the machine, form into a very flat disk, wrap in plastic wrap, and refrigerate for at least 2 hours or until firm enough to roll into balls. The dough may be refrigerated overnight. You may freeze the dough for up to 1 month; defrost in the refrigerator overnight before proceeding.

2) Position racks in the upper and lower third of the oven. Preheat the oven to 350°F. Line 2 jelly roll pans with parchment paper.

3) Roll the dough between your palms with lightly floured hands into 1-inch balls and place on the prepared pans 2 inches apart. Gently flatten just enough so that they don't roll around the sheet.

4) Bake for 18 to 22 minutes, or until just turning light golden brown around the edges and on the bottoms. Cool on the pans set on racks for 5 minutes, then sift the remaining 1 cup confectioners' sugar over the warm cookies. After the cookies have cooled completely, roll them in the confectioners' sugar on the cookie sheet to cover completely. Store at room temperature in an airtight container for up to 2 weeks, along with the confectioner's sugar. Roll them around again right before placing on a serving tray.

¾ cup shelled unsalted green pistachios, rubbed clean of papery skin, lightly toasted (see page 22)

1½ cups sifted confectioners' sugar, divided

¼ teaspoon salt

1 cup (2 sticks) unsalted butter, at cool room temperature, cut into pieces

1 teaspoon almond extract

2 cups all-purpose flour

chocolate chunkochino
cookies MAKES ABOUT 28 COOKIES

The name of these chocolate- and espresso-filled cookies is meant to be evocative of the corner coffee bar where the combination of chocolate and coffee is often on display. This is a chocolate chip–style batter, with dark brown sugar as well as the addition of freshly ground espresso and chocolate nibs. Your choice of chocolate for the chunks is very important. I like Valrhona Caraïbe for these. This recipe features a quick and easy step that will make your cookies look like they are bursting with chocolate chunks—it is a food stylists' trick. Some of the chocolate chunks are reserved and then pressed onto the top of the cookies right before baking. They remain on the surface and give the cookies that look of chocolate abundance.

12 ounces bittersweet chocolate, cut into chunks, such as Valrhona Caraïbe (66%) or Callebaut (71%)

1½ cups all-purpose flour

½ teaspoon baking soda

¼ teaspoon salt

½ cup (1 stick) unsalted butter, at room temperature, cut into pieces

½ cup firmly packed dark brown sugar

½ cup sugar

2 tablespoons cacao nibs, such as Scharffen Berger

1 tablespoon freshly ground coffee, such as French or Italian roast

1 teaspoon vanilla extract

1 large egg, at room temperature

1) Set aside about ½ cup of the chocolate chunks for later use.

2) Whisk the flour, baking soda, and salt together in a small bowl to aerate and combine; set aside.

3) In the bowl of a stand mixer, beat the butter with the flat paddle attachment on medium-high speed until creamy, about 2 minutes. Add both sugars gradually and continue beating until light and fluffy, about 3 minutes more, scraping down the bowl once or twice; beat in the nibs, ground coffee, and vanilla. Beat in the egg. Add the flour mixture, mixing just until some floury streaks still remain. Add the larger amount of chocolate chunks and beat just until combined. Chill the dough for at least 2 hours or overnight. The dough may be frozen for up to 1 month, well wrapped in plastic wrap and placed in a zipper-top plastic bag; defrost in the refrigerator overnight before proceeding.

4) Position racks in the upper and lower third of the oven. Preheat the oven to 375°F. Line 2 jelly-roll pans with parchment paper; set aside.

5) Drop by generously rounded tablespoon (I use a Zeroll #40 scoop) 2 inches apart on the prepared pans. Using the reserved chocolate chunks, press pieces of chocolate on top of each cookie. Bake for 10 to

12 minutes, until light golden brown. The cookies will be a little soft in the center and firmer around the edges. Cool on the pans set on racks for 5 minutes, and then slide the parchment onto the racks to cool the cookies completely. Store at room temperature for up to 3 days in an airtight container in single layers separated by parchment paper.

making gorgeous, round, bakery-style drop cookies

Whether you buy cookies at a bakery or from the supermarket in a box, chances are they are all uniform in size and shape. Professionals have some easy techniques that you can employ at home so that your cookies will be as perfectly formed. Many drop cookie recipes call for cookies to be formed by generous or rounded "teaspoons" or "tablespoons." After years of baking, it finally occurred to me that these ever-present instructions were not very clear. Are we supposed to use a cereal teaspoon? A measuring teaspoon? Are we supposed to measure the dough flush with the top of the spoon? I know my mom taught me to gather up a generous amount of chocolate chip cookie dough with a cereal teaspoon, scraping it off with another teaspoon. But the blobs of dough were much larger than the teaspoon itself, so while calling this a "generous" or "rounded teaspoon" measure was somewhat descriptive, my cookies might very well have been quite different from what was expected. This is important for three reasons: First, the yield of a recipe depends on how a cookie batter or dough is measured. If you are expecting 2 dozen cookies, it is very disappointing to end up with a different amount, especially if it's less! Second, if cookies are measured to the correct size, not only will you get the appropriate yield, but they also will bake in the suggested time frame, which of course is geared toward that particular size cookie. Properly baked cookies depend on precise baking times. Third, if you use the right measure you will be rewarded with a batch of cookies that are all round, beautifully formed, and pretty much the same size and shape, which looks much more professional on the cookie tray. I use ice-cream–style scoops (also called food dishers) to form drop-style cookies. In my recipes that call for rounded teaspoons, I use a Zeroll #100 scoop; for rounded tablespoons I use a Zeroll #40. To use these tools, I scoop up cookie batter and scrape off the dough to be flush with the top of the scooper's bowl. See Ingredients and Equipment (page 17) for more information on these very useful kitchen tools. Larger sizes are also great for placing batter into muffins and cupcake tins.

TIP When you read this recipe you might think, "Oh this is just a glorified chocolate chip cookie." I say there is nothing wrong with that! The thing is that, as with so many cookie recipes, the preparation is fairly simple, but then our tendency is to throw them in the oven and lose focus. Baking time is very important here. Just 30 seconds to 1 minute too long and you will lose any chew this cookie has to offer, and it will become crispy. No less tasty, perhaps, and maybe you want them crispy, but the point is that by simply juggling the timing by about 1 minute you can control the outcome. I have written the recipe so that there will still be a bit of chewiness left to them even after cooling.

fruit desserts

FROM STONE FRUITS to berries, cherries, apples, pears, and bananas, the world of fruit has much to offer. While I certainly love to sink my teeth into a juicy peach or crunchy apple as a simple snack, there are times when a little embellishment can elevate fruit into a spectacular dessert. The key to any fruit dessert is to work with fruit at its peak, in season. Farmers' markets and greenmarkets are flourishing, and if you have one near you, shop for your fruit there; not only will your fruit be the freshest it can be, but you will be supporting your local farmers as well. And they usually don't mind, and even encourage, tasting beforehand. You want to start with fruit that tastes fabulous on its own.

Do take note, however, that some recipes require ripe fruit, while others work best with fruit that is still firm, perhaps a day or two before its ultimate peak ripeness. Individual recipes will tell you what you need.

Here you will find fritters, crisps, shortcakes, and fools, to name just a few, as well as what I believe is the ultimate biscuit-style strawberry shortcake.

ginger shortcakes
with caramelized nectarines and sour cream

The fruit in this shortcake is caramelized, which simply means exposing fruit to high heat so that the natural sugars in the fruit, as well as the sugars added, caramelize and provide that rich caramel-like flavor. The use of brown sugar accentuates the caramel flavors even further. This is worlds apart from the more expected strawberry shortcake, somehow more sophisticated, yet appreciated by traditionalists at the same time.

for the shortcakes Position a rack in the middle of the oven. Preheat the oven to 400°F. Line a jelly-roll pan with parchment paper; set aside.

1) In a large bowl, combine the flour, sugar, baking powder, ginger, and salt. Cut in the butter with two knives or a pastry blender until the butter is the size of flat raisins. Whisk the milk and egg in a small bowl to blend. Add the milk mixture to the dry ingredients and begin stirring with a wooden spoon to combine. Quickly add the crystallized ginger and stir just until a dough forms. Turn the dough out onto a lightly floured surface. Knead gently until the dough is smooth, about 5 turns. Pat out the dough to a 6 × 4-inch rectangle about 1 inch thick. Cut into 8 equal pieces; use your hands to shape each into a round biscuit. Arrange the biscuits on the prepared pan, spacing 2 inches apart.

2) Bake for 12 to 17 minutes or until a toothpick inserted in the center tests clean when removed. The tops will be light golden brown and the bottoms a tad darker. Cool on the pan set on a rack until lukewarm, about 10 minutes. The biscuits may be used warm at this point. Alternatively, store at room temperature for up to 8 hours,

SHORTCAKES

2 cups all-purpose flour

¼ cup sugar

1 tablespoon baking powder

1 teaspoon ground ginger

¼ teaspoon salt

½ cup (1 stick) chilled unsalted butter, cut into pieces

½ cup whole milk

1 large egg

¼ cup finely chopped crystallized ginger

FILLING

2 pounds peeled, pitted nectarines, thinly sliced (about 10 medium fruit to yield 6 cups sliced)

⅔ cup firmly packed light brown sugar

1 tablespoon freshly squeezed lemon juice

CREAM TOPPING

3 cups full-fat sour cream

⅔ cup sugar

loosely wrapped in foil. Rewarm for 10 minutes at 350°F before serving, if desired.

for the filling Combine the nectarines, brown sugar, and lemon juice in a large sauté pan over medium heat. Cook, stirring occasionally, until the nectarines give off juice and the sugar dissolves. Continue to cook, tossing frequently, for about 10 minutes, or until the fruit softens and the juices begin to caramelize. If there is a lot of juice, remove the fruit and reduce the juice to a thick syrup. Recombine the fruit and syrup if necessary. The filling may be held at room temperature for 2 hours.

for the topping Gently whisk together the sour cream and sugar in a small bowl until smooth, but not too loose. Let sit for 5 minutes to dissolve the sugar. This may be made 1 hour ahead and refrigerated in an airtight container.

for the assembly Right before serving, cut the shortcakes in half horizontally. Place the bottom halves, cut side up, in 8 shallow dessert bowls. Top each with the nectarines, and then the sour cream topping, and crown with a shortcake top, cut side down.

TIPS You actually have a choice here as to whether to peel the nectarines or not. Peeled fruit will give you a slightly more elegant look and texture. I actually like the skin, and if the fruit is very fresh with a nice thin skin, I have been known to leave it on; it's your choice. Also, when halving the shortcakes, try to pry the two halves apart with a fork, as opposed to slicing them in half with a knife. The slightly uneven texture created by this method will hold in the juices and soak up the cream even better.

spiced plum
pavlovas

In the mid-1920s, Russian ballerina Anna Pavlova toured Australia and New Zealand and made such an impression that a namesake dessert began appearing in restaurants. It is a slightly chewy meringue round topped with cream and fruit, usually served as one large dessert to be divided among diners. The original was said to be as light and airy as the dancer's quality of movement. The meringue was meant to mimic the shape of her tutu, the cream was reminiscent of its lacy frills, and the original fruit used, kiwi, was supposed to represent the green silk roses on her costume. This recipe offers individual pavlovas and uses lightly spiced red-fleshed plums.

for the pavlovas Position a rack in the middle of the oven. Preheat the oven to 350°F. Line a jelly-roll pan with parchment paper; set aside.

1) In the clean, grease-free bowl of a stand mixer, whip the egg whites on low speed using the wire whip attachment until frothy. Add the cream of tartar and turn the speed to medium-high. When soft peaks form, add the superfine sugar gradually. Continue whipping until stiff, glossy peaks form. Beat in the cornstarch, vinegar, vanilla, and cardamom. Drop the meringue mixture onto the prepared pan in 6 mounds, evenly spaced apart. Use the back of a spoon to make a depression in the center of each pavlova. Put the pavlovas in the oven and immediately reduce the temperature to 250°F.

2) Bake for 45 to 55 minutes, or until the pavlovas are dry on the outside and have taken on a pale straw color. The centers will still be soft. They should easily lift off the parchment without breaking. Cool completely on the pan set on a rack. The pavlovas are ready to serve or may be stored at room temperature in an airtight container for up to 2 days.

for the plum filling Put the plums, sugar, lemon juice, and cardamom in a large skillet. Cook over medium-high heat, tossing occasionally,

PAVLOVAS
4 large egg whites

¼ teaspoon cream of tartar

1 cup superfine sugar

2 teaspoons cornstarch

½ teaspoon apple cider vinegar

½ teaspoon vanilla extract

¼ teaspoon ground cardamom

PLUM FILLING
7 to 9 medium, ripe red or purple plums, pitted and cut into eighths (to yield 4 cups), such as Black Beauty, Santa Rosa, or Cassleman

½ cup sugar

1 tablespoon freshly squeezed lemon juice

½ teaspoon ground cardamom

CREAM TOPPING
1½ cups crème fraîche

2 tablespoons sugar

until the sugar dissolves, about 5 minutes. Cook until the plums are tender but still hold their shape, stirring occasionally, about 3 minutes longer. Cool to room temperature. The plums are ready to serve or may be refrigerated for up to 2 days in an airtight container. Bring to room temperature before serving.

for the topping Beat the crème fraîche and sugar in a medium bowl with a large balloon whisk until soft peaks form. Let sit for 5 minutes to dissolve the sugar. The topping may be made 1 hour ahead and refrigerated in an airtight container. Rebeat to stiffen, if necessary.

for the assembly Place the pavlovas on serving plates. Spoon the plum mixture into the center depressions and any juice around the pavlovas on the plate. Top the plums with the cream topping and serve immediately.

mango, banana, and pineapple
chocolate crisp SERVES 6

Apple crisp is a fall classic. I have always loved the crunchy brown sugar–oat topping and wondered how it would work with tropical fruit. And being a fan of chocolate-dipped bananas, I figured, why not add cocoa to the topping? It works. This is delicious and unexpected. But I have to tell you, it is not much to look at. The cocoa-enhanced crisp is dark and plain looking. However, when I made 17 desserts at once for a massive tasting, this was the only dessert that was finished, the baking dish scraped clean. Score one for the plain Janes of the food world. Expect an unassuming look but with a huge payoff in flavor and texture.

1) Position a rack in the middle of the oven. Preheat the oven to 375°F. Coat a 9½ X 1½-inch pie plate or decorative ovenproof dish with nonstick spray. Place the baking dish on top of a parchment-lined jelly-roll pan (to catch drips).

for the topping In a medium bowl, stir together the brown sugar, oats, flour, cocoa, cinnamon, and salt. Sprinkle the butter pieces over the top of the dry ingredients. Cut in using a pastry blender, two knives, or your fingers until the crisp topping resembles a chunky granola. You do want it to be in clumps, not loose. Squeeze the clumps together with your fingers, if necessary. The topping may be frozen in a zipper-top bag for up to 1 month; just defrost as the oven preheats.

for the filling Toss all of the filling ingredients together in a medium bowl. Scrape into the prepared baking dish. Scatter the topping evenly over the fruit.

1) Bake for 35 to 45 minutes, or until the topping is crisp and lightly browned, and the fruit is bubbling around the edges. Let sit for 10 minutes before serving. It may be served warm or at room temperature but is best eaten the day it is made.

TOPPING

¾ cup packed light brown sugar
⅔ cup old-fashioned rolled oats (not quick or instant)
6 tablespoons all-purpose flour
3 tablespoons sifted natural cocoa
Generous ¼ teaspoon ground cinnamon
Scant ¼ teaspoon salt
6 tablespoons (¾ stick) chilled unsalted butter, cut into pieces

FILLING

3 large, ripe bananas
3 cups mango chunks (about ½-inch pieces, from 4 to 6 mangoes)
2 cups fresh pineapple chunks (½-inch pieces, from approximately half a pineapple)
¼ cup gold rum, such as Mount Gay Eclipse
¼ cup packed light brown sugar
3 tablespoons all-purpose four
2 teaspoons freshly squeezed lime juice

fruit desserts (97)

summer berry vacherin
with crème fraîche SERVES 8

A vacherin is a meringue confection, sometimes layered and filled with ice cream, sometimes with whipped cream. The name *vacherin* comes from its supposed visual similarity to the French cheese of the same name—the commonality being the fact that they are both round, somewhat white, and creamy. Since meringue by definition is so sweet, I like to pair it with a tangy whipped crème fraîche. The berries can be any combination that you like—I use strawberries, blueberries, and two colors of raspberries. The addition of golden raspberries raises the elegance factor. This dessert is a big, impressive affair, but with a casual look. It is comprised of two meringue disks piped with a star tip, which gives texture in look and feel. Two additional rings of meringue are also piped out and used to build up the top of the "cake," which is then filled with the cream and fruit. The vacherin improves in texture upon refrigeration for a few hours, as the crispy, chewy meringue, soft cream, and juicy fruit meld together to produce more than a sum of its parts. At this point, or upon serving, the meringue might crack, lending a rustic look that I think it is part of its charm. Think "shabby chic."

VACHERIN

1¼ cups sifted confectioners' sugar

1 tablespoon cornstarch

4 large egg whites

¼ teaspoon cream of tartar

¾ cup superfine sugar

Pastry bag

Large star decorating tip, such as Ateco #835 or Wilton #2110

for the vacherin Position racks in the upper and lower third of the oven. Preheat the oven to 275°F. Line 2 jelly-roll pans with parchment paper. Trace two 8-inch circles on each paper, situated so that they are spaced apart. Flip the paper over. You should be able to see the circles through the parchment.

1) Whisk together the confectioners' sugar and cornstarch in a medium bowl to aerate and combine; set aside.

2) In the clean, grease-free bowl of a stand mixer, whip the egg whites on low speed using the wire whip attachment until frothy. Add the cream of tartar and turn the speed to medium-high. When soft peaks form, add the superfine sugar gradually. Continue whipping until stiff, glossy peaks form. Fold in the confectioners' sugar mixture.

CREAM AND BERRIES

1 cup crème fraîche

1 cup heavy cream

¼ cup sifted confectioners' sugar

1½ cups blueberries

1½ cups raspberries, preferably half red and half golden

1½ cups sliced strawberries (about 6 ounces)

3) Scrape the meringue into the pastry bag fitted with the star tip. Using two of the traced circles as a guide, begin in the middle of the circle and pipe a spiral to create two solid 8-inch disks. Pipe a ring along the outer 8-inch border for each remaining traced circle.

4) Bake for 45 to 55 minutes, or until the meringues are dry on the outside. They should easily lift off of the parchment without breaking. Cool completely on the pan set on a rack. The meringues are ready to assemble or may be stored at room temperature for up to 2 days in an airtight container.

for the cream and berries At least 1 hour before serving, and up to 4 hours ahead, whip the crème fraîche, heavy cream, and confectioners' sugar with the wire whip attachment on medium-high speed until soft peaks form. Watch very carefully at this point and whip on medium speed just until stiff peaks form. Toss the berries together gently in a bowl; set aside.

1) Place one meringue disk, top side up, on a serving platter. Top with a little less than half of the cream, spreading in an even layer with an offset spatula. Scatter a little less than half of the berries on top of the cream. Top with the second meringue disk, top side up. Spread with a thin layer of cream and place one meringue ring on top. Spread a little cream on top of the first ring, and then place the second ring on top (the cream will act as "glue"). Scrape the remaining cream within the rings and top with the remaining berries. Refrigerate for at least 1 hour and up to 4 hours. Serve cold.

TIP Superfine sugar is just what it sounds like. Its extra-fine texture dissolves more readily than regular granulated sugar. Sometimes it is used for its attractive, unique, sparkly, visual appeal, such as when used to make sugared fruit, and in these cases, you should purchase it. However, when it is to be incorporated into a recipe, such as here, you may make your own. Simply put granulated sugar in a food processor bowl fitted with the metal blade attachment and process until the sugar granules are reduced in size, but stop short of creating a powdery texture. Measure after processing.

mango fool

with blackberry-lime crush MAKES 4 FOOLS

Fools are fruit purees thickened with whipped cream. The proportion in my recipe is skewed toward the mango puree, to focus on the fruit. The pale orange cream is topped with a dark purple crush of half cooked, half fresh blackberries, sparked with a squeeze of fresh lime juice. Additional diced pieces of sunset-colored mango crown the very top. The recipe can easily be doubled. This dessert is best shown off in clear goblets, to appreciate the brilliant, contrasting colors. Indonesian Ataulfo mangoes are the most fiber-free and therefore have the best texture for this dish.

for the blackberry-lime crush Put half of the blackberries in a saucepan. Sprinkle with the sugar and add the lime juice. Mash well with a potato masher and bring to a simmer over medium heat. Once the mixture comes to a simmer, cook, stirring frequently, until the mixture exudes juice and then thickens, about 5 minutes. Remove from the heat and immediately stir in the remaining berries. Cool to room temperature. Refrigerate until cool or overnight in an airtight container.

for the fool Have ready 4 clear 10-ounce wineglasses. Peel the mangoes and discard the pits. Dice enough flesh to make ½ cup and set aside for garnish, refrigerated in an airtight container. Puree the remaining mango in a food processor fitted with the metal blade attachment until very smooth. Press through a strainer and measure out ¾ cup of puree; discard the solids. Any extra puree can be stirred into yogurt for breakfast or used to top a bowl of ice cream.

1) In the bowl of a stand mixer, whip the cream and sugar until soft peaks form. Thoroughly but gently fold in the mango puree. Divide the mango fool between the glasses and refrigerate for at least 1 hour or up to 6 hours. Top with the blackberry crush and garnish with the diced mango right before serving.

BLACKBERRY-LIME CRUSH

3 cups fresh blackberries, divided

4½ tablespoons sugar

1¼ teaspoons freshly squeezed lime juice

MANGO FOOL

6 small or 4 large ripe mangoes

½ cup heavy cream

1 tablespoon sugar

thousand leaves
with blackberry pastry cream MAKES 8 PASTRIES

The "thousand leaves" refers to the many-layered puff pastry in this dessert, which is traditionally called *mille-feuille* in French. This version features three shatteringly crispy mille-feuille layers interspersed with two layers of lavender-colored blackberry pastry cream. Sweetened blackberry puree, a few fresh blackberries, and a shower of confectioners' sugar finish off the presentation.

for the pastry cream and puree Puree 1½ cups of the blackberries in a food processor fitted with the metal blade attachment until smooth. Scrape into a fine-mesh strainer set over a clean bowl and press as much pulp through as possible; discard the seeds. Set the puree aside.

1) Make the pastry cream as described on page 10 without using the vanilla bean, but do add vanilla extract. Whisk in 2 tablespoons of the blackberry puree along with the extract and butter. Cool and chill as directed. This pastry cream is best if used within 2 days. The flavor and color will mute if it sits longer.

2) Put the remaining blackberry puree in a saucepan and stir in the sugar. Bring to a simmer and cook for a few minutes until the sugar is dissolved and the puree has slightly thickened. Cool. Refrigerate for up to 2 days in an airtight container.

for the puff pastry Cut a piece of parchment to fit a jelly-roll pan; place the parchment on a work surface.

1) Roll out the pastry directly on the parchment to fill up the dimension of the parchment. Use a sharp knife to trim the pastry with clean edges to a 16 × 11-inch size. Lift the parchment carefully and place back on the pan. Prick the pastry evenly all over. Chill the pastry while the oven preheats.

**PASTRY CREAM AND
BLACKBERRY PUREE**

3 cups fresh blackberries, divided

½ recipe Light Pastry Cream
(page 10; see below)

2 tablespoons sugar

¾ recipe Blitz Puff Pastry (page 4),
chilled and ready to roll out

½ cup sifted confectioners' sugar

2) Position a rack in the middle of the oven. Preheat the oven to 400°F. Place another piece of parchment on top of the pastry and top with a second jelly-roll pan.

3) Bake for 12 to 17 minutes, or until the pastry is beginning to dry and color. Remove the top pan and parchment and bake for 5 to 10 minutes more, rotating the pan front to back at the halfway point, or until the pastry is an even golden brown. Check the bottom of the pastry to make sure it is golden as well. If not, carefully flip the pastry over and bake for another minute or two until the bottom (now on top) is browned. Cool completely on the pan set on a rack.

for the assembly Prepare to assemble the dessert within 2 hours of serving. Slide the parchment paper with the pastry onto a cutting board. Cut into a 6 X 4 grid; quarters along the short side, sixths along the long side.

1) Work on top of a jelly-roll pan for the following assembly technique. Use a small offset spatula to spread about 1 tablespoon of pastry cream evenly on top of 16 of the pastry pieces. To assemble each pastry, stack 2 of these pieces on top of one another and crown with a piece of plain pastry. You should have 8 pastries comprised of 3 pieces of pastry and 2 layers of pastry cream, with the top piece being a plain piece of pastry. Put the confectioners' sugar in a strainer and generously sift over the tops of the pastries. Drizzle some of the reserved puree on each serving plate and place a pastry on top or alongside. Scatter some fresh berries on each plate and serve immediately or refrigerate for up to 2 hours.

strawberry biscuit
shortcakes MAKES 6 SHORTCAKES

When I did a poll of favorite fruit desserts, this American classic came up more than any other. The combination of buttery, flaky biscuit pastry, the fresh dairy flavor of softly whipped cream, and the dark red color and fruity sweetness of strawberries is hard to beat, and for many this dessert defines the taste of summer. Make these only when you have access to absolutely perfect juicy, ripe, flavorful berries, preferably ones that have never been refrigerated. Try the farmers' market and taste before you buy, if possible. The reduction of half of the fruit and juices concentrates the flavor, while the other half of the fruit, left raw, gives you the fresh aspect of the dish that is so memorable.

These biscuits were tested and retested more than any other in the book. I was determined to retain the texture and flavor qualities of baking powder biscuits, which I love, while adding just enough sugar to help the biscuits blend well with the other components. I also wanted the biscuits' texture to be soft enough to not fight your fork and to readily absorb the fruit juices. As far as the cream is concerned, while I sometimes like to whip cream with confectioners' sugar for its stabilizing capacity, in this instance I use granulated sugar. It will have to be whipped right before assembling the dessert, but the flavor of the final whipped cream will be that much purer.

for the shortcakes Position a rack in the middle of the oven. Preheat the oven to 425°F. Line a jelly-roll pan with parchment paper; set aside.

1) In the bowl of a stand mixer, add the flours, sugar, baking powder, and salt and mix briefly on low speed using the flat paddle attachment to combine. Grate the chilled butter on the large holes of a box grater directly into the bowl. Mix on low-medium speed until the butter is distributed evenly, but there are still pockets of butter, which is desirable. Slowly add the milk, with the mixer running, and mix until the dough comes together in large clumps and there is no dry mixture left on the bottom of the bowl. Do not overmix.

BISCUIT SHORTCAKES

1¼ cups all-purpose flour

1 cup sifted cake flour

2 tablespoons sugar

1 tablespoon baking powder

½ teaspoon salt

6 tablespoons (¾ stick) chilled unsalted butter

1 cup whole milk

FILLING

1½ pounds strawberries, preferably small to medium, divided, stems removed

¼ cup plus 1½ teaspoons sugar, divided

1½ teaspoons freshly squeezed lemon juice

TOPPING

2 cups chilled heavy cream

2 tablespoons plus 2 teaspoons sugar

TIP I like to split the biscuits with a fork rather than a knife. This creates more texture within the cut surfaces to catch the juices.

2) Turn the dough out onto a lightly floured surface. Knead very gently just until the dough comes together. Pat it gently into a flat rectangle ¾ to 1 inch thick. Use a bench scraper to fold one half of the dough over the other; pat down again. Fold and pat down again to a ¾- to 1-inch thickness. Use a 2½-inch sharp round biscuit cutter to cut out 6 biscuits. You might get 4 to 5 biscuits initially and then have to gently reform the dough to cut out the last biscuit or two. Arrange the biscuits on the prepared pan, evenly spaced apart.

1) Bake for 12 to 15 minutes, or until a toothpick inserted into center tests clean when removed. The tops and bottoms should be very lightly colored. Cool on the pan set on a rack until lukewarm, about 10 minutes. The biscuits may be used warm at this point. Alternatively, store at room temperature for up to 8 hours, loosely wrapped in foil. Rewarm for 10 minutes at 350°F before serving, if desired.

for the filling Roughly chop half the berries and combine with 3 tablespoons of the sugar in a saucepan. Stir well to combine and cook over medium heat, stirring frequently, until the fruit is bubbling and juicy, about 5 minutes. The juices should darken and concentrate. Cool completely. Halve or quarter the remaining berries (you want them to be bite-size). Toss with the remaining sugar and the lemon juice in a bowl and allow to sit, stirring occasionally, until the juices exude and the sugar dissolves, about 15 minutes. Fold the two berry mixtures together. Refrigerate for up to 3 hours in an airtight container.

for the assembly Right before serving, combine the cream and sugar for the topping in the bowl of a stand mixer. Beat with the balloon whip attachment on medium-high speed just until it is visibly thickening, and then reduce the speed and continue to whip until very soft peaks form.

1) Pry the shortcakes in half horizontally with a fork. Place the bottom halves, cut side up, on 8 dessert plates or, preferably, shallow bowls. Spoon over a good quantity of strawberries and juice, top with a generous dollop of cream, and crown with the top of the biscuit. Allow to sit for about 5 minutes for the juices to penetrate the biscuit.

banana-walnut baklava
with honey-cinnamon syrup MAKES 18 BAKLAVA

This is my take on the classic Middle Eastern dessert baklava. Mine features walnuts, cardamom, honey, and cinnamon—and, of course, layers of flaky phyllo dough—but what sets this one apart is a layer of sliced bananas in the middle. The inspiration came when I was thinking about my enjoyment of bananas and walnuts together. The bananas add a creamy, fruity moistness to the traditional pastry. Make sure your cardamom is very fresh, as its flavor becomes quite muted if the spice is old, while conversely, when fresh, it adds an elegant, intoxicating accent to this dish.

If you delve into the preparation of baklava, you will find proponents of adding hot syrup to cold pastry, hot syrup to hot pastry, and cold syrup to hot pastry. Each camp declares that its technique produces the least soggy result. After experimentation, I have fallen into the first camp. There is an alchemy that seems to happen before your eyes as you pour the hot syrup over the cold pastry. The heat of the syrup seems to penetrate the pastry and melds the flavors and textures together in an optimum way. Also, you might notice that my baklava is cut into triangles, as opposed to the often seen diamonds; it's your choice. Triangles result in no waste, hence my preference.

Don't be put off by the seemingly confusing instructions for layering the phyllo. When you actually have the phyllo in hand and follow along as you prepare the dessert, it will make sense.

for the pastry Position a rack in the middle of the oven. Preheat the oven to 350°F.

1) Toss together the chopped nuts, sugar, cardamom, and cinnamon in a bowl; set aside.

2) Unroll the phyllo dough and cover with a damp towel. (Keep the phyllo covered with the towel as you work). Lightly brush the bottom and sides of a 9-inch square pan with melted butter. Lay one piece of phyllo along the bottom of the pan, lining up one side with the edge of the pan; it will cover the bottom and overhang the opposite side, as it is larger than the pan. Lightly brush the phyllo along the bottom

PASTRY

2 cups walnut halves, finely chopped

¼ cup sugar

½ teaspoon ground cardamom

½ teaspoon ground cinnamon

½ pound phyllo dough, such as Athens brand, defrosted

13 tablespoons (1 stick plus 5 tablespoons) melted unsalted butter

2 medium, ripe bananas

banana–walnut baklava (*continued*)

SYRUP

1 cup sugar

⅔ cup water

1½ tablespoons freshly squeezed lemon juice

1 tablespoon plus 1 teaspoon honey

1 teaspoon finely grated lemon zest

½ teaspoon ground cinnamon

of the pan with butter, then fold the excess overhang over that piece. It will not cover the entire bottom. Take the next piece of phyllo from your covered stack and align it with this last piece to cover the bottom completely; this piece will now overhang the other side. Continue layering and buttering the phyllo until you have 10 layers of phyllo in the bottom of the pan, ending with a light brushing of butter.

3) Scatter the nut mixture evenly over the pastry. Peel the bananas and slice into ½-inch-thick rounds directly over the nuts. The slices will overlap somewhat. Top with the remaining phyllo sheets, repeating the technique of layering and buttering as described above. Butter the top of the last piece. Use a sharp knife to cut into 9 squares (3 × 3), and then cut each square in half into 2 triangles.

4) Bake for 30 to 35 minutes, or until golden brown. Cool completely in the pan set on a rack.

for the syrup After the pastry has cooled, prepare the syrup. Put all the syrup ingredients in a saucepan and stir to combine. Heat over medium-high heat until boiling, swirling the pan once or twice, making sure the sugar is dissolved and the mixture is boiling quite readily. Turn the heat down and simmer for a few minutes, until the syrup just begins to visibly thicken. Immediately pour the syrup over the pastry, concentrating along the cut lines and edges. Allow the pastry to sit and absorb the syrup for at least 4 hours. Store in the pan at room temperature, covered with aluminum foil, for up to 3 days.

TIPS Here are a few tips for cutting the pastry. If the top layers of phyllo are moving around, chill the pastry briefly. The butter will solidify and eliminate that problem. Also, you might have to place one hand on the top of the pastry to brace it as you cut; take care not to press down and compress the pastry. I find a small, thin, serrated blade works best. Use a gentle sawing motion and it will go smoothly. Make sure to allow the full 4 hours for the syrup to be absorbed by the pastry—it is a key step. Be patient and you will be rewarded with sticky, sweet, yet still crispy baklava.

honey-glazed banana fritters

with sesame seeds SERVES 6

When I was growing up in New York City in the 1960s and 1970s, it seemed as though many upscale Chinese restaurants had this dessert on the menu. There is something about the hot, creamy banana center surrounded by crispy fritter batter and a coating of sticky, caramelized honey that was, and is, irresistible. These must be fried right before serving; as with all deep-fried foods, they are best eaten as close to preparation time as possible. You can serve these with vanilla ice cream, but I think they just need a plate and a fork. To make the very cold ice water, fill a 1-cup measuring cup with water and add several ice cubes. Allow to chill for a few minutes; pour off extra water to measure 1 cup for the recipe.

1) Toss the sesame seeds in a small hot skillet for a few minutes until lightly toasted. Set aside.

2) Spread a double layer of paper towels next to the stove. Pour enough oil into a deep-fat fryer or pot to reach a depth of 3 inches. Clip on a thermometer and bring to 350°F.

3) Meanwhile, scrape the honey into a small, narrow saucepan (you want the honey to be deep) and bring to a boil over medium-high heat. Cook until the honey just begins to darken. Turn off the heat, but keep the honey warm and fluid.

4) Gently whisk the flour and ice water together to make a smooth batter. Drop the banana chunks into the batter one by one and toss gently back and forth using two spoons until they have a thin, even coating. Carefully drop a few at a time into the hot oil and fry for a few minutes or until golden brown; flip them over at least once during frying. Remove from the oil with a slotted spoon and drain briefly on the paper towels to absorb excess oil. Drop one by one into the honey and toss to coat. Immediately place on dessert plates, sprinkle with the sesame seeds, and serve. Use bowls if you are adding a scoop of ice cream.

2 tablespoons hulled white sesame seeds

Flavorless vegetable oil, such as canola or sunflower

1½ cups honey

1 cup self-rising flour

1 cup ice water

4 medium to large ripe bananas, peeled and cut crosswise into fourths

red wine–poached cherries
with chocolate-flecked shortcakes MAKES 8 SHORTCAKES

When you bring these to the table, just try and keep the guests at bay. Picture shortcakes flecked with chocolate, split and filled with deep red wine–poached cherries and whipped cream, the entire creation drizzled with chocolate ganache. I have two words for you: Dig in! If you have a cherry or olive pitter, this recipe will go more quickly.

CHERRY FILLING

2 cups slightly fruit red wine, such as Merlot

1 cup water

1 cup sugar

2 teaspoons freshly squeezed lemon juice

2 pounds (about 6 cups) sweet cherries, such as Bing, stemmed, pitted, and halved

SHORTCAKES

2 cups all-purpose flour

¼ cup sugar

1 tablespoon baking powder

¼ teaspoon salt

3 ounces semisweet chocolate, grated on largest holes of a box grater, such as Ghirardelli (45%), Callebaut (52%), or Bissinger's (60%)

½ cup (1 stick) chilled unsalted butter, cut into pieces

½ cup whole milk

1 large egg

for the filling Stir together the wine, water, sugar, and lemon juice in a large saucepan. Bring to a simmer over medium-high heat and stir until the sugar dissolves. Add the cherries and simmer until the cherries are just tender but still hold their shape. Remove the cherries with a slotted spoon to a bowl. Turn the heat to high and boil the liquid until very thick and syrupy. Pour over the cherries and cool to room temperature. The cherries are ready to use; or refrigerate for up to 2 days in an airtight container. Bring to cool room temperature before using.

for the shortcakes Position a rack in the middle of the oven. Preheat the oven to 400°F. Line a jelly-roll pan with parchment paper; set aside.

1) In a large bowl, combine the flour, sugar, baking powder, and salt. Toss in the grated chocolate. Cut in the butter with two knives or a pastry blender until the butter is the size of flat raisins. Whisk the milk and egg in a small bowl to blend. Add the milk mixture to the dry ingredients and begin stirring with a wooden spoon to combine. Turn the dough out onto a lightly floured surface. Knead gently until the dough is smooth, about 5 turns. Pat out the dough to a 6 × 4-inch rectangle. Cut into 8 equal pieces; use your hands to shape each into a round biscuit about 1 inch thick. Arrange the biscuits on the prepared pan, spacing 2 inches apart.

2) Bake for 12 to 17 minutes or until a toothpick inserted into the center tests clean when removed. The tops and bottoms should be very lightly colored. Cool on the pan set on a rack until lukewarm, about 10 minutes. The biscuits may be used warm at this point. Alternatively, store at room temperature for up to 8 hours, loosely wrapped in foil. Rewarm for 10 minutes at 350°F before serving, if desired.

for the topping and assembly Right before serving, make sure the ganache is fluid and ready to use. Whip the cream and sugar until soft peaks form. Pry the shortcakes in half horizontally with a fork. Place the bottom halves, cut side up, on 8 dessert plates or, preferably, shallow bowls. Use a slotted spoon to scoop up the cherries and divide them on top of the shortcake bottoms. A little cherry juice will be included, which is perfect; just do not overly soak the biscuits. Top with the whipped cream and shortcake tops. Drizzle the tops with the warm chocolate ganache. If desired, spoon some extra cherry juice around the shortcakes. Serve immediately.

TOPPING

½ recipe Dark Chocolate Ganache (page 7), slightly warm and fluid

2 cups chilled heavy cream

3 tablespoons sugar

six-fruit gazpacho
with crystallized mint SERVES 6

This dessert is a takeoff on the classic tomato-based chilled soup. Instead of the traditional additions of cucumbers, bell peppers, and onions, here you will find tropical fruits and berries in colors ranging from purple to red to orange to yellow to green. The colors burst forth and beckon you to dig into this clean, crisp, refreshing dessert. The trick with this recipe is to have a very consistent size of dice for all the cut fruit. The refrigeration period is necessary for the flavors to meld. You can serve this in wide, shallow soup bowls, but I also like to present this in tall iced tea glasses, or even goblets accompanied with a long-handled spoon. If you want to add a little something extra, consider a scoop of the vanilla ice cream or mango sorbet.

1) Gently toss all of the fruit together in a bowl. Add the juices and mint (to taste) and fold gently into the fruit. Cover and refrigerate for 2 hours or up to 6 hours. Divide between 6 soup bowls or glasses. Top each with a sprig of crystallized mint and serve immediately.

TIP Mint sprigs as omnipresent garnish are a pet peeve of mine, except where mint is integral to the recipe, as it is here. Please consider garnish options that are related to the recipe. If your lemon dessert seems to need something to gussy it up, consider some candied lemon peel or a shower of lemon zest. If your cake features chocolate, chocolate curls or shards would be perfect—you get the idea.

1¼ cups small to medium fresh blueberries

1 cup crushed canned pineapple (not drained)

1 cup diced fresh strawberries

2 ripe green kiwi, peeled and diced

2 small or 1 large ripe mango, peeled and diced

1 ripe strawberry papaya, peeled, diced, and seeds reserved

½ cup freshly squeezed orange juice

1 teaspoon freshly squeezed lemon juice

1 teaspoon to 1 tablespoon very finely chopped fresh mint

Crystallized mint leaves (see page 262)

cakes

THIS CHAPTER HOLDS a special place in my heart—I love the process of baking and decorating a cake. Whether it is simple or spectacular to behold, I truly enjoy the creative aspect of developing cake recipes. I have written two books on wedding cakes, so you might think that elaborate cakes are where my preferences lie, but even in those books, I always stressed flavor as the most important feature. This chapter is no different. You will find cakes both straightforward and elaborate, cakes that take very little time and effort and some that demand serious attention to detail, but they all taste fabulous.

how to bake unforgettable cakes

* Use high-quality cake pans, such as Wilton's Decorator Preferred or Magic Line, for the most evenly baked cake layers.

* Use an oven thermometer to make sure that your oven is calibrated properly.

* Do not overbake your cakes. Use time cues and visual cues, both of which are given in recipes. The visual cues are the most important, and I usually suggest baking until a wooden toothpick shows a few moist crumbs. There will be residual pan heat after you remove the cakes from the oven, so do not bake your cakes until the toothpick tests completely clean unless the recipe makes that suggestion.

* Cool cake pans on cooling racks for proper air circulation. After the initial cooling, run an icing spatula around the edges of the cake, pressing out against the pan so as not to shave off any cake. Then, unmold onto the racks themselves, remove the parchment, if applicable, and cool thoroughly. (Exceptions are noted in specific recipes.) Proper cooling helps your cake's texture be as good as it can be.

* Most of these cakes can be made up to 1 day before filling/frosting/assembling. Place the cake layers on cardboard rounds of the same size (purchased at craft or cake-decorating stores), then double-wrap in plastic wrap and store at room temperature. Refrigeration will dry them out.

* Follow the storage instructions in individual recipes. If a cake is refrigerated, make sure to bring it to room temperature before serving, except where noted. The butter in many of these cakes and frostings must soften to allow the best texture and flavors to come through.

chocolate-glazed marzipan cake
with cognac-soaked apricots SERVES 12 TO 14

We all need a few cakes in our repertoire to rely on for special occasions, and this one fits the bill. This cake was created for my cousin Rachel Jackson's high-school graduation, but it would work well for important birthdays, anniversaries, and other significant times of life. It is elegant, sophisticated, and actually improves in texture and flavor if made a day or two in advance. It features almond paste in the batter, which is added for flavor and moistness; minced apricots are soaked in cognac and folded into the cake along with bittersweet chocolate shavings. The top is covered with a layer of marzipan and then glazed with chocolate ganache. Roses made from marzipan and apricots embellish the top—it is a showstopper. Rachel's father, Larry, actually proclaimed that even if I never created another dessert in my entire life, I had justified my existence with the invention of this cake!

CAKE

1 cup minced dried Blenheim apricots

½ cup cognac

¾ cup plus 1 tablespoon all-purpose flour

1½ cups blanched sliced almonds, toasted (page 22)

¼ teaspoon salt

2 ounces semisweet chocolate, in block form, such as Valrhona Equitoriale (55%)

½ cup plus 2 tablespoons (1¼ sticks) unsalted butter, at room temperature, cut into pieces

6½ ounces almond paste, crumbled into pieces

¾ cup sugar

for the cake Combine the apricots and cognac in a small saucepan and bring just to a simmer over medium heat; remove from the heat and let sit for 10 minutes. Alternatively, combine in a microwaveable bowl and heat on high power for 1 to 2 minutes, or until very hot. Remove from the microwave and let sit for 10 minutes. Set aside. In either case, take care to not allow the liquor to ignite.

1) Position a rack in the middle of the oven. Preheat the oven to 325°F. Coat two 8 x 2-inch round cake pans with nonstick spray, line the bottoms with parchment rounds, and then spray the parchment.

2) Put the flour, almonds, and salt in the bowl of a food processor fitted with the metal blade attachment. Process until the almonds are ground to a very fine meal; set aside. Grate the chocolate using the largest holes on a box grater; set aside.

3) In the bowl of a stand mixer, beat the butter with the flat paddle attachment on medium-high speed until creamy, about 1 minute. Add the almond paste and beat until combined. Add the sugar

gradually and continue to beat until very light and fluffy, about 3 minutes more. Beat in the vanilla and almond extracts. Add the eggs one at a time, beating well after each addition. Add the flour mixture and pulse the mixer on and off, taking care not to overmix. Fold in the shaved chocolate and apricots with any liquid with a few broad strokes. Divide the batter evenly in the pans and smooth the tops with an offset spatula.

4) Bake for 20 to 25 minutes, or until a toothpick inserted in the center shows a few moist crumbs when removed. The cake will be tinged light golden brown around the top and edges and will have begun to come away from the sides of the pan. Cool cakes in the pans on racks for 5 minutes. Unmold, peel off the parchment, and place directly on the racks to cool completely. Trim the layers to be level, if necessary. The layers are ready to fill and frost. Alternatively, place the layers on cardboards and double-wrap in plastic wrap; store at room temperature if assembling within 24 hours.

for the syrup Combine the water and sugar in a small pot. Stir to wet the sugar. Place over medium heat and bring to a simmer. Cook until the sugar dissolves, swirling the pot once or twice. Remove from the heat, cool to room temperature, and stir in the cognac.

for the assembly Have all the components ready to use. Place one cake layer, bottom side down, on a cardboard round of the same size and place on a cake turntable. Brush with half the syrup, then spread the apricot spread evenly over the cake. Top with the second cake layer, bottom side up, and brush with the remaining syrup. Roll out the marzipan on a work surface lightly dusted with confectioners' sugar or cornstarch to a thickness of ¼ inch. Using the cake pan as a guide, cut out an 8-inch circle. Place the marzipan circle on top of the cake. Cover the top and sides of the cake with a smooth, even, thin layer of buttercream. Chill until the buttercream is firm, about 1 hour.

1) Place the cake on a rack set over a clean pan. Pour all of the liquid ganache over the center of the cake; it will spread out and begin to drip down the sides. Gently facilitate this process with an icing spatula, covering the entire cake. Any excess ganache that drips

1 teaspoon vanilla extract

1 teaspoon almond extract

5 large eggs, at room temperature

SYRUP

1 tablespoon sugar

1 tablespoon water

1 tablespoon cognac

FILLING

⅓ cup 100% apricot fruit spread

4 ounces Marzipan (page 14), or use purchased

1½ cups Italian Meringue Buttercream, vanilla variation (page 8)

1 cup Dark Chocolate Ganache (page 7), fluid and ready to pour, made with Valrhona Equitoriale (55%) or Valrhona Caraque (56%)

APRICOT ROSES

20 dried Blenheim apricots

6 marzipan roses of various sizes (page 15)

12 marzipan leaves of various sizes (page 15)

3 marzipan tendrils of appropriate size for roses (page 15)

down to the pan can be reused. Chill briefly to set the ganache, for about 1 hour or up to 1 day.

for the apricot roses Halve each apricot if necessary. You want round, solid "halves." Place between 2 pieces of parchment paper and flatten lightly with a rolling pin. Take one half and roll it tightly into a rose "center." Use additional halves, wrapped around the center, each over-lapping the one before, to make "petals." Depending on the size of the apricots, you might have to trim the halves; always make sure a rounded uncut edge is toward the top to form the rounded petal shape. Keep adding petals until the rose is the size you want. You might only need 4 or 5 halves per rose. Use a toothpick with a pointed end to hold them together if they are unfurling. You do need to press the petals together firmly to adhere. Store for up to 1 day in an airtight container.

for the decoration Place the cake on a display plate. Arrange a few marzipan roses, leaves, and tendrils and apricot roses as desired. The cake may be served immediately or refrigerated for up to 2 days in an airtight container. Bring to room temperature before serving.

TIPS There are several key components to this recipe. The almonds ground for the batter must be blanched or they will darken the color of the cake and also make the cake a bit drier. Sliced almonds give the proper measurement. I use American Almond Products almond paste (see Resources, page 287) for the cake batter, for its superior flavor and texture. Do not substitute any premade marzipan for this step or the al-mond paste that comes in a tube often found in the supermarket. Dried apricots come from various sources, typically Turkey and California. I highly recommend California Blenheim apricots. They have an intense flavor and vivid, bold color. The cognac that you choose to plump the apricots with should be one that you like to drink as is. The cake layers are filled with an apricot spread that is 100 percent fruit, as opposed to a jam or preserve, both of which are laden with sugar; we are using the spread for added flavor and moistness, not sweetness. Fruit spreads can be found near jams and jellies in the supermarket. These are not the same as spreads made with sugar alternatives.

how to decorate unforgettable cakes

* My approach to decorating cakes is to bring decorative elements to the outside of the cake that relate to the flavors of the cake. Cakes containing chocolate might sport chocolate curls or a dusting of cocoa; lemon cakes could be crowned with candied lemon peel; cakes with a coffee flavor could be embellished with chocolate-covered coffee beans—you get the idea. Along the same lines, I never put a mint leaf garnish on a cake that doesn't contain mint. It makes no sense to me and is in fact a bit of a pet peeve . . . now a white chocolate–mint creation with a mint leaf would be fine.

* When frosting a cake, there are six key points:

  * Use a cake turntable and cardboards of the same size and shape as the cake (for a 9-inch cake, use a 9-inch cardboard), and have icing spatulas at hand.

  * Make sure the frosting is soft and spreadable. If it is just a little bit too cold or stiff, it will not apply well. A consistency between peanut butter and mayonnaise is just right.

  * Always keep the icing spatula gliding on top of the frosting and do not let it touch the cake (or you will bring crumbs up into the frosting).

  * With Italian Meringue Buttercream (page 8), always make a thin crumb-coat to seal in crumbs. The final frosting layer will apply much more easily.

  * Use the cardboard edge to help guide your icing spatula for crumb-coats and smooth final coats.

  * If using a pastry bag, fill only halfway and make sure the frosting is soft and creamy enough to flow smoothly through your chosen tip.

toasted coconut cake

with lime cream and mount gay rum SERVES 12 TO 14

The inspiration for this cake came from the tropical flavors of coconut, lime, and gold rum. The yellow cake is made with pure coconut milk as its liquid and has sweetened coconut folded into the batter. Lime cream is spread between the cake layers that have been brushed with a full half-cup of rum. A lightly sweetened whipped cream frosting covers it all, and then it gets a complete cloak of toasted and untoasted coconut. The cake is very moist and even improves in texture and flavor if made a day before serving.

for the cake Position a rack in the middle of the oven. Preheat the oven to 350°F. Coat two 9 × 2-inch round cake pans with nonstick spray, line the bottoms with parchment rounds, and then spray the parchment.

1) Whisk together the flour, baking powder, and salt in a medium bowl to aerate and combine; set aside.

2) In the bowl of stand mixer, add the butter and beat with the flat paddle attachment on medium-high speed until creamy, about 2 minutes. Add the sugar gradually and continue to beat until very light and fluffy, about 3 minutes more. Beat in the vanilla. Add the eggs one at a time, beating well after each addition. Add the flour mixture in three additions, alternately with the coconut milk. Begin and end with the flour mixture; add 1 cup of the coconut and beat briefly until smooth. Divide the batter evenly in the pans and smooth the tops with an offset spatula. Reserving 1¼ cups of coconut, spread the remaining 1¼ cups coconut out in a single layer on a jelly-roll pan.

3) Toast the coconut in the oven, shaking the pan once or twice, until it is golden, about 5 minutes. Put the cake layers in the oven at the same time and bake for 20 to 25 minutes, or until a toothpick

CAKE

3 cups sifted cake flour

1 tablespoon baking powder

¼ teaspoon salt

1 cup (2 sticks) unsalted butter, at room temperature, cut into pieces

1½ cups sugar

1 teaspoon vanilla extract

4 large eggs, at room temperature

1 cup 100% pure coconut milk (not sweetened cream of coconut)

3½ cups sweetened flaked coconut, divided

¾ cup gold rum, such as Mount Gay Eclipse

LIME CREAM

6 tablespoons sugar

4½ tablespoons freshly squeezed lime juice

3 large egg yolks

3¾ tablespoons unsalted butter

¾ teaspoon finely grated lime zest

toasted coconut cake (*continued*)

FROSTING

½ cup (more or less) 100% pure coconut milk

3 tablespoons sugar

1½ cups chilled heavy cream

1 tablespoon confectioners' sugar

shows a few moist crumbs when removed. The cakes will be tinged light golden brown and will have begun to come away from the sides of the pans. When the cakes are done, place the pans on racks and immediately poke the cakes all over with a bamboo skewer. Brush the cakes evenly and equally with half of the rum. Cool the cakes completely in the pans on racks. Unmold, peel off the parchment, and brush this bottom side (now on top) with the remaining rum. Trim the layers to be level, if necessary. The layers are ready to fill and frost. Alternatively, place the layers on cardboards and double-wrap in plastic wrap; store at room temperature and assemble within 24 hours. Cool the toasted coconut in the pan on a rack as well. Set this toasted coconut aside for decorating the outside of the cake.

for the lime cream Put the sugar, juice, and yolks in the top of a double boiler. Whisk together to break up the eggs. Add the butter. Place over the bottom of a double boiler filled with hot water that is just touching the bottom of the bowl. Place over medium heat and bring the water to a simmer.

1) Whisk the mixture frequently over simmering water for about 12 minutes, or until the mixture reaches 180°F. (The temperature is more important than the time it takes, and the curd itself should not simmer.) The curd will thicken and form a soft shape when dropped from a spoon. Stir in the zest after removing from the heat. Let cool to room temperature, scrape into an airtight container, and refrigerate overnight or for up to 1 week.

for the frosting Put the coconut milk and sugar in a small saucepan. (Chances are that you will have a little over $^1/_2$ cup of coconut milk left if you have used one 14-ounce can for the cake. Use it all to be efficient. It will be somewhere between $^1/_2$ cup and $^7/_8$ cup; that's okay.) Stir to combine, bring to a simmer over medium-high heat, and simmer until reduced by half. Cool completely.

1) Put the heavy cream, reduced coconut milk, and confectioners' sugar in a mixer bowl. Whip with the wire whip attachment until

stiff peaks form, but do not overbeat. The frosting should be used immediately.

for the assembly Toss together the $1\frac{1}{4}$ cups toasted coconut with the reserved $1\frac{1}{4}$ cups coconut in a large bowl.

1) Place one cake layer on a 9-inch cardboard round, bottom side down. Spread the top of the cake layer with the lime cream; top with the second cake layer, bottom side up. Frost with the whipped cream frosting. Press the toasted coconut mixture all over the top and sides. Refrigerate for at least 4 hours or overnight. Bring to room temperature before serving.

TIPS Pure unsweetened coconut milk can be found in Asian markets and the international aisle of the supermarket. It has no sugar added; cream of coconut cannot be substituted. A typical can is 13 to 14 ounces and will give you enough for the cake as well as the frosting. If you are comfortable making citrus curd, you can make it over direct heat—I do all the time. Just don't walk away, and take care not to scorch or boil it.

rum raisin–chocolate roulade
with whipped chocolate ganache SERVES 8

This cake takes the form of a log shape filled with rich chocolate whipped cream and rum–soaked raisins rolled up inside in a spiral fashion. The exterior is covered with an even richer deep, dark chocolate glaze. The filling and glaze start out with the same recipe, so there are actually fewer components than you would think. The chocolate and rum flavors are quite prominent, so save this for an adult dinner party. Also, the choice of rum will greatly affect the final flavor. I have made this with many different rums, and I like it with gold rum. Mount Gay Extra Old rum makes this cake particularly decadent—a mature rum for a mature crowd.

RUM RAISINS

¾ cup dark raisins

⅔ cup gold rum, such as Mount Gay Extra Old

GANACHE FILLING AND GLAZE

1¾ cups heavy cream, divided

9 ounces semisweet chocolate, finely chopped, such as Valrhona Equitoriale (55%)

3 tablespoons unsalted butter, softened

COCOA ROULADE

¼ cup whole milk

2 tablespoons unsalted butter

½ cup sifted cake flour

¼ cup sifted Dutch-processed cocoa, plus extra

1 teaspoon baking powder

¼ teaspoon salt

for the rum raisins Put the raisins in a small bowl and cover with very hot tap water. Plump for 5 minutes, drain, and put in a small saucepan. Add the rum, heat over medium-high heat, very carefully tip the pan toward the flame source, and stand back. The mixture will ignite and flambé. (Or ignite with a long match if you have an electric stove.) Cover and remove from the heat. The flame will subside. Cool completely. The raisins are ready to use or may be stored at room temperature for up to 2 days in an airtight container.

for the ganache Put 1 cup of the cream in a medium saucepan and bring to a boil over medium heat. Remove from the heat and immediately sprinkle the chocolate into the cream. Cover and allow to sit for 5 minutes. The heat of the cream should melt the chocolate. Gently stir the ganache until smooth. If the chocolate is not melting, place over very low heat, stirring often, until melted, taking care not to scorch the chocolate. Whisk in the butter until smooth. Cool to room temperature. The ganache is ready to use or may be refrigerated for up to 1 week in an airtight container. (Rewarm until fluid if chilled before proceeding.) Remove ¹/₂ cup of the ganache for glazing the cake; set aside.

for the roulade Position a rack in the middle of the oven. Preheat the oven to 350°F. Coat a jelly-roll pan with nonstick spray, line with parchment, and then spray the parchment.

3 large eggs

3 large egg yolks

1 cup sugar

1) Put the milk and butter in a small saucepan over medium heat to melt the butter, or melt together in a microwave. Set aside, keeping warm.

2) Whisk together the flour, ¼ cup cocoa, baking powder, and salt in a small bowl to aerate and combine; set aside.

3) In the bowl of a stand mixer, whip the eggs, yolks, and sugar on high speed using the wire whip attachment until light and fluffy and a ribbon forms, about 2 minutes. Sprinkle the flour mixture over the egg mixture and fold it in using a balloon whisk; combine just until no streaks of flour remain. Slowly drizzle the butter mixture over the batter and continue folding with the whisk, finishing off with a large rubber spatula. Scrape into the prepared pan; rap the flat bottom of the pan on the counter to release any air bubbles.

4) Bake for 8 to 12 minutes, or until slightly puffed and a toothpick inserted in the center tests clean. Do not overbake or it will lose its flexibility. Cool completely in the pan on a rack. Use a knife tip to loosen all the edges. Place a clean piece of parchment on your work surface, sprinkle with some extra cocoa, and invert the cake onto it. Remove the pan and very gently peel off the parchment.

for the assembly Have ready a large flat serving platter at least 14 inches long and 6 inches wide that can fit in your refrigerator.

1) Put the larger amount of room-temperature ganache in the bowl of a mixer and freeze for 15 minutes. Add the remaining ¾ cup chilled cream and beat with the wire whip attachment on medium-high speed just until soft peaks form.

2) Drain the raisins, reserving the liquid. Brush any liquid over the cake. Remove 2 tablespoons of the raisins; set aside. Fold the larger amount of raisins into the whipped chocolate cream.

cutting cakes

Different cakes require different cutting techniques, but the end result we strive for is always the same—we want even, clean cuts so that the cake is presented to its best advantage. Some cakes work best with a thin-bladed slicing knife, others with a serrated knife, but in all cases it really helps if the knife is wiped clean between cuts with a warm, damp cloth. Also, in general, cakes cut more easily and cleanly when cold, but if they are to be served at room temperature, you have to weigh whether it is more important to present the whole room-temperature cake to the guests or if you can slice the cake ahead of time while cold and just present the individual slices, already plated. (In the latter case, cover them with plastic wrap while they come to room temperature so that they don't dry out.)

3) Spread the chocolate-raisin filling evenly over the cake using an offset spatula. Leave a $\frac{1}{2}$-inch border along one of the short sides. Beginning with the opposite end, begin to firmly roll the cake. Use your fingers to facilitate the initial turn, then pick up the parchment to help roll the cake. Once rolled, drape parchment over the cake and use your hands to firmly shape the roll.

4) Carefully transfer the roll onto a serving platter, cover with plastic wrap, and refrigerate for at least 1 hour, or until the filling has firmed up.

5) Remove the cake from the refrigerator. Trim the ends if desired; they will be left unglazed. The remaining $\frac{1}{2}$ cup ganache should be fluid, but not hot. Sprinkle the remaining raisins over the top of the roll. They can be haphazard in design. Pour the fluid ganache straight down the center top of the roll and allow it to begin to drip down all sides. Use a small offset spatula to cover the entire roll (except the ends), raisins and all. Chill the cake until the glaze is firm, at least 1 hour. Bring to room temperature before serving. The cake may be served immediately or refrigerated overnight. (This cake is an odd shape, so if you do not have a large cake dome, simply drape loosely with foil.)

fruits and flowers
flan SERVES 10

This fresh and fancy cake begins with a base of a vanilla butter cake brushed with orange juice and Grand Marnier. Then vanilla pastry cream cushions an abundant crowning of fresh, colorful fruit and a scattering of rose petals. The cake is very easy to prepare and is best if made in a special flan pan (see alternative pan suggestions below in Tip). I use the Kaiser La Forme flan pan, which is 12 inches across and 2 inches deep, has fluted edges, and, most importantly, has a depression in what becomes the top of the cake. This area is ultimately filled with pastry cream and fruit. What makes this recipe special is the selection, preparation, and arrangement of the fruit; I think an array of different colors and shapes is best. Use the photo for inspiration, but also let what is available be your guide. Buy the most vividly colored, peak-of-flavor, and perfectly formed fruit you can find.

for the syrup Combine the sugar and juice in a small saucepan. Stir to wet the sugar. Place over medium heat and bring to a simmer. Cook until the sugar dissolves, swirling the pot once or twice. Remove from the heat, cool to room temperature, and stir in the Grand Marnier. The syrup is ready to use, or refrigerate for up to 1 week in an airtight container.

for the cake Position a rack in the middle of the oven. Preheat the oven to 350°F. Coat a 12-inch nonstick fluted flan pan with nonstick spray.

1) Whisk together the flour, baking powder, and salt in a medium bowl to aerate and combine; set aside.

2) In the bowl of a stand mixer, beat the butter with the flat paddle attachment on medium-high speed until creamy, about 2 minutes. Add the sugar gradually and continue to beat until very light and fluffy, about 3 minutes more. Beat in the vanilla. Add the eggs one at a time, beating well after each addition. Add the flour mixture in

SYRUP

½ cup sugar

⅓ cup orange juice, freshly squeezed or not-from-concentrate

⅓ cup Grand Marnier

CAKE

2 cups plus 2 tablespoons sifted cake flour

1¼ teaspoons baking powder

¼ teaspoon salt

½ cup plus 2 tablespoons (1¼ sticks) unsalted butter, at room temperature, cut into small pieces

1½ cups sugar

2 teaspoons vanilla extract

4 large eggs, at room temperature

⅓ cup whole milk

TOPPING

6 cups assorted fruit such as blueberries; red, gold, or black raspberries; blackberries; red, black, or white currants or seedless grapes; whole black, red, or Rainier cherries with the stem; Cape gooseberries; sliced apricots, bananas, gold or green kiwis, mangoes, nectarines, papayas, peaches, pears, plums, pluots, or strawberries; quartered fresh figs; pomegranate seeds

¾ cup water

1 tablespoon freshly squeezed lemon juice

1 recipe chilled Light Pasty Cream, (page 10)

Fresh, unsprayed rose petals

three additions, alternately with the milk. Begin and end with the flour mixture and beat briefly until smooth. Scrape the batter into the pan.

3) Bake for 20 to 25 minutes, or until a toothpick shows a few moist crumbs when removed. The cake will be tinged a light golden brown and will have begun to come away from the sides of the pan. Place the pan on a cooling rack, poke holes all over the cake with a bamboo skewer, and brush half of the syrup evenly over the cake. Cool until just warm, about 20 minutes. Unmold onto a serving platter. Poke the top with a skewer several times and brush with the remaining syrup. Cool completely.

for the topping Sort, clean, and slice the fruit, if necessary. Combine the water and lemon juice and dip any fruit that might need it into this acidulated water to prevent discoloration (such as sliced bananas or pears).

for the assembly Spread the pastry cream evenly on top of the cake, filling the recessed area. Arrange the fruit as desired, creating depth and interest with the color, texture, and size of various fruit. The cake is ready to serve, or refrigerate for up to 3 hours. This cake is best served as close as possible to assembly. Bring to cool room temperature before serving. Scatter the rose petals over the cake immediately before serving.

TIP The Kaiser flan pan is versatile and a good one to have at your disposal. However, if you would prefer not to buy it, you can use a 10-inch springform pan. Bake the cake until done using visual cues as suggested, and then cut and scrape out a slight depression about 1 inch deep in the center top of the cake; proceed as directed.

ricotta cheesecake
with clementine–cranberry marmalade SERVES 12

I used to be a die-hard New York–style cheesecake fan. There is something incomparable about the dense, creamy-smooth texture, but I find that it is sometimes too rich. Ricotta cheesecakes never appealed to me—until I made one with fresh ricotta cheese. It is much smoother in texture and has a much fresher dairy flavor than supermarket ricotta. You will most likely have to go to a cheese store or a good cheese department, such as at Whole Foods. A thermometer is helpful for the marmalade.

MARMALADE

4 clementines, scrubbed clean

⅔ cup water

1¼ cups sugar

½ cup fresh cranberries

CRUST

⅔ cup all-purpose flour

2 tablespoons sugar

1 teaspoon very finely grated lemon zest

½ teaspoon salt

5 tablespoons chilled unsalted butter, cut into pieces

1 large egg yolk

2 teaspoons water

½ teaspoon vanilla extract

FILLING

2 pounds fresh whole-milk ricotta cheese

¾ cup plus 2 tablespoons sugar

1 tablespoon Grand Marnier

½ teaspoon vanilla extract

for the marmalade Bring a deep medium pot filled with water to a boil over high heat. Add the clementines and bring back to a boil for 1 minute. Drain. Slice in half through the stem end, then slice crosswise as thinly as possible. Put the clementines, the ⅔ cup water, and the sugar in the same pot, stir to combine, and bring to a simmer over medium heat. Simmer uncovered, stirring often, until the mixture reaches 220°F—or check for the following visual cues. Begin checking after 5 to 10 minutes by placing a teaspoonful on the chilled plate. Hold the plate vertically and see if the mixture "gels" and slowly moves down the plate in a jellied state. It should not be completely fluid, and it should not be so firm as to completely hold its shape. Err on the side of looser rather than firmer. The total simmering time will be 10 to 15 minutes.

1) Stir the cranberries into the marmalade and cook for 2 minutes more or until they just begin to pop open. Cool completely. Refrigerate for up to 2 weeks in an airtight container. Bring to room temperature before using.

for the crust Position a rack in the middle of the oven. Preheat the oven to 350°F. Coat a 9-inch springform or loose-bottomed pan with nonstick spray.

1) Whisk together the flour, sugar, lemon zest, and salt in a medium bowl to blend. Add the butter and cut in using a pastry blender or two knives until the fat is cut into ⅛-inch pieces. Whisk together the egg yolk, water, and vanilla and add to the flour mixture; toss with your fingers or a fork until evenly moistened and the dough just holds together if squeezed. Press the dough in an even layer all over the bottom of the prepared pan. Prick all over with a fork. Bake for 20 to 25 minutes, or until just beginning to turn light golden brown. Cool in the pan on a rack while you make the filling.

for the filling In the bowl of a stand mixer, beat the ricotta with the flat paddle attachment on medium-high speed until smooth, about 1 minute. Beat in the sugar, scraping down the bowl once or twice. Beat in the Grand Marnier and vanilla. Beat in the eggs one at a time, scraping down after each addition and allowing each egg to be absorbed before continuing. Beat in the flour and salt. Scrape the batter on top of the prepared crust and smooth into an even layer.

1) Bake for 45 to 55 minutes. The edges might rise higher than the center and tinge lightly with color. The center will still jiggle when you gently shake the pan. Remove from the oven and run a very thin, sharp knife around the edge of the cake to release it from the pan's sides; this should help prevent cracks from forming. (Even if they do they will be covered with the marmalade, so don't worry.) Cool completely in the pan on a rack. Refrigerate for 6 hours or overnight.

2) Unmold the cheesecake and place on a display plate. Spread the room-temperature marmalade over the top of the cheesecake right before serving.

4 large eggs
3 tablespoons all-purpose flour
⅛ teaspoon salt

TIPS The marmalade makes a generous amount. If you do not want to use all of it on top of the cheesecake, it is excellent spread on toast for breakfast. This cheesecake is perfectly delectable without the topping. In that case, however, I would make a few alterations. At the very least, increase the vanilla in the filling to 1 teaspoon. Then, if you like, add 2 tablespoons each finely chopped candied orange peel and finely chopped candied lemon peel to the filling. Bake as directed. If you want to try this cheesecake and cannot get fresh ricotta, you could try supermarket whole-milk ricotta and buzz it briefly in a food processor fitted with metal blade to smooth it out. It will not be the same but will be better than using it straight from the container.

clementine-chocolate-almond torte
with chocolate lace, candied zest,
and caramelized fruit SERVES 10 TO 12

This very elegant, visually stunning cake was created in honor of my friend Alison Buck's 55th birthday. The two 8-inch layers of cake are textured from the ground blanched almonds, and very moist and flavorful from the clementine zest and pulp. The baked layers are placed in a 9-inch springform pan and filled and topped with thick, generous layers of moist, lightly whipped chocolate ganache. Valrhona Manjari chocolate is a great choice here for its highly acidic flavor profile. The whole is encased in a lacy dark chocolate band and crowned with candied clementine peel and glossy, crackly, caramelized sugar–coated clementine sections. There are several components, but many can be made ahead, so read the recipe thoroughly and take advantage. This is a cake to make in the winter when clementines are at their peak.

for the candied zest Remove the clementine peels in large pieces. Wrap the peeled fruit tightly in plastic wrap and refrigerate for up to 2 days; you will be able to use them for the caramelized segment component. Cut the peel into strips 1¼ inch wide and at least 2 inches long. Put the strips in a small pot and add cold water to cover. Bring to a boil over high heat, and then drain. Repeat 2 more times.

1) Line a jelly-roll pan with aluminum foil and lightly coat with non-stick spray; set aside. Stir together 1¾ cups of the sugar, the water, and the corn syrup in a small pot to moisten the sugar. Bring to a simmer over medium heat. Add the peel and maintain a low simmer until the peel is translucent, 1 to 1½ hours. The sugar syrup will not be totally absorbed; it will lessen in volume and toward the end of cooking the bubbles will cover the surface and possibly look a bit foamy. Drain the peel, discarding any syrup. Spread the pieces out on the prepared pan so that they are not touching and let sit at room temperature overnight. Toss the strips one at a time with the remaining ¼ cup

CANDIED ZEST

3 clementines, scrubbed clean

2 cups sugar, divided

1½ cups water

¼ cup light corn syrup

CAKE

1 clementine

1 cup plus 2 tablespoons blanched sliced almonds, very finely ground

1 cup sifted cake flour

1 teaspoon baking powder

½ teaspoon baking soda

⅛ teaspoon salt

½ cup (1 stick) unsalted butter, at room temperature, cut into small pieces

¾ cup sugar

½ teaspoon almond extract

2 large eggs, at room temperature

½ cup whole milk, at room temperature

CHOCOLATE GANACHE

3 cups heavy cream

12 ounces bittersweet chocolate, finely chopped, such as Valrhona Manjari (64%)

Pastry bag

½-inch plain round decorating tip, such as Ateco #806, Wilton #1A, or a standard coupler

CHOCOLATE LACE

3 ounces bittersweet chocolate, finely chopped, such as Valrhona Manjari (64%)

CARAMELIZED SEGMENTS

Segments from 3 clementines

Bamboo skewers

2½ cups sugar

½ cup water

¼ cup light corn syrup

sugar until coated. Store at room temperature for up to 1 week in an airtight container.

for the cake Position a rack in the middle of the oven. Preheat the oven to 350º F. Coat a 8 x 2-inch round cake pan with nonstick spray, line the bottom with a parchment round, and then spray the parchment. Also have on hand a 9-inch springform pan.

1) Very finely zest the clementine over a small bowl. Slice the fruit in half and use a hand reaming tool to extract the juice and pulp directly into the same bowl; set aside. If there are any seeds (there shouldn't be), simply pick them out and discard.

2) Whisk together the ground nuts, flour, baking powder, baking soda, and salt in a medium bowl to aerate and combine; set aside.

3) In the bowl of a stand mixer, beat the butter on medium-high speed until creamy with flat paddle attachment, about 2 minutes. Add the sugar gradually and beat until very light and fluffy, about 3 minutes more, scraping down the bowl once or twice. Beat in the almond extract. Beat in the eggs one at a time, scraping down after each addition and allowing each egg to be absorbed before continuing. Beat in the reserved clementine zest, pulp, and juice. The mixture will be very fluid. Add the flour mixture in three additions, alternately with the milk. Begin and end with the flour mixture and beat briefly until smooth. Scrape the batter into the prepared pan and smooth the top with an offset spatula.

4) Bake for 25 to 30 minutes, or until a toothpick inserted in the center shows a few moist crumbs when removed. The cake will be light golden brown and will have begun to come away from the sides of the pan. Cool cake in the pan on a rack for 8 to 10 minutes. Unmold, peel off the parchment, and place the layer directly on the rack to cool completely. Trim the layer to be level, if necessary. The layer is ready to fill and frost. Alternatively, place the layer on a cardboard round and double-wrap in plastic wrap; store at room temperature and assemble and serve within 24 hours. The cake may be frozen for

up to 1 month, well wrapped in plastic wrap and sealed in a zipper-top bag.

for the ganache Put the cream in a large saucepan and bring to a boil over medium heat. Remove from the heat and immediately sprinkle the chocolate into the cream. Cover and allow to sit for 5 minutes. The heat of the cream should melt the chocolate. Gently stir until smooth. Refrigerate for at least 6 hours or up to 3 days in an airtight container.

for the initial assembly Have the 9-inch springform pan assembled. Have the ganache chilled and scraped into a medium bowl. Use a large balloon whisk to gently soften and whip the ganache. It will be thick, and you are not trying to incorporate air as much as soften it a little bit. Just a few rotations of the whisk will do it, and do not over-handle, or the ganache will become grainy and stiffen. Scrape about half of the ganache into the prepared pastry bag.

1) Slice the cake layer in half horizontally. Center one half in the bottom of the 9-inch pan. Spread a good thick layer of ganache on top using an offset spatula, then use the pastry bag to pipe it around the edge of the cake, filling any space (remember you have an 8-inch cake, but a 9-inch pan). Smooth the ganache; you should not see any cake or any gaps between the ganache and pan sides. Center the second cake layer in the middle and repeat with the remaining ganache, smoothing the top well. Dip an offset spatula in warm water to make it easy to smooth the ganache. Cover the top of the pan with plastic wrap and refrigerate the cake for at least 2 hours or overnight.

for the chocolate lace Measure out a piece of aluminum foil to 35 inches long; do not use heavy-duty aluminum foil. In fact, the cheaper, thinner brands are better here, as they are more flexible. Fold it in half lengthwise. Make a mark with a pen at the 32-inch point. Measure the finished height of your cake, add $1/2$ inch, and make a mark at that point as well (most likely the cake will be around 2 inches tall). Trim the long open edge along that mark. Place flat on a work surface and smooth out the wrinkles.

1) Melt the chocolate in the top of a double boiler or in the microwave and scrape into a parchment cone; snip a small opening. Pipe
a thick, lacy design all over the foil within your marked area. Go
up and down and side to side to make the lace very interconnected,
which will give it strength and structure. Let sit to firm up partially
while you proceed.

for the final assembly Have a flat display plate ready; it must be flat
or you will not be able to apply the chocolate lace band. To unmold
the cake, dip an icing spatula in very hot water and run it between
the cake and the pan, pressing out toward the pan so that you do
not shave off any of the ganache or cake. Open the springform, remove the cake, and place on the display plate in front of you. Pick
up the aluminum strip from both short ends and place the center of
the strip, chocolate side in, at the center rear of the cake (the side
away from you). Make sure the bottom of the strip is aligned with
the base of the cake. Bring the two ends of the foil around the cake
and toward you. The slightly tacky chocolate will adhere the strip to
the moist ganache; keep the strip as even as possible, aligning the
bottom of the strip with the bottom of the cake. Position the short
end that has the chocolate on it so that it lies flat against the cake.
The other short end, with the extra clean foil, should be left sticking
out, by about 1 inch. Place in the refrigerator until the chocolate
lace hardens, at least 30 minutes. Meanwhile, make the caramelized
tangerine segments.

for the caramelized segments This is a bit of a production, and there
are several aspects to consider. First, separate the segments and strip
them of white strings and pith as best you can. Pat dry with paper towels. Insert skewers into the segments. Line a jelly-roll pan with aluminum foil and coat with nonstick spray. Stir together the sugar, water,
and corn syrup in a small, deep pot to moisten the sugar. Have ready
a bowl of ice-cold water that is large enough to accommodate the
bottom of your pot. Bring the sugar mixture to a boil over medium
heat and cook to 310°F. Immediately plunge the bottom of the pan

into the ice water to stop the cooking. Quickly dip a piece of fruit into the sugar syrup, lightly scrape the bottom of the fruit against the pan rim to remove excess syrup, and place on the prepared pan. Repeat with the other sections. Take care to make a thin coating (reheat the sugar gently if necessary to retain fluidity), and space the fruit apart on the pan so the pieces are not touching.

1) After the sugar hardens on the fruit, twist the skewers gently and remove. Use the fruit as soon as possible (although on a dry, cool day, I have held these for up to 6 hours). Remove the cake from the refrigerator; carefully peel the foil away from the chocolate band, starting with end that is firmly against the cake. Take care as you reach other end, where the chocolate lace will not be supported by cake. After all the foil is removed, place the palm of your hand against the lace that is still sticking out. The heat from your hand will soften the chocolate slightly. This could take 10 seconds or up to a minute. Once the chocolate softens slightly, use your palm to coax it gently into place against the cake, and the band will slightly overlap as well. Arrange the pieces of candied peel around the edge of the cake, inside the band, which will be a little higher than the edge of the cake. Cluster the caramelized segments in the center of the cake and serve immediately.

TIP   If the lacy band cracks or for whatever reason does not work for you, don't worry. Just break it up into large pieces (at least 2 to 3 inches wide) and simply press them against the sides of the cake until they stick. Don't mention to the guests what you had originally intended. No one will know, and it will look spectacular in its own right.

chocolate ganache cake
with armagnac-soaked prunes SERVES 8 TO 10

Prunes get a bad rap. They seem to still be associated with nursing homes, the elderly, and staying "regular." Well, have you ever thought about what a prune is? It's a dried plum, and plums are a fabulous, sweet, juicy fruit. In their dried form they are classically combined with Armagnac, a type of cognac, in French cuisine. The addition of chocolate makes for a moist, elegant, very adult-oriented chocolate cake.

FILLING

2¼ cups moist dried plums (prunes)

½ cup Armagnac or cognac

WHIPPED GANACHE

3 cups heavy cream

10 ounces semisweet chocolate, finely chopped, such as Valrhona Equitoriale (55%) or Ghirardelli (45%)

CAKE

6 large eggs, separated

½ cup sugar, divided

7 tablespoons sifted Dutch-processed cocoa

¼ teaspoon cream of tartar

Pastry bag

Large star decorating tip, such as such as Ateco #835 or Wilton #2110

1½ ounces semisweet chocolate, finely chopped, such as Valrhona Equitoriale (55%) or Ghirardelli (45%)

for the filling Place the dried plums in a single layer in a wide saucepan. Add the Armagnac and cook over medium heat until it almost comes to a boil. Remove from the heat, cover, and steep for 15 minutes. They are ready to use, or they may be stored at room temperature for up to 4 days in an airtight container.

for the ganache Put the cream in a large saucepan and bring to a boil over medium heat. Remove from the heat and immediately sprinkle the chocolate into the cream. Cover and allow to sit for 5 minutes. The heat of the cream should melt the chocolate. Gently stir until smooth. Refrigerate for at least 6 hours or up to 3 days in an airtight container.

for the cake Position a rack in the middle of the oven. Preheat the oven to 350°F. Coat two 8 × 2-inch round cake pans with nonstick spray, line the bottoms with parchment rounds, and then spray the parchment.

1) Whisk together the egg yolks, ¼ cup of the sugar, and the cocoa in a medium bowl; set aside.

2) In the clean, grease-free bowl of a stand mixer, whip the egg whites on low speed using the wire whip attachment until frothy. Add the cream of tartar and turn the speed to medium-high. When very soft peaks form, add the remaining ¼ cup sugar gradually. Continue whipping just until stiff peaks form. Fold about one-quarter of this meringue into the egg yolk mixture to lighten it, then fold in

the remaining whites until the mixture is uniform. Divide the batter evenly between the pans and smooth the top with an offset spatula.

3) Bake for 12 to 15 minutes, or until a toothpick inserted in the center shows a few moist crumbs when removed. The cake will look puffed and be very light in texture, almost soufflé-like. Cool completely in the pans on racks. The layers are ready to fill and frost. Alternatively, double-wrap the pans in plastic wrap; store at room temperature if assembling within 24 hours.

for the assembly Remove 12 plump prunes from their liquid and set aside. Puree the remaining prunes and any liquid in a food processor fitted with the metal blade attachment until a thick, smooth paste forms.

1) Whip the ganache in a stand mixer using the wire whip attachment, or whisk by hand with a large balloon whisk. Either way, whip just until soft peaks form, which will appear quickly.

2) Run an icing spatula around the edges of one cake layer and unmold it on a flat display plate that is at least 12 inches across; peel off the parchment if necessary. Evenly spread the prune puree over the cake with a small offset spatula. Use a light hand so as not to tear the cake. Cover with a thick layer of whipped ganache. Run an icing spatula around the edges of the second cake layer and unmold it right on top of the ganache; peel off the parchment if necessary. Cover the top and sides generously with whipped ganache. Scrape the remaining ganache into the pastry bag fitted with the tip. Pipe 12 large rosettes on top of the cake, evenly spaced around the outer edge. You may decorate the cake with additional rosettes around the bottom of the cake, if desired. Refrigerate the cake for at least 1 hour to set the ganache.

3) Meanwhile, melt the 1½ ounces chocolate in a double boiler or the microwave. Spread a piece of aluminum foil on a dinner plate. Dip the reserved 12 prunes halfway in the chocolate and place on the foil-lined plate. Refrigerate briefly to set the chocolate. Right before serving the cake, nestle the chocolate-dipped prunes on top of each rosette on top of the cake.

TIPS The cake layers are so light that they are most safely stored right in the pans in which they are baked, if they are to be stored overnight before assembling. Also, I do not unmold them onto cardboard rounds, as they stick to the cardboard and are hard to serve from them. By the way, I once made the finished cake on a Wednesday, placed it inside an airtight cake dome, and froze it until that Sunday. I took it out and let it defrost overnight in the refrigerator, and it was party-perfect on Monday. This cake is so moist, there is very little that can dry it out.

24-karat
manjari lemon truffle heart SERVES 10 TO 12

There are so many things I love about this cake. First and foremost, it is an intriguing blend of fruity dark chocolate and lemon, a combination I was introduced to at a chocolate tasting at La Maison du Chocolat. You can get this cake into the oven in 15 minutes, no fancy techniques required. The cake can wait for you in the refrigerator for up to 4 days, or in the freezer for up to a week, before you cloak it with a shiny chocolate glaze. You can make it in an 8 x 3-inch round pan, if you like. Note that you do need an extra-deep pan. Both round and heart-shaped 3-inch-deep pans can be found at www.bakedeco.com.

GLAZE

1 cup heavy cream

8 ounces bittersweet chocolate, finely chopped, such as Valrhona Manjari (64%) or Scharffen Berger (70%)

1 tablespoon freshly squeezed lemon juice

CAKE

9 large eggs, at room temperature

1½ pounds bittersweet chocolate, finely chopped, such as Valrhona Manjari (64%) or Scharffen Berger (70%)

1½ cups (3 sticks) unsalted butter, at room temperature

2 tablespoons finely minced lemon zest

1 tablespoon freshly squeezed lemon juice

for the glaze Put the cream in a medium saucepan and bring to a boil over medium heat. Remove from the heat and immediately sprinkle the chocolate into the cream. Cover and allow to sit for 5 minutes. The heat of the cream should melt the chocolate. Gently stir the ganache until smooth. If the chocolate is not completely melted, place over very low heat, stirring often, until melted, taking care not to scorch the chocolate. Whisk in the lemon juice. The glaze is ready to use. Refrigerate for up to 1 week in an airtight container or freeze for up to 1 month. You may rewarm the glaze to its fluid state on low power in the microwave or over very low heat in a saucepan.

for the cake Position a rack in the middle of the oven. Coat an 8 x 3-inch heart-shaped pan with nonstick spray. Cut out a heart-shaped piece of parchment paper using the pan as a guide. Line the pan with the parchment and spray the parchment.

1) Put the eggs, still in their shell, in a bowl of warm water for 5 minutes. This will warm the eggs and allow for maximum volume when whipped. Meanwhile, melt the chocolate and butter together in the top of a double boiler or in a microwave; stir until smooth. Whisk in the lemon zest and juice. Put the chocolate mixture in a large bowl, if it isn't already in one. In the bowl of a stand mixer, beat

the eggs on high speed using the wire whip attachment until tripled in volume and the mixture forms a ribbon. Fold about one-quarter of the eggs into the chocolate mixture to lighten it, and then fold in the remaining eggs until completely blended. Scrape into the prepared pan. Place the pan in a larger roasting pan. Add hot water to come halfway up the outside of the pan.

2) Bake for 12 to 15 minutes, or just until the surface looks dull. When you tilt the cake pan slightly, the edges will come away from the sides of the pan. The cake will look like a warmed-over pudding. Remove from the roasting pan and cool completely in the pan on a rack. Cover with plastic wrap and refrigerate overnight or for up to 4 days, or freeze for up to 1 month (in the pan). Defrost in the refrigerator overnight, if necessary.

for the assembly Have the glaze fluid and ready to use. Cut out a cardboard heart, using the pan as a guide. Unwrap the pan. Invert the pan and hold it so that your fingers are looped around the open side, which is now the bottom. Run hot water over the solid bottom and sides of the pan. Run a thin icing spatula under the hot water and then use it to loosen the cake from the sides of the pan. Place the cardboard heart over the cake, then invert the pan again, this time onto a flat work surface with a nice hard rap. The cake should unmold. Repeat the above steps if it does not. Also, jiggling the cake back and forth a bit can help loosen the surface tension that is making it stick to the pan. Place the cake, on the cardboard, on a rack set over a clean jelly-roll pan. Pour about three-quarters of the glaze over the center of the cake and allow it to drip toward and over the sides. Use a small icing spatula and any remaining glaze to help cover the sides. Refrigerate the cake for at least 1 hour to set the glaze, or overnight.

for the decoration Put about ½ teaspoon gold luster powder in a tiny bowl. Add drops of vodka, stirring with a brush, until you reach a paint consistency. Paint a freeform design on top of the chilled glaze, such as making whorls and swirls. Use tweezers to pull off tiny bits of the gold leaf and place here and there among the painted gold. It will stick to the glaze. Bring the cake to a cool room temperature before serving.

DECORATION
Edible gold luster powder
Vodka
Small artist's brush
1 sheet gold leaf, at least 22 karat
Tweezers

walnut praline torte

with espresso buttercream SERVES 10

This torte might be short in stature, but it is long on taste and sophistication. The cake itself includes 2 whole cups of ground walnuts baked into the 9-inch layer. After cooling, the cake is cut in half and given a good soaking with Kahlúa. The pastry cream–based buttercream is not too sweet and gets its coffee kick from instant espresso powder. I like to add a layer of apricot spread for moistness and flavor.

CARAMELIZED WALNUTS

Flavorless vegetable oil,
such as canola or sunflower

1 cup sugar

3 tablespoons water

1 cup walnut halves

TORTE

2 cups walnut halves, toasted
(see page 22)

¾ cup soft white bread crumbs

¼ cup cornstarch

6 large eggs, separated

⅔ cup sugar, divided

Pinch of salt

½ teaspoon almond extract

½ teaspoon vanilla extract

⅛ teaspoon cream of tartar

BUTTERCREAM

1 tablespoon plus 1 teaspoon
instant espresso powder,
such as Medaglia d'Oro

1 tablespoon hot water

Scant 1 cup whole milk

for the caramelized walnuts Line a jelly-roll pan with aluminum foil; smooth out any wrinkles. Lightly coat the foil with flavorless vegetable oil using a pastry brush.

1) Put the sugar and water in a very small saucepan and stir to combine. Bring to a boil over medium heat and cook until it turns light amber in color. Immediately remove from the heat. Quickly drop 8 walnut halves into the caramel one at a time, and use two forks to help them submerge and become coated with caramel. Use the forks to remove from the caramel, allow the excess to drip off, and place right side up on the prepared pan. Quickly stir in the remaining walnuts, then scrape the mixture out onto the prepared pan (not touching the individual walnuts) and spread as thin as possible.

2) Allow the nuts to cool at room temperature and harden completely. Leave the 8 individual walnut halves as is. Break up the remaining walnut praline into large chunks and process in a food processor fitted with the metal blade attachment into a fine, sparkly praline. Store the whole nuts and ground praline separately for up to 3 days in airtight containers.

for the torte Position a rack in the middle of the oven. Preheat the oven to 350°F. Coat a 9 x 3-inch round springform pan with nonstick spray, line the bottom with a parchment round, and then spray the parchment.

1) This large amount of walnuts must be finely ground without letting them become oily and pasty. I find the best way to do this is to grate them through the fine holes of a food processor disk attachment, then remove the disk, insert the metal blade attachment, add the bread crumbs and cornstarch, and process again until the nuts are finely ground; set aside.

2) In a stand mixer bowl fitted with the wire whip attachment, beat the egg yolks, ⅓ cup of the sugar, and the salt on medium-high speed until thick and creamy. Beat in the extracts. Fold the nut mixture into the egg yolk mixture until combined; set aside.

3) In the clean, grease-free mixer bowl of a stand mixer, whip the egg whites on low speed using the wire whip attachment until frothy. Add the cream of tartar and turn the speed to medium-high. When very soft peaks form, add the remaining ⅓ cup sugar gradually. Continue whipping until soft, glossy peaks form. Fold about one-quarter of the whites into the batter to lighten it, and then fold in the remaining whites just until white streaks remain. Scrape into the prepared pan, and smooth the top with a small offset spatula.

4) Bake for 25 to 30 minutes, or until a toothpick inserted in the center shows a few moist crumbs when removed. The cake might be tinged light golden brown and will have begun to come away from the sides of the pan. Cool cake in the pan on a rack for 8 to 10 minutes. Unmold, peel off the parchment, and place directly on the rack to cool completely. The layer is ready to fill and frost. Alternatively, place the layer on cardboard and double-wrap in plastic wrap; store at room temperature if assembling within 24 hours.

for the buttercream Whisk together the espresso powder and hot water in a medium saucepan until dissolved. Add the milk and heat over medium heat until warm.

1) Meanwhile, whisk together the yolks, sugar, and cornstarch in a heatproof bowl until very smooth; set aside.

2) Drizzle about one-quarter of the warm milk over the egg mixture, whisking gently. Add the remaining warm milk and whisk to

3 large egg yolks
⅓ cup sugar
2 tablespoons cornstarch
1 teaspoon vanilla extract
1 cup (2 sticks) unsalted butter, very soft, cut into pieces

SOAKING SYRUP AND FILLING
2 tablespoons sugar
2 tablespoons water
2 tablespoons Kahlúa
¼ cup 100% apricot spread (not jam or jelly)

combine. Immediately pour the mixture back into the saucepan; whisk in the cornstarch mixture and cook over medium-low heat until it begins to simmer and bubbles appear. Whisk constantly to prevent scorching, cooking for about 1 minute. The pastry cream should be thick enough to mound when dropped from a spoon, but still satiny. Remove from the heat and whisk in the vanilla.

3) Allow the pastry cream to cool completely; stir occasionally to release the heat. The buttercream is ready to be finished; or, alternatively, when almost at room temperature, scrape into an airtight container, press plastic wrap directly onto the surface, snap on the cover, and refrigerate for up to 3 days. Bring back to room temperature before finishing the buttercream.

4) In the bowl of a stand mixer fitted with the wire whip attachment, briefly beat the room-temperature pastry cream on low speed to loosen it slightly. With the mixer running on medium speed, add the butter, a few tablespoons at a time, and beat until the butter is absorbed before adding more. Keep adding butter until all is added, and beat until perfectly smooth. The buttercream is ready to use and best if used immediately.

for the soaking syrup Put the sugar and water in a small saucepan and stir to combine. Bring to a boil over high heat, swirling the pot once or twice to help the sugar dissolve. Remove from the heat and cool to room temperature. Add the Kahlúa.

for the assembly Place the cake layer on a cardboard round (if not already), bottom side down. Slice evenly in half horizontally; place the top half to the side. Use a pastry brush to add half the soaking syrup to the bottom half of the cake. Spread the apricot spread evenly over the cake. Spread a $^1/_4$-inch layer of the buttercream over the apricot filling. Put the top cake half into place, cut side down. Use a pastry brush to apply the remaining soaking syrup. Apply the buttercream smoothly to the top and sides of the cake. Press the ground praline to the sides of the cake (you can just pick up the cake on the cardboard and hold over the bowl of praline mixture with one hand, and apply the praline mixture with your other hand). Arrange the whole caramelized walnuts evenly around the top of the cake. The cake may be served immediately or refrigerated overnight in an air-tight container. Bring to room temperature before serving.

unmolding springform and loose-bottomed cake pans

You are probably familiar with springform pans. They are comprised of a flat bottom and an expandable ring that goes around the base, forming the sides, which then closes and snaps into place. They are usually called for when making cheesecakes. A loose-bottomed pan has a one-piece solid ring (the sides of the pan) and a flat, loose bottom that goes down into the ring and fits snugly. The two types of pan can be used interchangeably. I prefer loose-bottomed pans, as the sides are solid and completely smooth. To unmold, here are some helpful techniques:

* Run a warm icing spatula around the edges of the cake, pressing out toward the pan. If you press inward, you might shave off some of the cake. This will begin loosening the cake from the pan.

* Warming the outside of the pan's sides is also helpful. Wrap a warm, wet towel around the outside for a minute to loosen the cake. Place the bottom of the pan on a smaller diameter base, such as a large canned good. For springform-style pans, unhinge the springform, open it wide, and bring it down and away from the cake. For the loose-bottomed style, just pull straight down and away. If the cake is a cheesecake, you can try twisting it a bit if it resists.

* For either style, if the cake is resisting unmolding, you can apply heat from a hair dryer to the exterior of the pan's sides, or you can even use a propane or butane torch (such as the ones used for torching crème brûlée).

pomegranate-chocolate
mousse cake SERVES 10

This is replacing raspberries and chocolate as my favorite fruit-and-chocolate combination, and if you like the former, you will enjoy this as well. The tangy, fruity, acidic aspects of the pomegranate work wonderfully with milk and dark chocolate, in this case a chocolate cake brushed with pomegranate syrup, filled with a milk chocolate mousse, covered in a pale pink pomegranate buttercream, and topped with a pomegranate-chocolate ganache. Several of the components can be made ahead, so plan accordingly. You will need two pomegranate products: POM Wonderful 100 percent pomegranate juice, found in many supermarkets, as well as pomegranate molasses, found in specialty stores and stores featuring Middle Eastern ingredients. Both are integral to the recipe, so seek them out. Al Wadi pomegranate molasses has a very good flavor and is preferred.

MOUSSE

9 ounces dark milk chocolate, finely chopped, such as Valrhona Jivara (40%)

⅓ cup POM Wonderful 100% pomegranate juice

1½ cups chilled heavy cream

SYRUP

⅓ cup sugar

⅓ cup water

⅓ cup pomegranate molasses, such as Al Wadi

1 recipe Dark and Moist Chocolate Cake (page 6), layers baked and cooled

for the mousse Combine the milk chocolate and juice and melt together in the top of a double boiler or in a microwave; stir until smooth. Allow to cool until barely warm. Whip the cream until soft peaks form. Fold into the chocolate. Cover the bowl with plastic wrap and refrigerate until firm enough to spread, or refrigerate overnight in an airtight container.

for the syrup Put the sugar and water in a small saucepan and stir to combine. Bring to a boil, swirling the pot once or twice, and boil for about 1 minute or until the sugar dissolves. Cool, then whisk in the pomegranate molasses.

for the initial assembly Level each cake layer, if necessary. Split each layer in half horizontally into 2 equal halves; you should have 4 even layers. Place one layer, bottom side down, on a same-size cardboard round. Brush the layer with syrup, then spread generously with mousse. Top with another layer of cake, brush with syrup, and top with mousse. Repeat one more time with the third cake layer. Top with the final cake layer, bottom side up. Brush this top layer with syrup. Refrigerate the cake until the mousse is firm, about 1 hour.

1) Make sure the buttercream is silky smooth and soft; it should be the texture of mayonnaise. Apply a thin crumb coat of buttercream. Chill until the buttercream is firm, about 1 hour. Apply a final coat of buttercream, making a very smooth surface on the top and sides of the cake. Chill briefly while you make the ganache.

for the ganache Put the cream in a medium saucepan and bring to a boil over medium heat. Remove from the heat and immediately sprinkle the chocolate into the cream. Cover and allow to sit for 5 minutes. Gently stir until smooth. Gently whisk in the pomegranate molasses. Cool slightly, but it should still be fluid.

for the final assembly The aim is to create a solid layer of ganache on top of the cake and create attractive drips of the ganache down the sides of the cake; some of the buttercream on the sides should still show through. To best accomplish this, pour the ganache straight down onto the center of the cake and allow it to pool outward toward the edges where it will eventually drip over the edges and down the sides. You might have to encourage this by very gently moving the ganache out toward the edges with a small offset spatula. Use a very light hand and agitate the ganache as little as possible. You can also pick up the cake and tilt it this way and that. The drips will be asymmetrical, which is fine. Refrigerate until the ganache has firmed up, about 1 hour. The cake may be may be refrigerated for up to 2 days. Bring to room temperature before serving. If desired, peel and seed the fresh pomegranate and remove about 2 tablespoons of fresh seeds. Sprinkle the seeds on top of the cake and serve immediately.

½ recipe Italian Meringue Buttercream (page 8), made with POM Wonderful 100% pomegranate juice instead of water

GANACHE

1 cup heavy cream

9 ounces semisweet chocolate, finely chopped, such as Ghirardelli (45%), Callebaut (52%), Valrhona Equitoriale (55%), or Bissinger's (60%)

Heaping ¼ cup pomegranate molasses, such as Al Wadi

1 fresh pomegranate (optional)

chocolate mango
cloud cake   SERVES 8 TO 10

This is ethereal, decadent, and rich all at the same time. The base is a flourless chocolate cake, part cakey, part pudding-like. A layer of moist, fragrant mangoes tops the cake and sits under a "cloud" of softly whipped cream. It is a subtle textural delight. The choice of chocolate and fruit is important. Valrhona Manjari's acidic, fruity flavor profile brings out the same flavors in the mango. And as far as the fruit itself is concerned, I like the smaller, flatter, golden yellow Ataulfo mangoes for this recipe. They are extremely flavorful and sweet and creamy in texture, being much less fibrous than the larger, oval varieties. I often find ripe and inexpensive mangoes in Asian and Latin markets.

for the cake Position a rack in the middle of the oven. Preheat the oven to 350°F. Coat a 10-inch springform pan with nonstick spray.

1) Melt the chocolates and butter together in a microwave or the top of a double boiler; stir until smooth and allow to cool slightly.

2) In the bowl of a stand mixer, whip the eggs and sugar on high speed using the wire whip attachment until thick and a ribbon forms. Fold about one-quarter of the eggs into the chocolate mixture to lighten it, then fold in the rest. Fold in the cocoa powder. Scrape into the prepared pan.

3) Bake for 15 to 20 minutes, or until the top looks dry, the cake is slightly puffed, and the edges might have just begun to come away from the sides of the pan. A hairline crack may have formed, which is fine. Cool completely in the pan on a rack. The cake may be stored at room temperature for up to 24 hours, covered with plastic wrap.

for the fruit filling Cut each mango lengthwise on each side of the pit, as close to the pit as possible. You will have 2 cupped halves. Score ½-inch squares into the flesh, taking care not to cut through the skin. Turn each half "inside-out" by pressing up on the skin, exposing and

CAKE

4 ounces bittersweet chocolate, finely chopped, such as Valrhona Manjari (64%) or Scharffen Berger (70%)

4 ounces bittersweet chocolate, finely chopped, such as Valrhona Caraïbe (66%) or Callebaut (71%)

½ cup (1 stick) unsalted butter, at room temperature, cut into pieces

5 large eggs, at room temperature

1 cup sugar

½ cup sifted Dutch-processed cocoa, such as Valrhona

FRUIT FILLING

3 ripe mangoes (preferably Ataulfo), 7 or 8 ounces each

1 tablespoon sugar

2 teaspoons freshly squeezed lime juice

chocolate mango cloud cake (*continued*)

1¾ cups chilled heavy cream

3 tablespoons sifted confectioners' sugar

¼ teaspoon vanilla extract

separating all of the squares. Working over a bowl, use a spoon to scoop under the flesh, along the skin; the squares will pop right out. Sprinkle with the sugar and lime juice and toss to coat. The filling may be used right away or refrigerated for up to 1 hour.

for the topping and assembly Right before serving, combine the cream, confectioners' sugar, and vanilla in a large bowl and whip until soft peaks form.

1) Unmold the cake and place on a display plate. Use a slotted spoon to scoop up the mango and scatter evenly over the top of the cake. Use a rubber spatula to scrape all of the cream on top of the cake. Use a large spoon to create attractive whorls and peaks. Serve immediately, cut into wedges.

TIP When folding the egg mixture, chocolate mixture, and cocoa, I find a large balloon whisk is the best way to start the folding process; then I finish off with a large rubber spatula.

cassata with chocolate,
cherries, orange, and almonds   SERVES 10 TO 12

Fresh ricotta has an incomparable bright, clean dairy flavor and can be whipped until very smooth to create a classic, creamy filling for this take on *cassata Siciliana*. Traditionally, this cake is often covered with a fondant-type icing and/or marzipan. Mine has an emphasis on chocolate with a dark chocolate ganache glaze, but also includes all the expected and harmonious flavors of candied orange peel, almonds, chocolate, and maraschino liqueur. This incredibly aromatic liqueur is redolent of cherries, orange, almonds, and rose and creates a signature flavor profile for this cake, so do not leave it out.

I created this version for a dear friend, Iris Kent, on her 88th birthday. This is a tall, substantial cake, suitable for such important occasions. Fresh ricotta truly makes this cake. There will be variations in their moisture content, so if yours is particularly moist, verging on wet, drain it for 15 minutes in a cheesecloth- or coffee filter–lined strainer set in the sink. To assemble the cake you will need a 9-inch diameter springform pan that is a full 3 inches high. Using the pan as a mold helps create the cake's symmetrical shape.

for the cake Position a rack in the middle of the oven. Preheat the oven to 350°F. Coat two 9 x 2-inch round cake pans with nonstick spray, line the bottoms with parchment rounds, and then spray the parchment.

1) Whisk together the flour, baking powder, and salt in a medium bowl to aerate and combine; set aside.

2) In the bowl of a stand mixer, beat the egg yolks and 1 cup of the sugar with the wire whip attachment on medium-high speed until thick and creamy. Beat in the extracts. Slowly drizzle the butter over the batter and fold in until combined, then fold the dry mixture into the egg yolk mixture until combined; set aside.

3) In the clean, grease-free bowl of a stand mixer, whip the egg whites on low speed using the wire whip attachment. Add the cream

SPONGE CAKE

1½ cups sifted cake flour

1½ teaspoons baking powder

½ teaspoon salt

6 large eggs, separated

1 cup plus 2 tablespoons sugar, divided

1 teaspoon vanilla extract

¼ teaspoon almond extract

6 tablespoons (¾ stick) unsalted butter, melted and slightly cooled

⅛ teaspoon cream of tartar

SOAKING SYRUP

⅓ cup sugar

⅓ cup water

⅔ cup maraschino liqueur

FILLING

3½ cups fresh whole-milk ricotta cheese

1 cup plus 1 tablespoon sifted confectioners' sugar

2 ounces semisweet chocolate, such as Valrhona Equitoriale (55%), Ghirardelli, (45%) or Callebaut (52%), grated on largest holes of a box grater

½ cup blanched sliced almonds, toasted (see page 23) and chopped

⅓ cup diced candied orange peel, finely chopped

⅓ cup dried tart cherries, finely chopped

1 recipe Dark Chocolate Ganache (page 7)

DECORATION

3 ounces marzipan (must be soft and pliable)

¼ cup blanched sliced almonds, toasted (see page 23)

2 tablespoons diced candied orange peel, finely chopped

⅓ cup dried tart cherries

of tartar and turn the speed to medium-high. When very soft peaks form, add the remaining 2 tablespoons sugar gradually. Continue whipping until soft, glossy peaks form. Fold about one-quarter of the whites into the batter to lighten it, and then fold in the remaining whites just until white streaks remain. Scrape into the prepared pans, smoothing the tops with a small offset spatula.

4) Bake for 20 to 25 minutes, or until a toothpick inserted in the center shows a few moist crumbs when removed. The cake will be light golden brown and will have begun to come away from the sides of the pan. Cool cakes in the pans on racks for 8 to 10 minutes. Unmold, peel off the parchment, and place directly on the racks to cool completely. Trim the layers to be level, if necessary. The layers are ready to assemble. Alternatively, place the layers on cardboards and double-wrap in plastic wrap; store at room temperature if assembling within 24 hours.

for the soaking syrup Put the sugar and water in a medium saucepan and stir to combine. Bring to a boil over medium-high heat and simmer until the sugar is dissolved. Remove from the heat and cool to room temperature. Add the maraschino.

for the filling Whisk the ricotta in a large bowl until smooth. Whisk in the confectioners' sugar, then fold in the grated chocolate, almonds, orange peel, and cherries.

for the assembly Slice each cake in half horizontally into 2 equal halves, creating 4 equal halves each about ½-inch thick. Place one layer, bottom side down, in the bottom of a 9 × 3-inch springform pan. Brush liberally with the soaking syrup and top with a third of the filling mixture, leveling the top with a small offset spatula. Repeat with the cake layers and filling, ending with a cake layer bottom side up, brushed well with syrup. Double-wrap very well with plastic wrap and refrigerate for at least 6 hours or overnight.

1) Have the ganache fluid but not hot. Unmold the cake and place on a rack set over a clean jelly-roll pan. Pour about 1 cup of ganache over the top of the cake and carefully spread it to cover the top of the cake and allow to drip down the sides. Use a small spatula to help the ganache cling to the sides. This entire coat will be thin. Refrigerate until the ganache is firm. Repeat the glazing with the remaining ganache creating an opaque layer of glaze on the top and sides of the cake. Refrigerate until the ganache is firm.

for the decoration Knead the marzipan to soften. Roll out on a work surface into long ropes the thickness of a pencil. Create a border around the top outer edge of the cake with the marzipan ropes. I like to allow a few inches of marzipan to be interspersed with loops of marzipan. Sprinkle the almonds along the outer edges of the cake, next to your marzipan, and gently press to adhere to the ganache. Sprinkle the orange peel and cherries over the center top of the cake. The cake is ready to serve or may be refrigerated for up to 1 day. Bring to room temperature before serving.

chocolate mousse meringue cake

with blueberries and cream SERVES 10

The sweet yet tart nature of blueberries pairs very well with dark chocolates, especially chocolates with slightly fruity flavor notes. This cake is comprised of three layers of crisp yet delicate cocoa meringue interspersed with a fresh blueberry jam, whipped cream, and fresh blueberries. The outside is textured, featuring small piped logs of chocolate meringue that adhere to the exterior coating of chocolate mousse. The visual of the cake is a tribute to the classic Lenôtre cake called Concorde, but this is a very modern version, with the addition of the fruit. This cake is elegant to behold and is one of those desserts that seems to be rich and light at the same time.

for the jam Put the blueberries, sugar, and lemon juice in a medium nonreactive saucepan. Cook over medium heat, stirring occasionally, until the sugar dissolves and the berries begin to give off juice. Roughly mash the berries with a potato masher or a fork. Continue to cook, stirring occasionally, until the fruit softens and the juices thicken and begin to evaporate, 10 to 15 minutes; when you draw a wooden spoon across the bottom of the pot, it should leave a trail where you can see the pot. Cool to room temperature. Refrigerate in an airtight container for about 4 hours, until cold and spreadable. The jam may be refrigerated for up to 2 days.

for the mousse Refrigerate 1 cup of the heavy cream. Heat the remaining ½ cup cream in a saucepan until hot but not boiling. Meanwhile, whisk the egg yolks and sugar in a heatproof bowl. Add the hot cream slowly, whisking constantly. Pour the mixture back into the saucepan and cook to 150°F, which will happen quickly, so don't walk away. Pour through a fine-mesh strainer. Set aside, whisking occasionally to release the heat.

1) Meanwhile, melt the chocolates in the top of a double boiler or in the microwave; stir until smooth. Combine the custard and chocolate and whisk occasionally until cooled to room temperature.

BLUEBERRY JAM

4 cups fresh blueberries

¼ cup sugar

2 teaspoons freshly squeezed lemon juice

CHOCOLATE MOUSSE

1½ cups heavy cream, divided

3 large egg yolks

2 tablespoons plus 1 teaspoon sugar

3 ounces semisweet chocolate, finely chopped, such as Valrhona Equitoriale (55%) or Ghirardelli (45%)

2 ounces bittersweet chocolate, finely chopped, such as Valrhona Caraïbe (66%), Valrhona Manjari (64%), or Scharffen Berger (70%)

COCOA MERINGUE

8 large egg whites

1 teaspoon cream of tartar

1¾ cups sugar

1 teaspoon vanilla extract

¼ cup sifted Dutch-processed cocoa

Pastry bag

½-inch plain round decorating tip, such as Ateco #806, Wilton #1A or a standard coupler that is a solid round, with no notch

FILLING AND TOPPING

1 cup chilled heavy cream

2 tablespoons sifted confectioners' sugar

1½ cups fresh blueberries, divided

1 tablespoon sifted Dutch-processed cocoa

1 tablespoon sifted confectioners' sugar

2) In the bowl of a stand mixer, beat the chilled 1 cup cream until firm peaks form (a little firmer than soft peaks, but not stiff). Fold about one-quarter of the cream into the chocolate to lighten, then fold in the remaining cream just until no white streaks remain. Scrape into an airtight container and refrigerate for at least 6 hours or until firm enough to spread. The mousse may be refrigerated overnight.

for the cocoa meringue Position three racks in the upper, middle, and lower third of the oven. Preheat the oven to 250°F. Line 3 jelly-roll pans with parchment paper. Using the bottom of an 8-inch cake pan, trace two circles on one pan, so that the circles are not touching. (They will just fit on 1 pan). Trace one circle on the second pan. Flip the papers over; you should still be able to see the circles through the parchment.

1) In the clean, grease-free mixer bowl of a stand mixer, whip the egg whites on low speed using the wire whip attachment until frothy. Add the cream of tartar and turn the speed to medium-high. When soft peaks form, add the sugar gradually. Continue whipping until stiff, glossy peaks form. Beat in the vanilla and then the cocoa until well combined. Scrape the meringue into the pastry bag fitted with the tip or coupler. Starting in the center of the traced circles, pipe a tight spiral until you create a disk that fills the traced area. Repeat with other 2 circles. You will have extra; pipe long, straight logs of meringue in the open space on the pan with one disk as well as on the third pan until you use up all of the meringue. Make sure that none of the meringue disks or logs touch one another.

2) Bake for 1 hour and 45 minutes to 2 hours, or until dry to the touch. You should be able to gently lift a meringue disk from the parchment. Cool completely on the pans on racks. The meringue is ready to assemble. Store at room temperature for up to 3 days in an airtight container; these must be kept completely dry.

for the filling Right before assembling, whip the chilled cream and sugar just until stiff peaks form.

for the assembly Place 1 meringue disk, bottom side down, on a flat display plate. Spread with half of the blueberry jam, going almost to the edge. Cover with half of the whipped cream and sprinkle with ½ cup blueberries. Top with the second meringue disc and repeat with the blueberry jam, whipped cream, and another ½ cup blueberries. Top with the remaining disk, bottom side up. Spread the mousse on top and cover the sides. (If the mousse is stiff, put in a bowl over hot water and stir until softened.) Break or cut up the meringue logs into approximately 2-inch pieces and press them here and there on the sides and top. They should be flat against the cake as well as jutting out 3-D at angles (see photo on page 154). Scatter the remaining ½ cup blueberries on top; the berries should nestle here and there between the "logs." You may also press the berries here and there along the sides of the cake. Refrigerate for at least 4 hours or up to 6 hours; the meringue will soften and the whole will improve in texture. The cake may be refrigerated overnight. Right before serving, sift the cocoa and then the confectioners' sugar over the cake.

TIP In humid weather, or if you are at all concerned about the meringue not being dried out enough, leave the pans in the oven after you turn the oven off, while the oven cools. They will continue to dry out. If I am making the meringue the night before, I just keep the disks and logs stored in the oven on their pans until needed. The jam can be made with defrosted frozen blueberries; however, I find that these give a slightly lower yield and a less tender texture. I do prefer using fresh.

the voluptuous chocolate-covered
strawberry ganache cake SERVES 10 TO 12

ncreasingly I have people asking me to develop desserts that fit certain dietary life-styles, and non-dairy and vegan are high on that list. I believe that we all deserve to occasionally indulge, so it was a welcome challenge to create a cake that would satisfy while still meeting the requested criteria. This cake is indeed vegan, but I didn't put that in the title, because I didn't want to scare away those not so inclined; this cake is delectable for any and all chocolate lovers. The cake itself is very easy to make and is actually found in the Basics chapter, as I use it in my daily life for many applications. It is moist and dark—and just happens to be vegan. The ganache is made from chocolate and soy milk. The choice of soy is important, as they differ widely in flavor and texture; I prefer not to use low-fat varieties. The strawberries add moisture, color, and flavor. I have made this cake just as successfully with fresh raspberries.

for the ganache Put the soy milk in a large saucepan and bring just to under a boil over medium heat. Remove from the heat and immediately sprinkle the chocolate into the soy milk. Cover and allow to sit for 5 minutes. The heat of the soy milk should melt the chocolate. Gently stir the ganache until smooth. If the chocolate is not melting, place over very low heat, stirring often, until melted, taking care not to scorch the chocolate. Allow to cool until it is a spreadable consistency, between peanut butter and mayonnaise. You may stir it over ice water to hasten chilling, if desired.

for the assembly Have all components ready to use. Save the best strawberry for the center top of the cake. Stem the remaining berries and slice thinly (about ⅛ inch) through the stem end. Save the most attractive sliced berries for the top of cake.

1) Slice each cake layer evenly in half horizontally. Place one layer, bottom side down, on a cardboard round. Spread with some of the ganache, then arrange a thin, even layer of sliced berries. Repeat with the remaining cake layers, more ganache, and sliced berries.

SOY GANACHE

1 cup unsweetened soy milk, such as Eden brand Edensoy Original (do not use low-fat or "light")

12 ounces semisweet or bittersweet chocolate, finely chopped, such as Scharffen Berger (62%), Valrhona Manjari (64%), or Ghirardelli (45%)

ASSEMBLY

2 pounds medium strawberries

1 recipe Dark and Moist Chocolate Cake (page 6), layers baked and cooled

2 ounces semisweet or bittersweet chocolate, finely chopped, such as Scharffen Berger (62%), Valrhona Manjari (64%), or Ghirardelli (45%)

The final cake layer should be bottom side up. Cover the top and sides of the cake with ganache and allow to firm up at room temperature for several hours, or refrigerate briefly. Once the ganache is firmed, melt the remaining ganache in the microwave or in the top of a double boiler until it is fluid. Pour the remaining ganache over the cake and down the sides and apply a smooth final coat. Stem the reserved beautiful strawberry and place stem end side down in the center top of the cake. Starting on the outer top edge of the cake, arrange the remaining sliced berries in concentric rings all the way to the center, so that they touch the center berry. Melt the 2 ounces of chocolate, and put in a parchment cone. Drizzle over the berries in a looping pattern, radiating out from the center—kind of like drawing petals of chocolate over the berries in big swooping loops that start at the center berry and go to the edge of the cake. Allow the chocolate to set. The cake may stand at room temperature for up to 4 hours before serving.

TIP   To make this cake ahead, complete it through the step where you apply the final coat of ganache. The cake may be refrigerated overnight at this point. Bring to room temperature before serving and complete the decoration within 4 hours of serving.

angelic chocolate–espresso mousse cake

with chocolate-dipped strawberries SERVES 12

Angel pies have a meringue crust, which adds other features to the expected textures and flavors of what we think of when it comes to pies. However, try as I might, forming them in pie plates has never worked for me. I then set my sights on forming the crust in a springform pan, but that was not up to par either. Both techniques left me with malformed crusts that were hard to unmold and serve. As so many meringue recipes call for piping or forming meringue directly on a pan, I decided to try this approach, and it worked perfectly—and also brought the "pie" into a more stately "cake" dimension. It does crumble a bit when cut, but that is part of its charm. Meringue is very sweet, and the bitter edge of espresso in the dark chocolate mousse tempers that sweetness, while also adding a sophisticated edge. It is quite potent, though, so make this for coffee lovers. The chocolate-dipped strawberries add flavor and color and bring this cake into the realm of "Unforgettable."

for the crust Position a rack in the middle of the oven. Preheat the oven to 275°F. Line a jelly-roll pan with parchment paper. Trace one 9-inch circle on the paper; flip the paper over. You should be able to see the circle through the parchment.

1) Whisk together the confectioners' sugar and cornstarch in a small bowl to aerate and combine; set aside.

2) In the clean, grease-free mixer bowl of a stand mixer, whip the egg whites on low speed using the wire whip attachment until frothy. Add the cream of tartar and turn the speed to medium-high. When soft peaks form, add the superfine sugar gradually. Continue whipping until stiff, glossy peaks form. Beat in the vanilla. Fold in the confectioners' sugar–cornstarch mixture.

3) Use a large soupspoon to dollop large scoops of the meringue within the borders of the circle on the pan. Use the back of the spoon to create a flat, wide center and a high border all around, with

ANGEL MERINGUE CRUST

Scant 1 cup sifted confectioners' sugar

2¼ teaspoons cornstarch

3 large egg whites (save yolks for filling)

¼ teaspoon cream of tartar

Heaping ½ cup superfine sugar

½ teaspoon vanilla extract

CHOCOLATE-ESPRESSO MOUSSE FILLING

¼ cup hot water

1 tablespoon instant espresso powder, such as Medaglia d'Oro

9 ounces semisweet chocolate, finely chopped, such as Valrhona Equitoriale (55%) or Ghirardelli (45%)

cakes (161)

¼ cup Kahlúa

3 large egg yolks

¾ cup chilled heavy cream

CHOCOLATE-DIPPED
STRAWBERRIES

12 medium to large fresh, firm strawberries, stems intact

6 ounces semisweet chocolate, finely chopped, such as Valrhona Equitoriale (55%) or Ghirardelli (45%)

TOPPING

1 cup chilled heavy cream

2 tablespoons sifted confectioners' sugar

¼ teaspoon vanilla extract

attractive peaks here and there. Make sure the center is wide and flat and allows enough space to hold the forthcoming mousse. It might seem improbable that you can make this meringue structure right on the pan, but the meringue is very thick and holds its shape, and the shell comes together quite easily.

4) Bake for 1 hour to 1 hour and 30 minutes, or until the meringue is dry. It should easily lift off of the parchment without breaking. Cool completely on the pan on a rack. The meringue is ready to assemble or may be stored at room temperature for up to 2 days in an airtight container.

for the mousse Have the meringue shell on a flat display plate. Stir together the hot water and espresso powder in the top of a double boiler or in a microwave-safe bowl. Add the chocolate and Kahlúa and melt; stir until smooth, and cool to warm room temperature. Whisk in the egg yolks, one at a time. Whip the cream just beyond soft peaks and fold into the chocolate mixture until thoroughly combined. Immediately scrape into the meringue shell, gently smoothing the top. Refrigerate for at least 4 hours or overnight.

for the chocolate-dipped strawberries Line a jelly-roll pan with aluminum foil and smooth out any wrinkles. Very lightly coat with nonstick spray. Wash and thoroughly dry the strawberries. Melt the chocolate in the top of a double boiler or in a microwave and stir until smooth. Transfer the chocolate to a narrow, deep container such as a measuring cup. Holding the berries one at a time by the stem, dip a berry into the chocolate all the way to the "shoulder" of the berry. You want to leave some of the red berry and the stem exposed. Remove the berry and gently shake back and forth to encourage excess chocolate to drip back into the container. You want to create as thin a coating as possible. Place the berry, broad side down, on the prepared pan. Repeat with the remaining berries, and then refrigerate until the chocolate firms up, at least 1 hour. Refrigerate for up to 6 hours, but no longer.

for the topping and assembly Right before serving, whip the cream, confectioners' sugar, and vanilla until soft to firm peaks form. Pile the whipped cream on top of the dessert, covering the surface of the mousse, and creating attractive peaks here and there.

1) Place the berries evenly around the cake right where the whipped cream topping meets the meringue. Serve immediately. Use a sharp knife as well as a sharp triangular serving spatula to serve wedges. There will be some crumbling, but believe me, no one is going to complain. Make sure each person gets a chocolate-dipped berry.

TIPS   There are raw yolks in the mousse. Use pasteurized eggs, if concerned. To save room in the refrigerator, once the chocolate is set on the berries, you can peel them off the aluminum foil and transfer to a smaller plate or container; just keep in a single layer.

black cocoa
blackout cake SERVES 10

The visual of this cake, with its shaggy coating of dark cake crumbs, harkens back to Ebinger's Blackout Cake, beloved in the New York area. The bakery closed its doors in the early 1970s and the original recipe was never published; my version uses "black" cocoa, which is a specialty product that you can order from The Baker's Catalogue (see Resources, page 287). It has the color and flavor of the cocoa in Oreo cookies, and when combined with natural cocoa in this recipe, it gives the cake an extra-deep chocolaty boost. The filling and frosting is a rich pudding, which was one of the hallmarks of the original cake. Use the cocoas and chocolates suggested for best results. The pudding component is best made a day ahead. By the way, this impressive-looking cake is very easy to make. Don't tell anyone—people will think you slaved over it.

PUDDING

¼ cup sifted cornstarch

2 cups whole milk

1 cup heavy cream

1¼ cups sugar

6 ounces unsweetened chocolate, finely chopped, such as Scharffen Berger (99%)

¼ teaspoon salt

1½ teaspoons vanilla extract

CAKE

3 cups all-purpose flour

2 cups sugar

⅓ cup sifted black cocoa

⅓ cup sifted natural cocoa

1 tablespoon instant espresso powder, such as Medaglia d'Oro

2 teaspoons baking soda

for the pudding Put the cornstarch in a small bowl. In a large measuring cup or bowl, combine the milk and cream. Drizzle a few tablespoons of the milk-cream mixture over the cornstarch and whisk until smooth. Pour the remaining milk-cream into a medium pan, then add the cornstarch slurry, sugar, chocolate, and salt. Cook over medium-low heat, whisking often, until the chocolate melts, then watch carefully as you bring it to a gentle boil. Whisk often as it thickens and takes on a pudding consistency; it should simmer for about 2 to 3 minutes. The pudding should be thick and glossy and leave whisk marks on top. Remove from the heat and whisk in the vanilla. Scrape into an airtight container; cool to warm room temperature. Press plastic wrap directly onto the surface, snap on the lid, and refrigerate for at least 6 hours or preferably overnight.

for the cake Position a rack in the middle of the oven. Preheat the oven to 350°F.

1) Coat two 8 x 2-inch round cake pans with nonstick spray, line the bottoms with parchment rounds, and then spray the parchment.

2) Whisk together the flour, sugar, both cocoas, espresso powder, baking soda, and salt in a large bowl to aerate and combine. Whisk together the water, oil, vinegar, and vanilla in a medium bowl. Pour the wet ingredients over the dry mixture and whisk well until combined and very smooth. Divide the batter evenly between the 2 pans. Firmly tap the bottom of the pans on the work surface to dislodge any bubbles.

3) Bake for 30 to 35 minutes, or until a toothpick inserted in the center shows a few moist crumbs when removed. Cool cakes in the pans on racks for about 10 minutes. Unmold, peel off the parchment, and place directly on the racks to cool completely. Trim the layers to be level, if necessary, reserving the scraps. The layers are ready to use. Alternatively, place the layers on cardboards and double-wrap in plastic wrap; store at room temperature and assemble or serve within 24 hours.

for the assembly Have all the components ready to use. Slice both cake layers evenly in half horizontally. Three layers will be used to assemble the cake. The fourth should be crumbled by hand into a bowl along with any scraps; this will be used for the exterior of the cake. Place one cake layer on a serving plate, bottom side down. Cover with a thick layer of pudding, then top with the second cake layer and another layer of pudding. Top with the third cake layer, bottom side up. Cover the top and sides generously with pudding, which will be thick enough to stick to the cake. Use your fingers and palms to completely cover the cake top and sides with cake crumbs, pressing them into the pudding to adhere. Refrigerate for at least 1 hour and up to 8 hours before serving.

1 teaspoon salt

2 cups warm water

⅔ cup flavorless vegetable oil, such as canola or sunflower

2 tablespoons apple cider or distilled white vinegar

1 tablespoon vanilla extract

crème fraîche cheesecake

with rhubarb compote SERVES 10 TO 12

I adore cheesecakes in all of their guises, from ricotta-based Italian-style to dense, creamy New York–style to this unique ethereal version based largely on the sweet yet slightly tangy crème fraîche. Some cheesecakes are baked slowly in water baths or low-temperature ovens. This one is initially baked at a high heat, which gives it a distinguished brown top crust, while the center stays light and moist. This is all about the crème fraîche, so make sure it is very fresh. I use Vermont Butter & Cheese Company brand, which has a consistently good flavor and texture.

I had this cake in France, where it was barely sweetened, and was much more of an adjunct to the cheese course than a dessert. I have sweetened it up a bit and suggest serving it with a sweet-tart rhubarb compote. Take care when poaching the rhubarb so that it retains its shape; you do not want it breaking down into shreds. This makes a lovely Easter or other early-spring dessert. While many cheesecakes that contain cream cheese freeze well, I think the delicate texture of this one is best enjoyed within a day or two of baking.

COMPOTE

2 cups sugar

1 cup water

1 pound fresh rhubarb, preferably very red, cut into 3 x 1-inch pieces (you may or may not need to cut it lengthwise, depending on the width of the stalks)

CRUST

2 cups very finely ground shortbread cookie crumbs, such as Lorna Doone cookies (one 10-ounce box)

3 tablespoons unsalted butter, melted

for the compote Stir the sugar and water together in a medium sauté pan. Bring to a simmer over medium heat and cook until the sugar dissolves. Add the rhubarb and simmer just until tender, about 10 minutes. Set aside to cool. The compote may be used immediately, or carefully transfer to a shallow, wide, airtight container, taking care to keep the rhubarb in whole pieces. Refrigerate for up to 3 days.

for the crust Position a rack in the middle of the oven. Preheat the oven to 350°F. Generously butter the insides of a 9-inch springform or loose-bottomed pan.

1) Combine the cookie crumbs and melted butter in a small bowl, then press into an even layer on the bottom of the prepared pan. Bake for 15 to 20 minutes or until dry and just turning light golden brown. Cool in the pan on a rack while you prepare the filling. Increase the oven temperature to 500°F.

for the cheesecake In the bowl of a stand mixer, beat the cream cheese with the flat paddle attachment on medium-high speed until creamy, about 3 minutes. Add the sugar gradually and beat until very light and fluffy, about 3 minutes. Scrape down the bowl once or twice. Beat in the vanilla. Beat in the eggs one at a time, scraping down after each addition and allowing each egg to be absorbed before continuing. Beat in the crème fraîche and flour very gently and just until combined. Scrape the cheesecake batter over the crust in the prepared pan and smooth into an even layer.

1) Bake for 10 minutes, then turn the oven down to 275°F and open the oven door so that the oven cools down to 275°F as quickly as possible. Close the oven and continue baking at 275°F for 45 to 55 minutes, or until the top is tinged golden brown, the cake is puffed, and the center jiggles if gently shaken. Cool completely in the pan on a rack. Cover with plastic wrap and refrigerate overnight or for up to 2 days. Unmold the cake and place on a display plate. Serve cold, cut into wedges, with the compote alongside.

CHEESECAKE

1½ pounds cream cheese (not low-fat), at room temperature, cut into pieces

¾ cup plus 2 tablespoons sugar

2 teaspoons vanilla extract

4 large eggs, at room temperature

2 cups crème fraîche, at room temperature

1 tablespoon all-purpose flour

pies and tarts

THIS CATEGORY OF desserts is so versatile, encompassing everything from a double-crusted apple pie using various textures of
apples and a lattice-crusted pear pie rich with brown butter and
vanilla bean to a pecan-coconut-chocolate tart that is rich as a candy bar
and a smooth, silky custard pie with the flavors of banana and caramel.
Generally speaking, fruit pies and tarts are best eaten soon after they
are made—a warm apple pie on a fall day has much to be said for it. I
have given you many do-ahead tips in the sidebar on page 189; make
sure to read them through and take advantage of any steps that can be
completed ahead of time. Also, please note that pie plates and tart pans
come in many sizes, and the recipes suggest specific ones; you can read
more about this in the sidebar on page 202.

how to bake unforgettable pies

* Make the piecrust dough well ahead so that it has time to chill; it will roll out more easily.

* Lightly flour your work surface for rolling; too much flour will toughen the piecrust.

* Use the proper size pie plate as suggested in each recipe; they are not interchangeable.

* Coat the pie plate with nonstick spray to make serving easier.

* Make sure the oven is preheated properly. Many pies need a very hot oven in order to set the crust quickly.

* Take advantage of do-ahead steps so that fruit pies can be baked as close to serving time as possible.

* To save time, crusts can be rolled out on parchment, rolled up, wrapped well in plastic wrap, then frozen or refrigerated—this is a huge time saver.

latticed browned butter—
vanilla bean pear pie SERVES 8

This has become highly anticipated by my guests on my Thanksgiving table. It is a lattice-top pie filled with juicy pears tossed in browned butter, fragrant vanilla beans, and sweet golden raisins, which add a pleasant chewiness. Either Anjou or Bartlett pears work well.

FILLING

2 tablespoons unsalted butter

1 moist and plump vanilla bean

4 pounds ripe but firm pears, peeled, cored, and cut into ½-inch wedges

⅔ cup golden raisins

½ cup firmly packed light brown sugar

1 tablespoon all-purpose flour

1 teaspoon freshly squeezed lemon juice

1 recipe Double-Butter Piecrust (page 2), chilled and ready to roll out

TOPPING

2 teaspoons whole milk

1 tablespoon sugar

1) Position a rack in the middle of the oven. Preheat the oven to 375°F. Coat a 9 × 1¼-inch tempered glass pie plate with nonstick spray. Line a jelly-roll pan with parchment, set aside.

for the filling Put the butter in a small saucepan and melt over medium heat. Cut the vanilla bean in half crosswise, then slit each piece lengthwise and scrape all the seeds into the butter using a butter knife or small teaspoon. Add the empty pods to the butter as well. Continue cooking the butter and vanilla until the butter is golden brown but not burned, about 5 minutes. Remove from the heat and cool slightly.

1) Gently fold together the pear slices, raisins, brown sugar, flour, and lemon juice in a medium bowl. Remove the vanilla bean pods from the butter and discard. Pour the butter over the pear mixture and fold gently to combine.

2) Roll out one dough disk on a floured surface to a 12-inch round. Transfer to the pie plate. Scrape the filling into the crust. Roll out the second dough disk to a 12-inch round and cut into 1-inch-wide strips using a straight edge or fluted pastry wheel. Weave a lattice crust on top of the filling, trimming the strips and bringing the bottom crust up and over the strip's edges to seal. Crimp decoratively.

for the topping Brush the lattice with the milk and sprinkle with the sugar. Place the pie on the prepared pan. Bake for 55 to 65 minutes, or until the crust is golden brown and the filling is bubbling. Cool the pie plate directly on a rack for 30 minutes to allow the juices to thicken. Serve warm or at room temperature. Store at room temperature overnight, loosely covered with foil, if desired.

how to bake unforgettable tarts

* Make sure you have the correct size tart pan. I measure across the bottom. Many tart pans are European and may have odd metric sizes, which can throw off these recipe.

* Coat tart pans with nonstick spray to make serving easier.

* Make sure the oven is preheated properly. Many tarts need a hot oven in order to set the crust quickly.

* If baking blind, line the crust with aluminum foil, smooth it along the bottom and along the crust's edges with your fingers, then fill with pie weights.

* When baking blind, bake until the crust is beginning to set before removing the foil.

    After removing the foil, bake the crust just until it begins to color and/or is somewhat dry, or bake until done as the recipe dictates.

* Many tarts necessitate a chilling time before serving; make sure to follow the recommendations in individual recipes.

* Keep tarts in their pans until serving time to protect the crust.

* To create the most even crumb-style crust, use the bottom of a flat-bottomed, straight-sided glass or measuring cup to press against the crumbs. To create neat "corners," nestle the bottom edge of the cup up against the crumbs along the sides of the pan and press against them.

* If you transport the tart somewhere, don't forget to retrieve your tart bottom after serving! Many get misplaced this way.

cheesecake tart with . . .

SERVES 10

Cheesecakes never go out of style, and with good reason. They are rich and creamy and lend themselves to all sorts of variation. Oftentimes, however, if served after a meal, they can be quite heavy. My solution is to keep all of the flavor and texture, but shrink its size and turn it into a tart. Classic New York–style cheesecakes often come with a graham cracker crust; but using crisp oatmeal cookies offers a whole new flavor profile while maintaining the ease of a pat-in-style crust. The title of the recipe is meant to indicate how you can customize the tart to your liking, as it can be topped in many different ways, or even left as is. I have provided some topping ideas for you, but feel free to come up with your own.

CRUST

1¾ cups very fine crisp oatmeal cookie crumbs (without raisins)

¼ cup (½ stick) unsalted butter, melted

CHEESECAKE

1 pound regular or low-fat Neufchâtel cream cheese, at room temperature, cut into pieces

⅔ cup sugar

1 large egg

¼ teaspoon vanilla extract

½ cup sour cream (not low-fat)

1) Position a rack in the middle of the oven. Preheat the oven to 350°F. Coat a 10-inch loose-bottomed fluted tart pan with nonstick spray.

for the crust Stir the cookie crumbs and butter together in a small bowl. Pat evenly into the pan, covering the entire bottom and sides. Bake for 12 to 15 minutes, or until very lightly browned. Cool in the pan on a rack.

for the cheesecake Beat the cream cheese in the bowl of a stand mixer with the flat paddle attachment until creamy and smooth, about 2 minutes. Add the sugar and continue beating until light and fluffy. Beat in the egg, then the vanilla. Briefly beat in the sour cream. Scrape into the tart shell.

1) Bake for 25 to 35 minutes; the filling will be slightly puffed and the center will still jiggle slightly. Cool the tart pan on a rack. Refrigerate tart for at least 3 hours. The tart is ready to serve as is, or cover it with the topping of your choice (see below). The "naked" tart may be refrigerated for up to 2 days, covered with plastic wrap.

tropical topping

1) In a small saucepan over medium-low heat, melt the guava jelly and gently brush over the top of the cheesecake. Peel and slice the kiwi into ¼-inch-thick rounds. Peel, seed, and cut the papaya into ¼-inch-thick slices. Peel and pit the mango and cut into ¼-inch dice. Place overlapping papaya slices around the outside of the tart, with one end of each slice pointing toward the center of the tart and the other touching the edge. Then form an inner circle of overlapping kiwi slices. Place a small center mound of diced mango inside the kiwi. Slice the passion fruit in half crosswise. Scrape the passion fruit seeds onto the very center. Serve immediately or refrigerate for up to 3 hours. This is best served the day it is assembled.

¼ cup guava jelly, such as Smucker's

2 ripe kiwi

1 large (about 28 ounces) ripe red-fleshed papaya

1 ripe mango

2 ripe passion fruit

classic strawberry topping

1) You will need 3 cups of berries. Set 2 cups aside; chop the remaining 1 cup berries and put in a medium saucepan. Stir in the sugar and lemon juice and allow to sit for 10 to 15 minutes, or until the juices begin to exude. Mash the berries with a potato masher and bring to a simmer over medium-high heat, stirring the mixture occasionally as it cooks. Cook, stirring frequently, for about 5 minutes. Meanwhile, dissolve the cornstarch in the water and stir into the simmering berries. Continue to simmer and stir until thickened and glossy, 1 to 2 minutes. Scrape the mixture into a sieve set over a bowl; press down on the berry sauce until the solids are as dry as possible. Discard the solids. Reserve the glaze, cooling slightly; the glaze should still be fluid. Thinly slice the remaining berries and arrange attractively on top of the tart (in any design you like). Brush with the glaze. Serve immediately or refrigerate for up to 3 hours. This is best served the day it is assembled.

1 quart fresh strawberries, stemmed

¼ cup sugar

1 tablespoon freshly squeezed lemon juice

2 teaspoons cornstarch

1 tablespoon water

lemon-blueberry topping

1⅔ cups fresh blueberries, divided

1½ teaspoons sugar

½ teaspoon water

¾ cup Lemon Cream (page 12), chilled and ready to use

1) Stir together $\frac{1}{2}$ cup of the blueberries, the sugar, and the water in a small saucepan and bring to a boil over medium heat. Mash with a potato masher or fork and cook until soft and juicy and the fruit has broken down into a thick, saucy mash. Remove from the heat and fold in the remaining fresh fruit. Cool completely.

2) Spread the Lemon Cream over the cheesecake, leaving a $\frac{1}{2}$-inch border of cheesecake around the edges. Spoon the berries along the outer edge, in the available space. Serve immediately or refrigerate for up to 3 hours. This is best served the day it is assembled.

the berries pie

SERVES 8

Food memories can be quite vivid and hold strong associations. For me the thought of blueberry pie, which is what my nana always made for me, takes me right back to summers in New England. When I considered what it was about that pie that engaged me, I realized it was the quality of the flavors and juices from the berries. They concentrate beautifully during the high-heat baking, especially when sealed with a solid top crust. That balance of tart and sweet and the slight thickening of the juices, but not too much so, is what makes a blueberry pie so unforgettable for me. It occurred to me that other berries, such as raspberries and blackberries, can cook down with similar qualities, and so the idea for this pie was born. The juices in this pie have a tendency to overflow, so do bake the pie on a jelly-roll pan as suggested, to catch drips. I think a scoop of vanilla ice cream on the side enhances this dish enormously.

1) Position a rack in the middle of the oven. Preheat the oven to 400°F. Coat a 9½ x 1½-inch tempered glass pie plate with nonstick spray. Line a jelly-roll pan with parchment paper; set aside.

for the filling Whisk together the sugar and cornstarch in a large bowl to blend. I use 4 tablespoons of cornstarch, which makes a very juicy pie; increase to 5 or 6 tablespoons if you want more body. Add the berries and toss to coat. Let stand for 10 minutes, tossing occasionally.

for the dough and assembly Roll out 1 dough disk on a lightly floured surface to a 12-inch round; transfer to the prepared pie plate. Spoon the filling into the dough-lined dish. Roll out the second dough disk to a 13-inch round. Drape the dough over the filling, and trim the overhang to ½ inch. Press the edges together to seal; fold the overhang under and crimp decoratively. Cut several small slashes in the top crust to vent. Brush the top crust with the milk and sprinkle with the sugar, if desired. Place on the prepared pan.

1) Bake for 50 to 60 minutes, until the crust is golden and the filling is bubbling. Cool the pie plate directly on a rack for 30 minutes to

FILLING

1 cup sugar

4 to 6 tablespoons cornstarch

3 cups fresh blackberries

3 cups fresh blueberries

3 cups fresh red raspberries

1 recipe Double Butter Piecrust (page 2), chilled and ready to roll out

TOPPING

2 teaspoons whole milk

1 tablespoon sugar, optional

TIPS The freshness of the fruit is imperative for this pie, as it is all about the fruit. You will notice that there is not even any lemon juice added—nothing to take away from the pure, unadulterated flavor of the berries. Taste the berries before you buy them, if you can. They should be sweet, ripe, and ready to eat. I like a juicy pie and use the lesser amount of cornstarch. If you like a pie that cuts more cleanly, use the larger amount. Do not be tempted to alter the ratio of fruit; the body that the blueberries give is important to the finished dish. Also, trimming the crust is an important step. You want there to just be enough bottom and top crust so that you can press them together well, tuck them underneath, and create a good seal. It is easier to work with a generous amount of dough, but after baking, that creates a thick, indelicate crust. This goes for all two-crusted pies.

allow the juices to thicken. Serve warm or at room temperature. The pie is best served the day it is baked.

measuring berries

Over the past several years I have noticed that strawberries, blackberries, raspberries, and blueberries are being packaged in a variety of ways, some new to the market. It used to be that there were simple pints and quarts. Now we have those as well as 6-ounce packages, 5-ounce packages, 5½-ounce packages, containers labeled as dry pints, others labeled just as pints, and packages that are obviously much larger or smaller than any of the more expected sizes. This is important to recipe developers because since what you will find at the market is no longer standard, it ceases to make sense for us to call for "1 pint raspberries" in an ingredient listing if what you find is anything but.

Because of this variability, I call for volume measures for blueberries, raspberries, and blackberries, because there is little variation in their size and also because I think that you can easily eyeball at the supermarket what 1 cup or 2 cups looks like. Measuring strawberries, however, is more problematic. They can be as small as a fingernail or larger than a golf ball. In the book you will find strawberries called for in a few different ways, as I have determined which makes most sense for that recipe. In general, I try to find well-flavored berries that are small to medium in size. For some recipes, it is the final sliced or chopped volume of strawberries that is most important, so you will see this kind of listing as well.

If you are wondering why this confusion in the supermarket exists, it is because of the bottom line. Strawberries are often now packaged in plastic clamshell baskets in 1-pound, 32-ounce, and even 4-pound sizes, because they are easier to ship; less fruit lost due to damage means more money for the farmer and supermarket. In the off-season, packages will often be smaller for all berries, so the overall cost does not seem so high, in the hopes that this will still tempt the consumer. Conversely, at farmer's markets, the "pints" and "quarts" will often be filled to the point of overflowing, offering you a much higher yield than same-size packages in the supermarket.

red and purple plum tart
with marzipan crumble   SERVES 10 TO 12

I like to use a variety of purple-skinned and red-fleshed plums for this tart. (Do not use prune plums.) Unlike many recipes, this one does take very kindly to variation—if you are lucky enough to find fresh ripe apricots, simply substitute them for the plums and you will have yet another extraordinary tart. The flavor of the almond paste works very well with both fruits. By the way, you should note that the recipe calls for almond paste, not marzipan per se; it's just that "marzipan" sounds better in the title.

for the crust Coat a 10-inch loose-bottomed fluted tart pan with non-stick spray.

1) Put the flour, almonds, sugar, and salt in the bowl of a food processor fitted with the metal blade attachment and pulse to combine. Add the butter and pulse on and off until it forms a very coarse meal; there might be pockets of butter that are larger, which is fine. Pulse in the egg yolk, then drizzle in the smaller amount of cream through the feed tube and pulse until the dough is moistened and just holds together if squeezed. Add additional cream only if necessary. Scrape the crust mixture into the prepared tart pan and press into an even layer along the bottom and sides, flouring your fingertips, if necessary. Freeze for 15 minutes or refrigerate for 30 minutes while you prepare the topping. Preheat the oven to 400°F.

for the topping Put the flour, almond paste, brown sugar, and melted butter in a small bowl. Toss with your fingertips or a wooden spoon until well combined. Toss in the almonds; set aside.

for the filling Toss the plums, sugar, and cornstarch together in a medium bowl until the fruit is evenly coated.

for the assembly Line a jelly-roll pan with parchment paper; set aside. Line the tart shell with foil and pie weights. Place the tart pan

CRUST
1 cup all-purpose flour

¾ cup natural or blanched sliced almonds

¼ cup sugar

Pinch of salt

½ cup (1 stick) chilled unsalted butter, cut into pieces

1 large egg yolk

1 to 2 tablespoons chilled heavy cream

TOPPING
¾ cup all-purpose flour

5 ounces almond paste, crumbled

½ cup firmly packed light brown sugar

6 tablespoons (¾ stick) unsalted butter, melted

¼ cup natural or blanched sliced almonds

red and purple plum tart (*continued*)

FILLING

12 to 14 medium, ripe plums,
pitted and cut into eighths
(to yield 5 cups)

½ cup sugar

3 tablespoons cornstarch

directly on the oven rack and bake for 15 minutes; remove the foil and weights and bake for 5 minutes more. The crust should be dry to the touch and just tinged light golden brown.

1) Reduce the oven temperature to 375°F. Place the tart on the prepared jelly-roll pan.Pour the filling into the crust and sprinkle the topping evenly over the filling. Bake for 40 to 50 minutes, or until the filling is bubbling and the topping is a light golden brown. Cool the tart pan on the jelly-roll pan set on a rack. The tart is best served the same day but may be loosely covered with foil and stored overnight at room temperature.

cranberry-apricot
linzer torte SERVES 12

The classic linzer torte is made with a ground nut lattice crust and a filling of red jam, such as raspberry or red currant. This version uses hazelnuts and has a particularly moist, flavorful, thick—and pretty—cranberry filling. I make this every Thanksgiving and have it on hand for dessert as well as for breakfast. Fresh or defrosted frozen cranberries can be used, and the canned apricots work beautifully; don't be afraid of using high-quality canned goods such as these. Just make sure to purchase the ones packed in juice, not sugar syrup.

1) Position a rack in the middle of the oven. Preheat the oven to 350°F. Coat a 10-inch loose-bottomed fluted tart pan with nonstick spray. Line a jelly-roll pan with parchment; set aside.

for the crust Combine the hazelnuts and 1 cup of the flour in a food processor fitted with the metal blade attachment. Pulse on and off until the nuts are finely ground. Add the remaining 1 cup flour, the sugar, baking powder, and cinnamon. Pulse on and off once or twice to combine. Add the butter and pulse on and off until the mixture is the texture of coarse meal. Pulse in the egg yolks, orange zest, and vanilla and process until the mixture clumps. Turn the dough out onto a work surface, knead together briefly, and divide in half. Form one half into a flat disk, wrap with plastic wrap and freeze. Press the remaining half of the dough into the prepared tart pan, covering the bottom and sides evenly (you might have to dip your fingers in extra flour). Place the tart shell on the prepared pan. Line tart with foil and pie weights and blind-bake for 10 minutes. Place jelly-roll pan on rack to cool while you make the filling.

for the filling Combine the cranberries, apricots, sugar, and orange juice in a saucepan and bring to a boil over medium heat, stirring often, until the cranberries break down and the mixture has thickened,

CRUST

1 cup skinned whole hazelnuts

2 cups all-purpose flour, divided

¾ cup sugar

1 teaspoon baking powder

1 teaspoon ground cinnamon

¾ cup (1½ sticks) chilled unsalted butter, cut into pieces

2 large egg yolks

1 teaspoon orange zest

1 teaspoon vanilla extract

FILLING

3 cups cranberries

Two 15-ounce cans apricot halves packed in juice, drained and roughly chopped

1 cup sugar

¼ cup orange juice, freshly squeezed or not-from-concentrate

cranberry-apricot linzer torte (*continued*)

2 tablespoons apricot jam

1 teaspoon water

about 12 minutes. Let sit at room temperature while you roll out the top crust.

for the assembly Remove the dough from the freezer and roll out to an 11-inch round between two pieces of lightly floured parchment paper. Cut into 1-inch-wide strips with a straight or fluted edge pastry wheel.

1) Scrape the filling into the tart and weave a lattice crust on top with the strips. Press the outer edges of the strips to the par-baked pastry as well as you can to seal.

2) Bake the tart for 30 to 40 minutes, or until light golden brown; the filling should be bubbling. Cool the tart pan on the jelly-roll pan set on a rack.

for the topping Whisk together the apricot jam and water in a small saucepan and bring to a boil over medium heat. Boil for 1 minute. Press through a fine-mesh strainer, then brush over the warm crust. Cut into wedges and serve warm or at room temperature. The tart may be made 2 days ahead and stored at room temperature, wrapped well in plastic wrap.

TIP Some friends have told me they occasionally have trouble with the dough. After thinking about this for some time, I have come to believe that the problem is the nuts. Nuts have natural oils and some will be "oilier" than others. Fresh nuts that have never been frozen have the most oils and perform best. So buy your nuts fresh for this recipe—and definitely roll out the well-chilled dough for the lattice between pieces of parchment paper.

pecan-coconut tart
with chocolate crust SERVES 14 TO 16

My inspiration for this tart was my desire for a chocolate pecan pie with a more elegant silhouette. By making it into a tart, I think the proportions of crust to filling are also improved. The brown sugar and coconut add another dimension and the whole is very sweet and almost candy-like. Make sure to use unsweetened coconut, often found in natural foods stores. A little slice goes a long way. Serve with unsweetened whipped cream.

1) Coat a 10-inch loose-bottomed fluted tart pan with nonstick spray. Line a jelly-roll pan with parchment; set aside.

for the crust Put the flour, cocoa, sugar, and salt in the bowl of a food processor fitted with the metal blade attachment and pulse to combine. Add the butter and pulse on and off until it forms a coarse meal. Whisk together the egg yolk and cream, then drizzle through the feed tube and pulse until the dough is moistened and just holds together if squeezed. Press over the bottom and up the sides of the prepared pan. Pierce all over with a fork. Chill for at least 2 hours or up to 1 day.

1) Position a rack in the middle of the oven. Preheat the oven to 375°F. Place tart pan on prepared pan. Bake for 8 to 10 minutes, or until just beginning to dry. Cool the tart pan on the jelly-roll pan set on a rack while you prepare the filling.

for the filling Turn the oven down to 325°F. Whisk together the melted butter, brown sugar, and corn syrup. Whisk in the eggs one at a time, and then stir in the vanilla, salt, coconut, chocolate morsels, and pecans. Scrape the filling into the crust.

1) Bake for 40 to 50 minutes, or until the filling is puffed and is firm along the edges but still soft in the center. You might be able to

CRUST

1¼ cups all-purpose flour

¼ cup sifted Dutch-processed cocoa

3 tablespoons sugar

Pinch of salt

½ cup (1 stick) chilled unsalted butter, cut into pieces

1 large egg yolk

2 tablespoons chilled heavy cream

FILLING

¼ cup (½ stick) unsalted butter, melted

1 cup firmly packed light brown sugar

1¼ cups light corn syrup

3 large eggs

2 teaspoons vanilla extract

¼ teaspoon salt

¾ cup unsweetened shredded coconut

½ cup miniature semisweet chocolate morsels

1½ cups pecan halves, toasted (see page 23)

TOPPING

2 ounces semisweet chocolate, such as Ghirardelli (45%) or Callebaut (52%)

2 tablespoons unsweetened shredded coconut

see that the edges have begun to take on a little color. The filling will firm up tremendously upon cooling. Cool the tart pan on the jelly-roll pan set on a rack

for the topping Melt the chocolate in a double boiler or a microwave and spread it in a 1-inch border around the edges using a small offset spatula, then sprinkle the coconut on top of the chocolate. Refrigerate for 10 minutes to set the chocolate. The tart is ready to unmold and serve. The tart may be covered with foil and refrigerated for up to 2 days. Serve at room temperature or chilled.

espresso black-bottomed pie
in a chocolate chip cookie crust SERVES 8

Sometimes you want comfort food for dessert . . . something familiar and soothing, simple and satisfying. This dessert is in that category; consider it a stepped-up version of a classic custard pie. It cuts beautifully, with very clearly delineated layers. The dark chocolate custard filling is enhanced with the flavor of espresso, as is the generous topping of café au lait–colored whipped cream. The crust is a modified chocolate chip cookie dough—the elimination of any egg or leavener allows the crust to keep its shape in the pie plate. I like the walnuts in the crust, but I have made them optional so that you can make this dish for those who cannot have nuts.

1) Position a rack in the middle of the oven. Preheat the oven to 350°F. Coat a 9½ × 1½-inch tempered glass pie plate with nonstick spray.

for the crust In the bowl of a stand mixer, beat the butter and sugar on medium-high speed with the flat paddle attachment until sandy and smooth, about 3 minutes. Add the flour, salt, and vanilla, and beat on medium speed until the mixture begins to come together; it might look crumbly, but if you squeeze it between your fingers, it will come together. Beat in the chocolate morsels and nuts, if using, until combined. Gather the dough together into a ball with your hands while it is still in the bowl. Press into the prepared pie plate in an even layer along the bottom and up the sides, creating an even, high rim.

1) Bake for 20 to 22 minutes. The crust should be tinged light brown along the edges, but the bottom will still be a little soft. Do not bake any further; it firms up tremendously upon cooling. Cool the pie plate on a rack. The crust may be used immediately or stored overnight at room temperature, wrapped in plastic wrap.

for the filling Whisk together the sugar, cornstarch, cocoa, espresso powder, and salt in a medium heavy-bottomed saucepan. Whisk in

CRUST

5 tablespoons unsalted butter, at room temperature, cut into pieces

⅓ cup firmly packed light brown sugar

1 cup all-purpose flour

¼ teaspoon salt

2 teaspoons vanilla extract

¼ cup miniature semisweet chocolate morsels

½ cup walnut halves, toasted (see page 23) and finely chopped, optional

FILLING

⅔ cup sugar

¼ cup cornstarch

2 tablespoons Dutch-processed cocoa

½ teaspoon espresso powder

Pinch of salt

6 large egg yolks

1¾ cups whole milk

¾ cup heavy cream

6 ounces bittersweet chocolate, finely chopped, such as Valrhona Caraïbe (66%)

1½ teaspoons vanilla extract

TOPPING

1 teaspoon instant espresso powder

1 teaspoon vanilla extract

1⅓ cups chilled heavy cream

¼ cup confectioners' sugar

1 ounce bittersweet chocolate, grated, such as Valrhona Caraïbe (66%), optional

the yolks until smooth, then whisk in the milk and cream until combined. Cook over medium heat, whisking frequently, until it comes to a boil. At that point, whisk constantly until the custard thickens, 1 to 2 minutes. Remove from the heat and immediately whisk in the bittersweet chocolate and vanilla until smooth. Cool for 15 minutes, whisking occasionally to release the heat. Scrape into the prepared crust and refrigerate until chilled and firm, for at least 4 hours or overnight.

for the topping Dissolve the instant espresso powder in the vanilla in a chilled mixer bowl. Add the cream and sugar and beat on medium-high speed with the wire whip attachment until firm peaks form. Spread over the top of the custard, mounding gently in the middle. Sprinkle with the grated chocolate, if desired. Serve immediately or refrigerate for up to 6 hours.

lemon meringue tart

SERVES 10 TO 12

I truly believe that this is an improvement on lemon meringue pie. The classic pie filling, tempered with cornstarch as a thickener, has never been lemony enough for me. Also, there was always the danger of soggy crust and weeping meringue. This recipe features a sweet crust that is baked blind, which retains its crispness. The filling is a very puckery lemon cream, cooked separately, so you can easily control its thickness and prevent that soggy crust. The egg whites for the meringue topping are cooked over a water bath and are quite stable and never weep. An added plus is that the crust and filling can be made ahead. A candy thermometer is necessary for this recipe.

for the filling Put the eggs, yolks, sugar, and lemon juice in the top of a double boiler. Whisk together to break up the eggs. Whisk in the butter and zest. Cook over simmering water in the bottom of the double boiler, whisking often; the mixture will remain quite liquid for several minutes. After 10 to 15 minutes, the mixture will begin to thicken and bubble around the edges; whisk frequently at this point until the mixture thickens and reaches 180°F. (The temperature is more important than the time it takes, and the cream itself should not boil.) The cream will thicken and form a soft shape when dropped from a spoon. Let cool to room temperature, stirring occasionally to release the heat. Scrape into an airtight container and refrigerate for at least 6 hours or up to 1 week.

for the topping Whisk together the egg whites and sugar in a stand mixer bowl. Create a double-boiler; put the bowl in a large pot with enough hot water added so that it touches the bottom of the mixing bowl. Bring the water to a boil; whisk the whites occasionally. As the temperature nears 140°F, whisk frequently until the mixture reaches 160°F. Remove the bowl from the heat and place on the stand mixer. Add the cream of tartar and whip on high speed with the wire whip attachment until a thick meringue forms. Keep beating until it cools

FILLING

8 large eggs

5 large egg yolks

1 cup plus 3 tablespoons sugar

1 cup plus 2 tablespoons freshly squeezed lemon juice

6 tablespoons (¾ stick) unsalted butter, at room temperature, cut into small pieces

1 tablespoon finely grated lemon zest

TOPPING

4 large egg whites

1 cup sugar

Heaping ¼ teaspoon cream of tartar

1 Sugar Tart Crust (page 3), baked and cooled

to a barely warm temperature, about 5 minutes. The meringue must be used immediately.

for the assembly Unmold the tart shell and place on a display platter. Spread the lemon filling in the tart shell in an even layer. Top with the meringue and create peaks all over the top with an icing spatula or the back of a spoon. Brown the top with a butane or propane torch, or under a preheated broiler (in which case, place display plate on a jelly-roll pan). The tart is ready to serve or may be refrigerated for up to 4 hours.

TIP This filling is a large-batch version of a lemon cream or lemon curd. Sometimes I make lemon creams over direct heat, with careful monitoring. I find that with this large amount it is too easy to scramble the eggs, so take your time and use the double boiler technique suggested above.

bittersweet chocolate-caramel tart

with espresso cream and chocolate tangle SERVES 14 TO 18

The flavors of dark chocolate and very dark caramel are sophisticated, luscious, and, in this case, easy to put together, and yet the resulting dessert is spectacular. A sweet, buttery crust is filled with one layer of dark, burnt sugar caramel filling and one of bittersweet chocolate ganache. The whole is topped with espresso whipped cream and showered with shards of crisp chocolate. It is a textural delight. The specific chocolates used are necessary for the desired texture of the finished dish. While there are several components, the crust, ganache, caramel, and "tangle" can all be made ahead, so take advantage of this and it will come together easily. This tart is very rich and can be served in very slim slices.

for the tangle Cover a jelly-roll pan with aluminum foil and smooth the foil as best as you can to eliminate any wrinkles; set aside. Melt the chocolate in the top of a double boiler. When it is three-quarters of the way melted, remove from the heat, remove from the bottom of the double boiler, and stir very gently until completely melted. Scrape into a parchment cone, snip a very small opening, and make squiggly, overlapping lines, this way and that, on the prepared pan. Refrigerate until completely firm. Break into large pieces; may be used immediately or refrigerated for up to 1 week in an airtight container in single flat layers separated by foil or parchment.

for the ganache Put the cream in a large saucepan and bring to a boil over medium heat. Remove from the heat and immediately sprinkle the chocolate into the cream. Cover and allow to sit for 5 minutes. The heat of the cream should melt the chocolate. Gently stir the ganache until smooth. If the chocolate is not melting, place over very low heat, stirring often, until melted, taking care not to scorch the chocolate. Cool to room temperature. May be refrigerated for up to 1 week in an airtight container or frozen for up to 1 month. Reheat on the stove top or in a microwave before using just until fluid, but not hot.

CHOCOLATE TANGLE

2 ounces bittersweet chocolate, finely chopped, such as Valrhona Guanaja (70%)

GANACHE

1⅓ cups heavy cream

12 ounces bittersweet chocolate, finely chopped, such as Valrhona Caraïbe (66%)

CARAMEL

1½ cups sugar

6 tablespoons water

¾ cup heavy cream

1 Sugar Tart Crust (page 3), fully baked and cooled

ESPRESSO CREAM

1 teaspoon instant espresso powder, such as Medaglia d'Oro

½ teaspoon vanilla extract
1 cup chilled heavy cream
2 tablespoons sifted confectioners' sugar

for the caramel Put the sugar and water in a large heavy-bottomed pot. Stir to moisten the sugar and cook over medium-low heat, without stirring, until the syrup begins to color. Wash down the sides of the pot once or twice with a damp pastry brush if necessary. When the syrup is a medium amber color, watch closely, as the color will deepen quickly. Within the next minute or so the caramel will turn a very dark mahogany brown, the bubbles will be tan, and wisps of smoke might appear. Immediately remove from the heat and swirl the pot to dissipate the heat. Place on a cool burner and slowly pour in the cream. The mixture may bubble up furiously; just let the bubbling subside and whisk until smooth. If the cream is too cool, it will cause the caramel to seize; just place the pot back over low heat and stir until the sauce liquefies. Cool to room temperature. Refrigerate for up to 1 month in airtight container. Reheat in a double boiler or microwave before using just until fluid, but not hot.

for the assembly Have ganache and caramel fluid, but not hot. Scrape the caramel into the prepared tart shell. Use a small offset spatula to help it spread into an even layer. Freeze or refrigerate briefly until it is firm. Scrape the ganache over the caramel layer, using a small offset spatula to help it spread into an even layer. Refrigerate until firm, at least 4 hours, or up to 1 day ahead.

for the espresso cream and assembly Remove the tart from the refrigerator about 15 minutes before serving to soften slightly. In the chilled bowl of a stand mixer, whisk together the instant espresso powder and vanilla until dissolved. Add the cream and confectioners' sugar and beat on medium-high speed with the wire whip attachment until almost firm peaks form. Pile billows of the whipped espresso cream on top of the tart and crown with the broken pieces of chocolate "tangle." The tart is ready to serve. This is best cut with a sharp, thin-bladed knife, dipped in warm water between slices.

how to always have freshly baked fruit pies

Throughout this book I have striven to bring you do-ahead tips to make your life easier in the kitchen and therefore make the baking process more pleasurable. I am a stickler when it comes to my fruit pies . . . apple, pumpkin, berry, whatever flavor, I want it to be as freshly baked as possible when I serve it. Here is my approach:

For Single-Crusted Pies:

* Prepare the pie pastry; chill.
* Roll out the crust.
* Form the crust in the prepared pie plate, crimp, and freeze.
* Once frozen, wrap well in plastic wrap, taking care not to crush the decorative crimping.
* Freeze or refrigerate the crust till needed.
* Defrost in the refrigerator overnight, if applicable.
* Make the filling while the oven preheats.
* Fill the crust, bake the pie, and voilà!

For Double-Crusted Pies:

* Prepare the pie pastry; chill.
* Roll out each crust on a large piece of lightly floured parchment paper. The bottom disk should be about 12 inches across; the top crust about 13 inches.
* Roll up each piece of parchment with the crust inside. Crimp the ends of the parchment, then wrap well in plastic wrap.
* I keep a 15-inch mailing tube handy to insert the rolled crusts, which protects them during storage.
* Freeze or refrigerate the crusts till needed, taking care not to let them be crushed.
* Defrost in the refrigerator overnight, if applicable.
* Unroll the bottom crust, and fit into the prepared pie plate.
* Make the filling while the oven preheats.
* Fill the crust, place the top crust, crimp, bake the pie, and voilà!

deep-dish sour cream–apple pie

with lemon-cardamom streusel SERVES 8 TO 10

This is extra deep, formed in a springform pan. The sides are more than 2 inches deep, so there is plenty of filling. The crunchy, buttery brown sugar crumb on top is lightly accented with cardamom and lemon and is the perfect foil to the lush, rich, sour cream and apple filling. When you slice a big wedge, it is picture-perfect; guests will think this came from a fancy bakery. There are several do-ahead steps, so take advantage, particularly with two chilling times for the crust.

for the crust Roll out half of the dough on a lightly floured surface to a 10-inch round. Use the bottom of a 9 × 3-inch round springform pan as a guide and cut out a 9-inch circle. Assemble the pan with the sides locked into place, and coat the inside with nonstick spray. Transfer the circle of crust to the bottom of the pan. Roll out the remaining dough and cut 2 long strips, each one 17 × 2 inches. Take one strip and fit it into the pan along the side; have the bottom slightly curve in over the bottom crust. Press the lower edge of the strip against the bottom crust to seal. Brush the short, vertical edges of the side strip with water and press the second strip into place, trimming to fit with about ½ inch of overlap. Press the overlapping edges well to seal. Refrigerate for at least 2 hours or overnight.

for the filling Position a rack in the middle of the oven. Preheat the oven to 400°F. Toss together the apple slices and sugar in a large sauté pan. Cook over medium heat, occasionally stirring gently, taking care not to crush the fruit pieces. Cook for about 5 minutes, just until the mixture begins to exude juices and the apples soften just a tiny bit. Remove from the heat, cool slightly, then sprinkle the flour over, and toss gently to coat.

1) Whisk the eggs in a large bowl, then whisk in the sour cream, zest, and vanilla. Fold into the fruit mixture.

1 recipe Sugar Tart Crust (page 3), chilled and ready to roll out

FILLING

9 cups peeled, cored and thinly sliced apples (about 10 or 11 apples); use a mixture of Cortland, Golden Delicious, and Granny Smith

⅔ cup sugar

6 tablespoons all-purpose flour

2 large eggs, at room temperature

2 cups sour cream (not low-fat)

1 teaspoon finely grated lemon zest

1 teaspoon vanilla extract

STREUSEL

1 cup all-purpose flour

½ cup (1 stick) unsalted butter, melted

½ cup firmly packed light brown sugar

1 teaspoon finely grated lemon zest

½ teaspoon ground cardamom

2) Remove the crust from the refrigerator and scrape the filling into the crust. It will come right up to the top of the crust. Bake for 15 minutes while you prepare the streusel.

for the streusel Combine all the ingredients until well blended.

1) After the pie has baked for 15 minutes, remove from the oven and turn the heat down to 375°F. Squeeze the streusel between your fingers and palms to create clumps ranging in size from small to large grapes and scatter all over the top of the pie. There is a lot of streusel; use it all, gently mounding it in the center.

2) Return the pie to the oven and bake for 15 minutes more. Turn the heat down to 350°F and continue baking for 20 to 30 minutes more, or until the streusel is evenly browned and the pie feels firm when gently pressed. If you can see any filling bubbling around the edges, that is a good sign of doneness, but most likely it will be completely covered with streusel.

3) Cool the pan on a rack to allow the filling to thicken and set. Serve at room temperature. Store at room temperature for up 1 day.

TIP Cardamom has a flavor that dominates in recipes where it is used; it typically does not fade to the background in a dish. For an alternative flavor, try this recipe with cinnamon in its place, and leave the lemon zest out of both the filling and crust. You will have a more typical apple-cinnamon flavor profile, which, while more expected, is equally welcomed.

caramelized banana cream tart

in pecan crust SERVES 10

Pecans, sugar, and butter make up the whole of this crust, with no flour to get in the way of a very crunchy, nutty base for this creamy pie. Bananas tossed in hot caramel create the bottom layer, topped by a vanilla bean pastry cream and then billows of vanilla whipped cream on top. Right before serving, scatter whole caramelized pecans on the very top. The contrast of textures really makes the dessert, so pay careful attention to the assembly instructions. Note that this recipe calls for the Light Pastry Cream on page 10 to be made right before you scrape it into the prepared crust; it cannot be made ahead.

for the caramelized pecans Line a jelly-roll pan with aluminum foil; smooth out any wrinkles. Coat lightly with flavorless vegetable oil using a pastry brush.

1) Put the sugar and water in a very small saucepan and stir to combine. Bring to a boil over medium heat and cook until it turns light amber in color. Immediately remove from the heat. Quickly drop the pecan halves into the caramel one at a time and use two forks to help them submerge and become coated with caramel. Use the forks to remove the nuts from the caramel, allow the excess to drip off, and place them right side up on the prepared pan. Repeat with the remaining pecan halves. If the caramel thickens, reheat gently until fluid. The caramel will continue to darken while you are dipping, which is okay. Allow the nuts to cool completely and harden at room temperature. Store for up to 3 days in an airtight container.

for the crust Position a rack in the middle of the oven. Preheat the oven to 350°F. Coat a 10-inch loose-bottomed fluted tart pan with nonstick spray; set aside.

1) Put the nuts and sugar in the bowl of a food processor fitted with the metal blade attachment and process until very finely ground.

CARAMELIZED PECANS
½ cup sugar

1 tablespoon plus 2 teaspoons water

½ cup pecan halves

CRUST
2½ cups pecan halves

¼ cup sugar

¼ cup (½ stick) unsalted butter, melted

CARAMELIZED FILLING
½ cup sugar

2 tablespoons water

2 large, ripe but firm bananas

1 recipe Light Pastry Cream (page 10), ingredients ready to use

caramelized banana cream tart (*continued*)

TOPPING

1 large, ripe but firm banana

1½ cups chilled heavy cream

3 tablespoons confectioners' sugar

¼ teaspoon vanilla extract

Pulse in the melted butter until well blended. Pat into the prepared pan, creating an even layer across the bottom and up the sides.

1) Bake for 8 to 9 minutes. The crust might look puffy; use the back of a soup spoon to press the crust down and back into shape along the pan's sides and bottom. Bake for 8 to 9 minutes more, or until very lightly colored. Cool the tart pan on a rack. Store at room temperature for up to 1 day, loosely covered with aluminum foil.

for the filling Prepare the filling and topping the day of serving. At least 4 hours before serving, stir the sugar and water together in a nonstick skillet. Bring to a boil over medium-high heat and cook until it turns a light to medium golden amber. Meanwhile, peel the bananas. Remove the skillet from the heat and immediately slice the bananas into $\frac{1}{2}$-inch rounds right into the skillet. Toss well with the caramel. Immediately scrape into the prepared crust and set aside. Prepare the pastry cream as directed in the recipe on page 10. Scrape the warm (not hot) pastry cream over the bananas and spread until smooth using a small offset spatula. Let the pastry cream cool slightly at room temperature, and then refrigerate for at least 6 hours or until firm enough to slice. After it chills, you may cover it with a piece of plastic wrap pressed directly onto the surface.

for the topping Up to 2 hours before serving, peel and cut the banana in half and slice lengthwise into thin slices. Place these along the edge of the tart, using the curve of the fruit to follow the shape of the tart. There should be one ring of banana slices going around the entire tart. Beat the cream, sugar, and vanilla in the bowl of a stand mixer on medium-high speed with the wire whip attachment until firm peaks form. Pile the whipped cream attractively on top of the tart. The tart may be served immediately or refrigerated for up to 2 hours. Sprinkle the caramelized pecans on top right before serving.

apple, pear, and quince pie

with cheddar crust SERVES 8

Quince is a fruit you might not be familiar with, but after a taste of this pie, I am convinced you will be enamored. They look somewhat like both a fat round pear as well as an apple, are typically a rich yellow when ripe, and will emit the most enticing, fragrant aroma. They smell floral and fruity at the same time, and a bowl of these in your home will scent the entire room, similar to the way narcissus flowers release their fragrance. They are not eaten raw, but are often combined with apples in desserts because they seem to bring out every positive quality apples have, even more so. Here, combined with apples, pears, and an extra-sharp cheddar crust, you have a not-too-sweet pie, perfect for the midwinter months when you will find quince available. In the market they might be labeled *pineapple quince*, and each one should weigh about 10 ounces.

CRUST

3 cups all-purpose flour

1⅓ cups grated extra-sharp cheddar cheese (about 4 ounces)

½ teaspoon salt

¾ cup (1½ sticks) chilled unsalted butter, cut into pieces

½ cup ice-cold water

FILLING

4 cups peeled, cored, and thinly sliced apples, (about 5 apples) preferably half Cortland and half Golden Delicious

3 cups peeled, cored, and thinly sliced ripe pears, (about 5 pears) such as Anjou or Bartlett

1½ cups peeled, cored, and coarsely grated quince (about 3 quince)

for the crust Put the flour, cheese, and salt in the bowl of a food processor fitted with the metal blade attachment and pulse to combine. Add the butter and pulse on and off until it forms a very coarse meal; there might be pockets of butter that are larger, which is fine. Drizzle in the water through the feed tube and pulse until the dough is moistened and just holds together if squeezed. Gather the dough into 2 balls and flatten into disks. Wrap the dough in plastic wrap and refrigerate for at least 2 hours or up to 2 days. May also be frozen for 1 month, in which case, protect further by placing in a zipper-top bag. Defrost in the refrigerator overnight. Let the dough soften slightly at room temperature before rolling out.

for the filling Position a rack in the middle of the oven. Preheat the oven to 375°F. Coat a 9½ x 1½-inch tempered glass pie plate with nonstick spray.

1) Toss together the apples, pears, quince, sugar, lemon juice, and flour (use the higher amount only if the fruit is very juicy) in a medium bowl.

2) Roll out 1 dough disk on a lightly floured surface to a 12-inch round. Transfer to the pie plate. Scrape the filling into the crust and dot with the butter.

3) Roll out the second dough disk on a floured surface to a 13-inch round. Drape the dough over the filling. Trim the dough overhang to ½ inch. Press the top crust and the bottom crust together at the edge to seal. Fold under and crimp the edge decoratively. Create steam vents in the top crust.

for the glaze Whisk the egg in a small bowl. Use a pastry brush to glaze the entire top crust with egg glaze.

1) Bake for 50 to 65 minutes, or until the crust is golden brown and the filling is bubbling. Cool the pie plate on a rack for 30 minutes to allow the juices to thicken. Serve warm or at room temperature. Store at room temperature for up to 6 hours.

½ cup sugar

1 tablespoon freshly squeezed lemon juice

3 to 4 tablespoons all-purpose flour

2 tablespoons unsalted butter

GLAZE

1 large egg

fresh coconut custard
cream pie   SERVES 8

> Many coconut cream pies are made with vanilla pastry cream with some coconut folded in. Here I use canned coconut milk instead of whole milk in the pastry cream for more coconut flavor in addition to the actual coconut. The first thing you notice about this pie is the shower of fresh coconut strips mounded over the top—they are remarkably easy to make, so do not be scared off by the use of fresh coconut. Make sure to use pure whole coconut milk for the pastry cream, not sweetened cream of coconut or reduced-fat coconut milk.

1 recipe Single Butter Piecrust (page 2), chilled and ready to roll out

FILLING

1 large fresh coconut

2⅔ cups canned 100% coconut milk

4 large egg yolks

¾ cup sugar

¼ cup plus 2 teaspoons cornstarch

¼ teaspoon salt

2 teaspoons vanilla extract

TOPPING

1¼ cups chilled heavy cream

3 tablespoons confectioners' sugar

1 teaspoon vanilla extract

for the crust Position a rack in the middle of the oven. Preheat the oven to 375°F. Coat a 9½ x 1½-inch tempered glass pie plate with nonstick spray.

1) Roll out the dough disk on a lightly floured surface to a 13-inch round. Transfer to the pie plate. Fold the edge under and crimp decoratively, making a high rim. Line with foil and weights and blind-bake for 10 to 12 minutes, or until the rim and bottom of the crust are beginning to set. Remove the foil and weights and bake until very light golden brown, about 10 minutes more. Cool the pie plate on a rack. Store at room temperature for up to 8 hours, loosely covered with foil.

for the filling Position a rack in the middle of the oven. Preheat the oven to 350°F.

1) Poke holes in at least two of the coconut's eyes using a sturdy skewer or large nail and a hammer. Drain the coconut water and discard (or drink, if desired). Place the coconut directly on the oven rack and bake for about 30 minutes, or until the outer brown shell cracks. Wrap the coconut in a clean kitchen towel and rap very firmly with a hammer to crack the shell further. Unwrap the towel and peel the outer brown shell away, exposing the brown-covered white flesh,

which you want to extract in large pieces. Use a sharp vegetable peeler and make large strips of coconut until you have $1\frac{1}{2}$ cups. Grate the remaining coconut on the large holes of a box grater and set aside.

2) Put the coconut milk and 1 cup of the grated coconut in a medium saucepan and heat over medium heat until warm; set aside. (If you have leftover grated coconut, reserve for another use.)

3) Meanwhile, whisk together the eggs yolks, sugar, cornstarch, and salt in a heatproof bowl until very smooth; set aside.

4) Drizzle about $\frac{1}{4}$ of the warm coconut milk mixture over the egg mixture, whisking gently. Add the remaining coconut milk and whisk to combine. Immediately pour the mixture back into the saucepan and cook over medium-low heat, whisking constantly to prevent scorching, until it begins to simmer and bubbles appear, about 1 minute. The pastry cream should be thick enough to mound when dropped from a spoon, but still satiny. Remove from the heat and whisk in the vanilla. Allow the pastry cream to cool slightly, 2 to 5 minutes, then scrape right into the prepared piecrust. Refrigerate for at least 4 hours or until the custard is set. May be made up to 1 day ahead; cover loosely with aluminum foil.

for the topping Within 4 hours of serving, beat the cream, sugar, and vanilla on medium-high speed in the chilled bowl of a stand mixer with the wire whip attachment until firm peaks form. Scrape onto the pie and cover the custard completely, creating attractive peaks here and there. Cover with the larger shavings of coconut, mounding decoratively. Serve or refrigerate until needed. Serve cold.

amaretto-almond crunch
pumpkin pie SERVES 8 TO 10

To use current parlance, my BFF is a fabulous woman named Juanita Plimpton. She is not a cook—but she is an amazing taster and is able to consistently give me extremely helpful critiques. On one occasion she provided me with an entire concept. "Why not," she asked, "create a pumpkin pie with the flavors of almond and amaretto?" I never would have come up with this myself—and she was right. This is sensational in flavor as well as texture. Picture a fairly classic pumpkin pie flavored with a shot of amaretto liqueur, topped with a crunchy blend of amaretti cookies and almonds—almost a streusel. The juxtaposition of creamy pumpkin custard and ultra-crisp topping is unexpected and exciting.

for the topping Crumble the cookies by hand into a small bowl. The pieces should be about ¼-inch chunks, more or less. Toss with the almonds; set aside.

1) Position a rack in the middle of the oven. Preheat the oven to 375°F. Coat a 9 x 1¼-inch tempered glass pie plate with nonstick spray.

2) Roll out the dough on a lightly floured surface to a 13-inch round. Transfer to the pie dish. Fold the edge under, and crimp decoratively into a high border. Line with foil and weights and blind-bake for 15 to 17 minutes, or until just beginning to color. Remove the foil and weights. Bake until the crust is tinged very light brown, pressing with the back of a fork if the crust bubbles, about 5 minutes longer. Transfer to a rack. Reduce the oven temperature to 350°F.

for the filling Scrape the pumpkin into a food processor fitted with the metal blade attachment. Process for 15 seconds; scrape down the sides and process for 15 seconds more. Pulse in the brown sugar, spices, and salt until combined. Pulse in the eggs one at a time until blended, scraping down once or twice if necessary. Pulse in the cream

TOPPING

20 Lazzaroni Amaretti di Saronno cookies

¼ cup blanched sliced almonds

1 recipe Double Butter Piecrust, (page 2), chilled and ready to roll out

FILLING

One 15-ounce can pure solid-pack pumpkin

¾ cup firmly packed light brown sugar

¾ teaspoon ground cinnamon

¾ teaspoon ground ginger

¼ teaspoon freshly grated nutmeg

¼ teaspoon salt

3 large eggs, at room temperature

1 cup plus 2 tablespoons heavy
cream
2 tablespoons Disaronno Amaretto

and liqueur. Finish off by processing for 5 seconds to smooth out the mixture. Pour the filling into the crust. Sprinkle the topping evenly over the filling.

1) Bake for 50 to 55 minutes, or until the filling is set around the edges, and quivers in the center when you gently shake the pie dish. Cool the pie plate on a rack. The pie is best served the day it is made. Store at room temperature, loosely covered with foil.

pie plates, tart pans, and tart rings

Pies are all baked and presented in pie plates, which are typically round with sloping sides, but the actual dimensions are a very important detail to which you must pay attention. It is typical to come across pie plates that measure 9 to 9½ inches across; they can vary in depth, often being 1¼ to 1½ inches. These seemingly small variations make a huge difference in the final dish. If the recipe is developed for a 9 x 1¼-inch pie plate and is made in a 9½ x 1½-inch dish, the pie will be too thin and scant and look quite meager. Conversely, if you try to make a recipe made for the larger dimension in the smaller plate, you will most likely get overflow—and a mess. I use Pyrex pie plates, as I find they give the most reliable results in terms of browning the crust evenly. I use two sizes: the larger deep-dish 9½ x 1½-inch size and the smaller 9 x 1¼-inch size. All the recipes in this book will clearly tell you in the beginning of the recipe which size pie plate to use, and I strongly suggest that you make sure you have the right size. It can make the difference between the pie working flawlessly—and not at all.

Tarts are made either in tart pans, with fluted edges and loose bottoms, or in simple rings, and again, precise dimensions are important. When I call for a 10-inch tart pan, I have measured it straight across the bottom, from outer edge to outer edge. This is important to note because most fluted-edge, loose-bottomed pans flare out toward the top, and if measured there would indicate a different diameter. Many imported tart pans do not come in standard inch sizes, as they are metric, so do measure your pans to make sure you have the correct size. Tart rings are exactly what they sound like; they are straight-sided rings without a bottom of any sort. They must be placed on a pan, such as a jelly-roll pan, in order to be used. Take care when forming tart dough in a ring; the ring will be lifted up and off of the tart, so no dough can overhang the top of the ring. The fluted-edge, loose-bottomed tart pans that I use are 1 inch high; the rings are ⅞ inch high.

pear frangipane tart

with red wine sauce SERVES 8 TO 10

> "What bakery did this come from?" was the question posed to my friend who presented this tart at a dinner party. Indeed it would look at home in a bakery window, and when you serve it with a drizzle of the sweet, syrupy, irresistible red wine sauce, the dessert slides pleasantly into the realm of "restaurant worthy." All that being said, there is nothing complicated about it. The almond frangipane takes mere minutes to make in the food processor, and the red wine sauce similarly takes just a few minutes on top of the stove.

for the pears Stir the sugar and water together in a medium, deep saucepan. Bring to a simmer over medium heat and cook until the sugar dissolves. Lower the pears gently into the sugar syrup and simmer until just tender, 6 to 10 minutes depending on ripeness. Remove from the syrup and Put in a bowl to cool, reserving the syrup. The pears and syrup maybe be refrigerated for up to 2 days in an airtight container (they may be recombined after cooling for storage).

for the frangipane Put the almonds and sugar in the bowl of a food processor fitted with the metal blade attachment. Pulse on and off until the nuts are roughly chopped, then turn the machine on and process until finely ground. Add the egg and process until smooth, scraping down the bowl if necessary. Add the butter and process until smooth. Pulse in the amaretto and flour. The frangipane may be refrigerated in an airtight container for up to 2 days, or may be used immediately. If refrigerated, bring to room temperature before spreading into the crust.

1) Position a rack in the middle of the oven. Preheat the oven to 350°F. Coat a 10-inch loose-bottomed fluted tart pan with nonstick spray; set aside.

2) Roll out the prepared crust on a lightly floured surface to a 13-inch round. Fit into the prepared pan, pressing into the corners and

PEARS

4 cups water

2 cups sugar

4 ripe but firm pears, peeled, such as Anjou or Bartlett

FRANGIPANE

1 cup sliced blanched almonds

½ cup sugar

1 large egg, at room temperature

½ cup (1 stick) unsalted butter, at room temperature, cut into pieces

2 tablespoons Disaronno Amaretto

1 tablespoon all-purpose flour

1 recipe Sugar Tart Crust (page 3), chilled and ready to roll out

RED WINE SAUCE

1 cup dry red wine

½ cup water

½ cup sugar

cutting off the top so that it is flush with the pan. Place in the freezer while the oven preheats.

3) Bake for 8 to 10 minutes, or until the crust is just beginning to dry. Cool slightly on a rack. Increase the oven temperature to 375°F.

for the assembly Spread the frangipane into the prebaked crust in a smooth, even layer. Slice the pears in half lengthwise and remove the core and stem, then slice into eighths. Arrange the pear slices in a decorative pattern on top of the frangipane, pressing them gently into the filling.

1) Bake for 25 to 30 minutes, or until the frangipane is set, a bit puffed, and golden. Cool the tart pan on a rack. The tart may be made up to 1 day ahead. Store at room temperature, loosely covered with foil.

for the sauce Right before serving, stir the wine, water, and sugar together in a small saucepan and bring to a simmer over medium-high heat. Cook until thickened and syrupy, about 5 minutes. Serve the tart sliced into wedges with a drizzle of sauce on and around each wedge.

blueberry crème fraîche tart

with poppy seed crust   SERVES 8 TO 10

This is an elegant tart featuring a sweet tart crust with the addition of poppy seeds, and I cannot stress how excellent it is. Try it with fillings of your own, such as lemon cream or pastry cream. The crust is covered with a quick-cooked fresh blueberry jam and a crème fraîche custard and topped with lightly glazed, glistening fresh blueberries made using a technique I borrowed from my good friend Rose Levy Beranbaum. Whenever I want to chat baking, I ring up Rose. I happened to call her the day I was working on this tart. After I hung up, I remembered her brilliant technique for creating a fresh blueberry tart topping; here is my version. If you like blueberries, I implore you to make this tart; you will be thrilled.

for the filling Combine all the ingredients in a small saucepan and bring to a boil over medium-high heat, stirring often. As soon as the mixture looks juicy, use a potato masher to crush the berries. Continue to boil, stirring often, for 6 to 8 minutes, or until the berries have broken down and the mixture has thickened slightly. Cool completely, stirring occasionally to release the heat. Meanwhile, make the crust.

for the crust Position a rack in the middle of the oven. Preheat the oven to 350°F.

1) Prepare the crust as directed, adding the poppy seeds along with the flour. Wrap the ball of dough and chill for about 1 hour or until firm enough to roll. Coat a 10-inch loose-bottomed fluted tart pan with nonstick spray. Roll out the chilled crust on a lightly floured surface to a 13-inch round. Fit into the prepared pan, pressing into the corners and cutting off the top so that it is flush with the pan. Place in the freezer while the oven preheats.

2) Bake for 8 to 10 minutes, or until the crust is just beginning to dry. Cool the tart pan slightly on a rack.

BLUEBERRY FILLING

2 cups fresh blueberries

¼ cup sugar

2 tablespoons water

CRUST

1 recipe Sugar Tart Crust (page 3), ingredients only

2 tablespoons poppy seeds

CRÈME FRAÎCHE CUSTARD

1 cup crème fraîche

¼ cup sugar

1 large egg

BLUEBERRY TOPPING

3 cups fresh blueberries

¼ cup plus 1 tablespoon sugar

1 tablespoon cornstarch

⅓ cup water

1 teaspoon freshly squeezed lemon juice

for the custard Scrape the crème fraîche into a small saucepan, whisk to loosen gently, and heat over low heat until warm, whisking occasionally. Set aside, keeping warm. Whisk the sugar and egg together in a medium bowl. Slowly whisk in the crème fraîche until the custard is smooth.

1) Spread the blueberry filling evenly over the bottom of the crust, and then slowly pour the custard over the fruit. Some of the fruit might come up through the custard, creating a marbled effect; that is fine.

2) Bake for 15 to 20 minutes, or just until the custard is set. It should lightly jiggle in the center when you gently shake the pan, but will be firmer around the edges. Cool the tart pan on a rack, then refrigerate until firm, at least 6 hours or overnight.

for the topping Put the blueberries in a heatproof bowl. Stir the sugar and cornstarch together in a small saucepan. Whisk in the water and lemon juice and bring to a boil over medium heat. Whisk often and boil until the mixture is clear, 30 seconds to 1 minute. Immediately scrape the mixture over the blueberries and toss gently to coat. Quickly and gently scoop the berries out of the bowl and arrange in an even layer over the chilled tart. Refrigerate for up to 4 hours. Allow to sit at room temperature for about 15 minutes before serving.

double-decker "key" lime pie

—two ways SERVES 8 TO 10

This is an improved version of a pie from an earlier book of mine, and I felt the refinements justified a reprint. First of all, you will notice the word *key* is in quotes, and that is because I find freshly squeezed lime juice from readily available supermarket Persian limes to be tangier and preferable to key limes. You must be a citrus lover to appreciate this pie, because lime is featured in four different components: lime zest in the graham crust; lime juice and zest in the creamy bottom layer made with condensed milk; lime juice and zest again in the somewhat translucent lime curd; and a shower of candied lime zest crowning the pillowy top of whipped cream. Use a Microplane zester for the grated zest and a classic citrus zester to create long, thin strips for the candied zest, which should be very thin and thread-like. All of the limes should be washed, scrubbed, and dried before using, since you will be using much of the zest. The "two ways" in the title refers to the fact that this pie is great right out of the refrigerator and equally as engaging served frozen; it's your choice.

CANDIED LIME ZEST

2 firm, fresh, bright green limes

¾ cup water plus more as needed

½ cup sugar

CRUST

1½ cups very fine graham cracker crumbs

6 tablespoons (¾ stick) unsalted butter, melted

2 tablespoons sugar

1 teaspoon grated lime zest

CREAMY LIME FILLING

One 14-ounce can sweetened condensed milk

½ cup freshly squeezed lime juice

for the candied zest Use a citrus zester to zest the limes. Put the zest in a small saucepan and cover with cold water. Bring to a boil, turn down the heat, simmer for 5 minutes, and drain. Stir the ¾ cup water and the sugar together in the same saucepan and bring to a boil over medium-high heat, swirling the pot once or twice, until the sugar is dissolved. Add the zest and simmer until the zest is tender and translucent, about 10 minutes, again swirling the pot once or twice during cooking. Cool and store in the syrup at room temperature for up to 2 days in an airtight container.

for the crust Position a rack in the middle of the oven. Preheat the oven to 350°F. Very lightly coat the inside of a 9 X 1¼-inch tempered glass pie plate with nonstick spray.

1) Put the graham cracker crumbs, melted butter, sugar, and zest in a bowl and stir to combine. Pour the mixture into the pie plate and press with your fingers to create an even layer on the bottom and up

the sides, creating a high rim. Use a flat-bottomed glass to facilitate pressing the crumbs along the bottom and to help with the edges; keep the glass flat and move toward the edges and it will press the crumbs along the sides, creating an even crust all around. Bake for 6 to 8 minutes, or just until the crust starts to color. Cool the pie plate on a rack. Meanwhile, prepare the filling.

for the lime filling Whisk together the condensed milk, lime juice, yolks, and zest. Pour the mixture into the prebaked crust. Bake for about 10 minutes; the filling will be set. Cool in the pan on a rack. Meanwhile, prepare the curd.

for the lime curd Put the sugar, lime juice, and egg yolks in a heavy nonstick saucepan; whisk well to combine. Cook over medium-low heat, whisking frequently, until the mixture is thick, looks somewhat translucent, and coats a spoon, about 15 minutes; it is okay if the mixture simmers. Remove from the heat, stir in the lime zest, and allow to cool slightly. Gently spoon the lime curd over the filling and spread to make an even layer. Cool the pie plate on a rack to room temperature, then refrigerate for at least 4 hours or overnight.

for the whipped cream For version #1 (refrigerated), whip the cream and sugar right before serving until medium-firm peaks form. Spread the whipped cream over the pie all the way to the edges, creating attractive peaks. Serve immediately. For version #2 (frozen), whip and apply the cream as described above, then freeze the pie overnight. Serve frozen directly from the freezer. It will remain just soft enough to slice.

4 large egg yolks
1½ teaspoons grated lime zest

LIME CURD
1 cup sugar
⅔ cup freshly squeezed lime juice
8 large egg yolks
1 teaspoon grated lime zest

WHIPPED CREAM
1½ cups heavy cream
5 tablespoons sugar

white peach and raspberry "blossom"
tartlets with pistachio and essensia

These individual tartlets look like open peonies in full bloom. The thinly sliced white peaches, with their sunset-colored skin still attached, are placed in concentric rows to form petals with a single raspberry nestled in the center. The pastry cream beneath is enhanced with the floral and fruity Essensia orange Muscat wine, and the crust is a pale green from the pistachios. Pistachios do have an assertive flavor; if you prefer, you may make this crust with blanched sliced almonds. You will need eight 4-inch flan rings for the clean, round shape of these tartlets. There is some last-minute assembly, but the crusts and pastry cream can be made ahead, so this is actually a very doable dessert for a dinner party.

PISTACHIO CRUST

1¼ cups all-purpose flour

½ cup sifted confectioners' sugar

½ cup shelled unsalted raw green pistachios, rubbed clean of papery skin

Scant ¼ teaspoon salt

½ cup (1 stick) chilled unsalted butter, cut into ½-inch cubes

2 large egg yolks

⅛ teaspoon almond extract

1 to 2 tablespoons heavy cream

1 recipe Light Pastry Cream (page 10), made without vanilla bean or extract; 2 tablespoons Quady Essensia orange Muscat wine added

for the crust Put the flour, confectioners' sugar, nuts, and salt in the bowl of a food processor fitted with the metal blade attachment. Pulse a couple of times to begin chopping the nuts, then process until the nuts are very finely ground. Add the butter, pulse a couple of times, and then process until the butter is cut in and blended. Pulse in the yolks and almond extract. With the machine running, drizzle in just enough cream so that the pastry comes together in a ball. Wrap in plastic wrap and refrigerate for at least 2 hours, or overnight.

1) Position racks in the upper and lower third of the oven. Preheat the oven to 350°F. Line 2 jelly-roll pans with parchment paper. Coat eight 4-inch flan rings with nonstick spray, then coat with flour and shake off excess. Place on the prepared pans, spaced evenly apart.

2) Cut the crust into 8 even pieces. Roll each piece out one at a time on a lightly floured work surface. Fit the pastry into each ring, pressing the bottom edges flat against the bottom edges of the rings. Trim the pastry about 1 inch higher than the top of the ring and

fold in. Press gently to create a thicker band around the top of the ring. Then take a sharp knife and trim the pastry flush with the top, making sure none overlaps toward the outside. (You need to be able to lift the rings up and off after baking.) Refrigerate while the oven preheats.

3) Bake the tartlets for about 10 minutes and check. If the pastry is bubbling up, or slipping down the sides, simply press back down or into place with the back of a spoon. Bake for 10 to 15 minutes more, or just until they are beginning to color. Cool the tart pans on the jelly-roll pans set on racks. The tartlets are ready to fill or may be stored at room temperature overnight in an airtight container.

for the assembly Right before serving, remove rings and place the tartlets on serving plates. Fill with the pastry cream, spreading gently with the back of a spoon to fill the tarts almost to the top. Use a very sharp paring knife to cut all the way around each peach, through the stem end. Separate the two halves and remove and discard the pit. Cut half-moon-shaped slices as thin as possible; no more than $1/8$ inch thick. The thinness and evenness of the peach slices will make all the difference in the look and texture of the tart. Starting at the outer edge of the tart, place a peach slice, skin side up, with the flesh part of the fruit lightly pressed down into the pastry cream (the piece will be practically vertical). Arrange each subsequent slice slightly overlapping with the previous one until you have created one complete outer ring of fruit. Continue to form concentric circles of "petals." Fill each tart up almost to the center, then place one plump berry, domed side up, in the middle. Serve immediately.

FRUIT TOPPING
8 medium, ripe but firm white-fleshed peaches
8 medium to large firm raspberries

TIPS Flan rings are simply round metal forms, about $7/8$ inch tall, with no bottoms. They are placed on a parchment-covered jelly-roll pan and the pastry is formed inside. They make a very clean, contemporary-looking pastry with straight sides, a nice alternative to using fluted pans. The clean look allows the "blossom" to be the star of this dessert. They can be found at well-stocked bakeware stores such as Beryl's and Kerekes (see Resources, page 287). Take care when cutting the peaches. The skins can be tough, but they add so much beautiful color. If you slice the peaches thinly enough, the skins won't be a problem and the "petals" will also be easier to form. If you prefer, you may peel the peaches, or even peel half of them for a two-toned effect. Also, if you would like to make the tarts a few hours ahead, you can melt and strain peach jam and brush it lightly over the fruit. This will preserve the fruit, but will also add sweetness and somewhat mask the fresh fruit effect. It is a trade-off, for sure.

melon ribbon tartlets

MAKES 8 TARTLETS

Translucent pastel ribbons of orange- and green-fleshed melons make these tarts exceedingly refreshing; they taste and look like summer on a plate. The two keys to this dessert are choosing fragrant, ripe melons and having a very sharp vegetable peeler with which to create the melon ribbons. I have also had some success making ribbons with flat cheese planes. You will be "shaving" thin ribbons of melon, so whatever you use, make sure the implement is sharp.

for the crust Position oven racks in the upper and lower third of the oven. Preheat the oven to 350°F. Line 2 jelly-roll pans with parchment paper. Coat eight 4-inch flan rings with nonstick spray, then coat with flour and shake off excess. Place on the prepared pans, spaced evenly apart.

1) Cut the crust into 8 even pieces. Roll each piece out one at a time on a lightly floured work surface. Fit the pastry into each ring, pressing the bottom edges flat against the bottom edges of the rings. Trim the pastry about 1 inch higher than the top of the ring and fold in. Press gently to create a thicker band around the top of the ring. Then take a sharp knife and trim the pastry flush with the top, making sure none overlaps toward the outside. (You need to be able to lift the rings up and off after baking.) Refrigerate while the oven preheats.

2) Bake the tartlets for about 10 minutes. If the pastry is bubbling up, or slipping down the sides, simply press back down or into place with the back of a spoon. Bake for 10 to 15 minutes more, or just until they are beginning to color. Cool the tart crusts set on jelly-roll pans on racks. The tartlets are ready to fill or may be stored at room temperature overnight in an airtight container.

for the assembly Right before serving, remove the rings and place the tartlets on serving plates. Fill with the pastry cream, spreading gently with the back of a spoon to fill the tarts almost to the top.

1 recipe Sugar Tart Crust (page 3), chilled and ready to roll out

1 recipe Light Pastry Cream (page 10), made without the vanilla bean; use vanilla extract and also add 2 tablespoons Midori melon liqueur

FRUIT TOPPING

1 small, ripe but firm orange-fleshed melon, such as cantaloupe or Persian

1 small, ripe but firm green-fleshed melon, such as honeydew, Galia, or Santa Claus

24 to 36 firm, fresh raspberries

3) Cut the melons in half. Wrap one half of each melon in plastic wrap and reserve for another use. Take the remaining halves and scoop out the seeds. Cut each half into 1-inch wedges. Use a sharp paring knife to remove the rind from each wedge. Use a sharp vegetable peeler to shave long ribbons from the cut sides of the melon wedges, placing them carefully on a cutting board until you are done. Take one ribbon at a time and place it in a freeform curling shape on top of a tartlet. Add additional ribbons, alternating colors. It should look like a tiny, delicate pile of multicolored ribbons on top of the tart. Nestle a few berries here and there within the curls of melon. Serve immediately.

TIP Choosing ripe melons is key to this dessert. Look for fruit that is heavy for its size, which indicates juiciness. Melons with smooth rinds should be the proper color for that variety. Melons with netting, such as cantaloupes, should not show too much green. All should emit fragrance to indicate ripeness; however, if they have been excessively refrigerated they might not be fragrant. If you can shop at the farmer's market in season, this is the best bet. And if you can taste before you buy, even better!

glazed fresh strawberry tart
with champagne sabayon SERVES 8 TO 10

When local strawberries appear in early summer, I flip right to this recipe. Picture a tart of fresh strawberries all set upright, brushed with a shiny, candy-apple-red glaze made from cooked, mashed, strained berry juice. The concentrated glaze gives this tart an impossibly glossy red color that looks artificial, but couldn't be more fresh and natural. A sprinkling of green pistachios on top is optional, but the contrast makes the red pop even more. Presented on a plate with a generous dollop of a creamy, fluffy Champagne sabayon, this dessert combines crispy, juicy, and creamy textures, while keeping the freshness of the strawberries in the forefront. Choose either small or medium strawberries; it is important that they are all the same size for the elegance of the visual presentation.

for the filling Fill the crust with berries, all perched upright, nestled closely together and filling the entire crust.

1) Chop the remaining berries and put in a medium saucepan; stir in the sugar and lemon juice and allow to sit for about 5 minutes, or until the juices begin to exude. Mash the berries with a potato masher and bring to a simmer over medium-high heat, stirring the mixture occasionally as it cooks. Cook until the juices begin to thicken and deepen in color, 3 to 5 minutes.

2) Immediately scrape into a strainer set over a clean bowl (or large measuring cup if you have it). Press as much liquid as possible through the strainer; discard the solids. Measure the liquid out to 1 cup, adding water if necessary, and pour into a small clean saucepan. Stir the cornstarch and water together in a small bowl, and then stir into the juice. Bring to a simmer over medium-high heat and cook for 1 to 2 minutes, whisking frequently, or until the juice thickens and becomes shiny. Immediately glaze the berries, using both a teaspoon and a pastry brush to fill gaps between the berries and cover the tops and sides of the fruit. Sprinkle with nuts, if desired, while the glaze

1 Sugar Tart Crust (page 3), baked and cooled

STRAWBERRY FILLING

2 quarts small to medium fresh strawberries, stemmed

⅔ cup sugar

2 teaspoons freshly squeezed lemon juice

1 tablespoon cornstarch

1 tablespoon water

2 tablespoons unsalted green pistachios, lightly toasted (see page 23) and chopped, optional

SABAYON

4 large egg yolks

⅓ cup Champagne or dry sparkling white wine

¼ cup sugar

½ cup chilled heavy cream

is still moist. Refrigerate the tart while you prepare the sabayon, or for up to 6 hours.

for the sabayon Whisk the egg yolks and Champagne together in the top of a double boiler (or deep bowl for a makeshift double boiler). Whisk in the sugar. Set over boiling water that just touches the bottom of the bowl and whisk constantly until very thick and almost tripled in volume. The mixture should form a ribbon when you lift the whisk; this will take 5 to 8 minutes. Remove from the heat and immediately set over a bowl of ice water. Whisk the mixture until it is completely cool. Whip the cream in a separate, clean bowl until soft peaks form, then fold into the egg mixture. The sabayon may be used immediately, or cover the bowl with plastic wrap and refrigerate for up to 8 hours. If it separates at all, simply whisk before using. You might lose a little volume, but it will be fine to use. Serve wedges of the tart with a generous dollop of sabayon partially on top, partially to the side.

TIPS Look for individual soda bottle–size Champagne bottles at the liquor store. Or, buy a regular-size bottle, use the small amount needed for the sabayon, then serve the rest with the tart. For the sabayon, make sure to whisk the yolks and Champagne together before adding the sugar. If you combine the yolks and sugar first, and pause even for a minute before adding the liquid, this amount of sugar might very well toughen the yolks, and you will be left with little hard bits of raw yolk and the sabayon will not come together properly.

custards, gelées, mousses, and puddings

THERE WAS A time when if you saw the term *mousse* on a menu it was a promise of something exotic, sophisticated, and enticing. And then, well, the term, and the namesake dishes, became kind of boring and expected. The fact is that mousses give us smooth, delightful sensations on our palates: sometimes airy, sometimes dense and creamy, but always comforting and soothing. I am here to bring mousses into the new millennium, along with their other smooth and slippery cousins. This is the chapter for mousses, lightly jelled gelées, puddings, and custards. You will find everything from a showstopping ring mold made with Champagne to rice pudding, a trifle, crème brûlée, and even a gigantic cream puff.

peekaboo hazelnut–espresso
crème brûlée SERVES 6

The "peekaboo" in the title refers to the crunchy brûléed sugar topping peeking from beneath a latticework of piped dark chocolate. Underneath this two-tone and textured topping is a creamy coffee-rich custard, further enhanced with the intense flavor of hazelnut paste. See the sidebar on brûléeing (page 220).

for the custard Put the cream and ground coffee in a medium saucepan and bring to a boil over medium heat. Remove from the heat and let steep for 15 minutes. Strain through a fine-mesh strainer, pressing all the cream through the grounds. Clean the saucepan. Discard the solids and return the cream to the saucepan. Reheat gently over low heat and whisk in the hazelnut paste until smooth and combined; keep warm.

1) Position a rack in the middle of the oven. Preheat the oven to 325°F. Arrange six 5-ounce shallow ramekins (mine are 1 inch high) in a larger roasting pan(s); set aside.

2) Whisk the yolks and sugar together in a small heatproof bowl. Drizzle some of the warm cream mixture over the eggs, and then whisk in the remaining cream. Strain again into a large measuring cup with a spout and divide between the ramekins. Fill the larger pan(s) with hot water to reach almost halfway up the outside of the ramekins.

3) Bake for 20 to 25 minutes, or until the edges of the custard are set but the center still quivers if shaken gently. It will firm up upon cooling. Remove from the oven and remove the ramekins from the pan. Cool the ramekins on a rack to room temperature. Refrigerate for at least 3 hours, or up to 2 days covered with plastic wrap, taking care not to touch the wrap to the surface.

CUSTARD

2½ cups heavy cream

3½ tablespoons Italian or French roast coffee beans, very coarsely ground

2½ tablespoons unsweetened hazelnut paste

5 large egg yolks

⅔ cup sugar

TOPPING

1½ ounces bittersweet chocolate, finely chopped, such as Callebaut (71%) or Ghirardelli (60%)

1 tablespoon sugar

for the topping Melt the chocolate in a double boiler or microwave; keep warm and fluid. Sprinkle the sugar in a thin even layer over each custard. Caramelize using a propane or butane torch or under a broiler. Allow to sit for a minute or two for the sugar to harden and cool. Scrape the melted chocolate into a parchment cone and snip a tiny opening from the point of the cone. Make a lattice pattern over the caramelized sugar, leaving gaps so that you can see the sugar crust. Refrigerate or freeze for a minute or two to set the chocolate. Serve immediately.

TIP Note that I suggest very shallow dishes for the crème brûlée. These will give you a large surface area on which to create your caramelized topping. While you can make this dish in ramekins that are deeper than they are wide (or about equal), you will lose that desirable proportion; also, the baking times will be different. Since the dishes are so shallow, it can be a challenge to bake them in a water bath. Take extra care when moving the larger roasting pan in and out of the oven that no hot water gets into the cremes.

brûléeing

The literal translation of *crème brûlée* is "burned cream"; the "burned" part refers to the crunchy caramelized sugar topping that crowns the classic creamy French custard. In professional kitchens we often take liberties, and it is not unusual to hear someone saying, "Go brûlée the top of that custard." So in this vein, we have what I refer to as "brûléeing," which is the action of creating that glassy sugar crust. To achieve the best possible results I prefer to use a handheld torch, either butane or propane, as opposed to brûléeing in the broiler, as there is more control. While you can find small butane-fueled torches in cookware specialty shops, you can also just go to the hardware store, as I did, and buy a classic blowtorch powered by propane. The major benefit to using a torch is that you can easily move the heat source around, making sure the sugar melts evenly and completely without burning, and also without heating up and possibly liquefying the custard. The benefit to the broiler is that you don't need to buy an extra tool. Either way, brûlée your dessert right before serving. Below are specifics to help you achieve the best possible brûléed results.

For either the torch or the broiler approach, make sure that custards are chilled. Spread the sugar for topping in a thin, even layer over the surface.

using a torch

* Depending on your specific torch, you might want to adjust the heat level to medium-high.

* Hold the flame just over the surface of the sugar and move slowly back and forth as the sugar bubbles and eventually caramelizes and turns amber brown and glassy. Sometimes it seems to work best if the flame is above the surface; sometimes it works best with it just touching. Experiment.

* You might have to go over sections repeatedly, which is fine.

* The caramelization can take seconds or minutes, depending on many factors. The timing doesn't matter as much as the appearance. The sugar should be evenly melted, glassy, and amber in color.

using a broiler

* Preheat the broiler to high. Position a rack on the highest setting.

* Place the ramekins in a roasting pan and fill with ice water to reach halfway up the ramekins. This will help prevent the custards from melting.

* Place the roasting pan in the oven and broil just until the sugar melts and caramelizes. Watch carefully, as it can caramelize quickly.

* If the sugar is melting unevenly, rotate the pan front to back.

creamy arborio rice pudding with lemon
cream, raspberry sorbet, and chocolate SERVES 6 TO 8

Warm rice pudding is layered in glass goblets with ribbons of lemon cream and bits of crunchy bittersweet chocolate, and topped with frosty raspberry sorbet. The combination of temperatures, textures, and colors is as surprising as it is delectable. The range of 6 to 8 servings simply reflects goblet size and how generous you would like to make the servings.

for the rice pudding Have ready six or eight 10-ounce clear wine-glasses.

1) Combine the water, rice, and salt in a saucepan. Bring to a boil, covered, over medium heat. Turn down the heat and simmer for 15 minutes, or until the water is absorbed.

2) Stir in the milk, sugar to taste (½ cup if you like sweeter desserts), cardamom, and cinnamon. Bring to a boil, stir well, turn down to a simmer, and cook uncovered, stirring often, for about 20 minutes. The pudding should be the texture of a thick soup. Do not dry it out too much; it should flow from a spoon. It will firm up tremendously upon cooling. Remove from the heat, and cool until just warm. The pudding may be used immediately. Alternatively, cool to room temperature, then refrigerate for up to 2 days in an airtight container. Warm gently in a double boiler or microwave before assembling.

for the assembly Spoon a few tablespoons of rice pudding into each goblet, and top with the lemon cream and a sprinkling of chocolate. Repeat this layering once and top with scoops of sorbet. Serve immediately.

RICE PUDDING

2 cups water

1 cup Arborio rice

⅛ teaspoon salt

4 cups whole milk

⅓ to ½ cup sugar

¼ teaspoon ground cardamom

¼ teaspoon ground cinnamon

½ cup Lemon Cream (page 12)

2 ounces bittersweet chocolate, finely chopped, such as Valrhona Manjari (64%) or Scharffen Berger (70%)

1½ cups raspberry sorbet, such as Häagen-Dazs

TIP If there is one mistake you can make in this recipe, it is cooking the pudding too much once the milk has been added; it will become dry. The unctuous, creamy texture of the pudding while it is still fluid makes this dish quite intriguing and delicious.

spiced pear—white chocolate
tiramisu trifle SERVES 12

The advantage of trifles, those layered concoctions of cake, custard, liqueur, and fruit, is that they not only can be made ahead, but they even benefit from an overnight sit in the refrigerator. This makes them great party desserts—and they serve a crowd. This dessert was originally developed for *Bon Appétit*, and I am proud to say it graced the December 2007 cover (so go take a peek, if you still have it, or go to www.epicurious.com). My assignment was to create a showstopping white dessert. Let me tell you, this was a challenge! But the result is an elegant mélange of whites and creams with the flavors of pear, ginger, mascarpone, vanilla bean, and Poire William. To make the dessert family friendly, replace the pear liqueur with water. (The wine in the poaching liquid mostly evaporates.) Use El Rey Icoa white chocolate for this dish for its full cocoa butter flavors and also because it makes luscious curls. Do not be put off by the length of this recipe. There are several components, but most are quite easy.

WHITE CHOCOLATE CURLS

1 pound white chocolate, in block form, such as El Rey Icoa

Sharp 3-inch round biscuit cutter

WHITE CHOCOLATE MASCARPONE MOUSSE

7 ounces finely chopped white chocolate, such as El Rey Icoa or Callebaut

⅓ cup clear pear brandy, such as Trimbach Poire William

¼ cup water

½ moist and plump vanilla bean

1 cup mascarpone cheese, such as Vermont Butter & Cheese Company brand

1 cup heavy cream

for the chocolate curls The chocolate should be one large block with a surface area at least 4 inches square. You will only use about half, but this size is easiest to work with. The chocolate needs to be very slightly warmed. You can hold it between your palms for a few minutes, or you can place it in a microwave for 5 to 10 seconds at high power (depending on the size of the chocolate and the strength of the microwave). Place the chocolate on a work surface (I place it on a piece of parchment paper) and hold with one hand. Grasp the biscuit cutter firmly with the other hand and, beginning at the top of the piece of chocolate, hold the biscuit cutter nearly flat to the surface of the chocolate, ever so slightly angling it down near the top, and apply pressure there (in this way, the top curve of the biscuit cutter is in contact with the chocolate). Firmly drag the cutter toward you. A curl should form and curl up over itself within the biscuit cutter. If the chocolate shatters, it is still too cold. If the chocolate is too soft, a curl will not form either. Adjust the temperature and make curl after curl until you have used about half of the chocolate. Gently place the curls as you make them into a large, flat, airtight container. Store at room temperature in an airtight container for up to 3 days.

for the mousse Melt the white chocolate, pear brandy, and water together in the top of a double boiler or in a microwave. Stir until smooth; it will be liquidy. Split the vanilla bean lengthwise, scrape the seeds into the mixture, and whisk to break them up and incorporate. Whisk in the mascarpone. Allow to cool slightly. Whip the cream just until soft peaks form and fold into the mascarpone mixture (if the mascarpone mixture is still too liquidy, begin incorporating the cream by using a large balloon whisk, then finish off by folding with a large spatula). Cover and refrigerate until firm, about 2 hours, or refrigerate in an airtight container overnight.

for the poached pears In a 6-quart (9½-inch diameter, 5-inch deep) nonreactive pot, combine the white wine, pear juice, sugar, and spices; stir well, cover, and bring to a simmer over medium-high heat. Add the pears and simmer covered for 30 to 35 minutes, or until the pears are just tender when pierced with a sharp knife. Cool the pears in the poaching liquid. Refrigerate the pears and liquid overnight in an airtight container

for the assembly Assemble the dessert the day before serving. Make sure you have room in the refrigerator for this large dessert. Have ready a clear glass trifle bowl that is 8 inches across and 5 inches deep. Remove the pears from the poaching liquid and set aside. Bring the liquid to a boil over medium-high heat and boil uncovered for about 10 minutes, or until reduced by half. (You should begin with about 3 cups and end up with 1½ cups. You need a total of 1¼ cups; if you have less, add more pear juice to make up the deficit. The syrup should still be fluid and not so condensed that it is caramelized, which can happen if reduced too much.) Strain and discard the spices. Set the liquid aside.

1) Cut the pears into ¼-inch-thick slices; discard the stems and cores. Scrape the mascarpone mousse into the pastry bag fitted with the tip.

SPICE-POACHED PEARS

One 750-ml bottle dry white wine

2 cups pear juice (100% juice; not sugar-sweetened), such as Ceres brand

1¼ cups sugar

Two 3-inch cinnamon sticks

12 pods cardamom, crushed open (use whole spice, pods and seeds)

4 quarter-size pieces of peeled fresh ginger, about ⅛ inch thick

5 firm but ripe pears, peeled, such as Anjou or Bartlett

Three 3-ounce packages of 3-inch soft ladyfingers, separated

TOPPING

2 cups heavy cream

Pastry bag

Large star decorating tip, such as Wilton #2110 or Ateco #835

1 tablespoon confectioners' sugar

¼ cup finely minced crystallized ginger, optional

2) Arrange the ladyfingers, rounded side down, in the bottom of the trifle bowl, covering the entire bottom; some may be slightly overlapped (I use about 15 per layer). Brush with ¼ cup of the pear poaching liquid, saturating the ladyfingers evenly. Pipe a layer of mousse to cover the ladyfingers, taking care to keep the mousse neat and even. (I begin with a ring around the edge against the glass and continue in a concentric spiral toward the middle.) Arrange pear slices on top of the mousse, nestling their curved edges neatly against the sides of the bowl; arrange them snugly to make a single layer. Repeat the ladyfinger, poaching liquid, mousse, and pear layering 2 more times. End with a fourth layer of ladyfingers and brush with poaching liquid (you may have a few ladyfingers left over). Cover with plastic wrap and refrigerate for at least 6 hours, or overnight.

for the topping Right before serving, whip the heavy cream until beginning to thicken. Add ¼ cup of the poaching liquid and beat just until soft peaks form. Using a clean pastry bag and star tip, pipe large rosettes of cream all over the top of the trifle. The trifle should be just about even with the top of the bowl at this point. Arrange the white chocolate curls all over the top of the trifle, sprinkle with confectioners' sugar (through a fine-mesh strainer), and finish off with a sprinkling of crystallized ginger, if desired. Ta-da! Present at the table with pride.

TIPS Ladyfingers can be located in the bakery department of large supermarkets. Do not substitute crisp ladyfingers. Making chocolate curls successfully is all about the texture of the chocolate, which depends on brand as well as temperature. I find El Rey Icoa white chocolate to be softer and the easiest for making curls. Poach the pears only just until tender. If they are overcooked they will fall apart when sliced. They can still be used, but the clean look of the delineated layers of the finished dish will be lost.

the giant cream puff

I live near Springfield, Massachusetts, and every fall, along with over one million like-minded folks, I visit The Big E (formally known as The Eastern States Exposition), which is our gargantuan regional fair. It originated in 1917, when it was largely agricultural, but at today's fair you can find daily Mardi Gras parades, live concerts, celebrity chef demonstrations, a circus, a live shark tank, horse shows, pig racing, rides, and crafts, as well as all your favorite fair food (I am a kettle corn fanatic). But one of the biggest draws remains The Big E Cream Puff. Over 47,000 cream puffs are consumed each year, and I have watched with fascination at the long line waiting for this airy, sweet, and creamy treat. Fans say their love stems from the fact that it is kind of fancy and simple and comforting at the same time. And it's big! So in tribute, here is my version: an almost crispy pâte à choux shell, a generous filling of vanilla-flavored whipped cream, and a shower of confectioners' sugar. Who knew so few and such simple ingredients could yield such a dramatic dessert! The bread flour makes a puff with great, crisp, dry texture. Assemble these right before serving.

for the pâte à choux Position a rack in the middle of the oven. Preheat the oven to 400°F. Line a jelly-roll pan with parchment paper.

1) Combine the water, butter, and salt in a medium saucepan. Bring to a rolling boil over medium-high heat and immediately remove from the heat.

2) Quickly stir in the flour all at once. Keep stirring with a wooden spoon until the dough comes together. Place over very low heat and keep stirring. You want the dough to dry out. This will take about 1 minute; the pâte à choux should come cleanly away from the sides of the saucepan. Scrape the dough into the bowl of a stand mixer fitted with the flat paddle attachment.

3) Turn on low-medium speed and add the eggs one at a time, allowing each egg to be absorbed before continuing. The batter should

PÂTE À CHOUX

1 cup water

6 tablespoons (¾ stick) unsalted butter, at room temperature, cut into pieces

¼ teaspoon salt

1 cup bread flour

4 large eggs, at room temperature

Pastry bag

½-inch plain round decorating tip, such as Ateco #806 or Wilton #1A

CREAM FILLING

Pastry bag

Large star decorating tip, such as Ateco #835 or Wilton #2110

2 cups chilled heavy cream

¼ cup sifted confectioners' sugar, plus more for dusting

¼ teaspoon vanilla extract

be smooth, a rich golden yellow, and firm enough to hold a shape when mounded with a spoon.

4) Scrape the dough into the pastry bag fitted with the round tip. Pipe out 6 puffs, about 4 inches across and 2 inches tall, evenly spaced on the baking pan. Dip your fingertip in water and lightly press down any peak that has formed on the puffs; you want them to have a rounded appearance.

5) Bake at 400°F for about 25 minutes; they should be light golden brown all over. Turn down the oven to 350°F and continue to bake for 10 minutes. Insert a sharp knife into the side of each puff to allow steam to escape, and continue baking for 10 more minutes. They should be high, round, golden brown, and very dry and crisp.

6) Cool completely on the pan set on a rack. The puffs are ready to use. Alternatively, place in zipper-top freezer bags and freeze for up to 1 month. Take care not to let them get crushed during storage. Defrost at room temperature.

for the assembly Fit the pastry bag with the star tip. In the chilled bowl of a stand mixer, beat the cream on medium-high speed with the wire whip attachment until it just begins to thicken. Add the confectioners' sugar and vanilla and beat just until firm peaks form. Scrape into the pastry bag. Pry (or slice) open each puff horizontally, creating a slightly larger bottom half. Pipe a very generous amount of cream onto each puff bottom. Crown with a puff top. Shake a generous amount of confectioners' sugar on top and serve immediately—with lots of napkins.

TIP Pâte à choux puffs often bake up in such a way so that you can simply pry them apart and they divide appropriately. This is most often the approach I take. If you are nervous about this technique, by all means, slice them in half. A serrated knife works best in this instance.

champagne-cassis mousse
with raspberries SERVES 16

This is a creamy, light-as-air mousse, the palest of pink, molded in a ring, the center filled with fresh raspberries. It is dramatic, with the smoothest, most comforting texture, yet has a kick from almost a full bottle of Champagne and a generous dose of deep purple crème de cassis, a black currant liqueur. The Champagne can indeed be a domestic sparkling wine. In fact, less expensive brands, with their often larger, less delicate bubbles, work even better in this recipe. I like Cook's California Blush. As with all gelatin-based desserts, this needs time to set up. It is perfect made 1 day ahead.

1) Have ready a 12-cup ring mold. I use a classic Bundt-style pan, as it provides a low profile and a large enough center hole for the berries.

2) Pour the cold water into a small bowl. Sprinkle the gelatin over and set aside for 5 minutes to soften the gelatin.

3) Meanwhile, stir together the Champagne and cassis. Remove 1 cup and set aside. Pour the remaining larger portion into a medium saucepan. Scrape the softened gelatin into the saucepan and heat over medium heat, stirring gently, until the gelatin dissolves. Pour into a bowl set over ice and stir occasionally until it begins to thicken. This could take 30 minutes. The time is not important—the texture is. You are aiming for the moment when it is just starting to thicken but is still fluid.

4) Meanwhile, in the chilled bowl of a stand mixer, beat the cream and confectioners' sugar on medium-high speed with the wire whip attachment until very soft peaks form; set aside in the refrigerator.

5) Check the gelatin mixture. When it just develops a somewhat gelatinous but still fluid texture and shows a faint shape when you drop some from a spoon, it is ready.

¼ cup cold water

1 tablespoons plus 2 teaspoons unflavored powdered gelatin

3 cups rosé Champagne or sparkling wine

2 cups crème de cassis, such as Guyot

4 cups heavy cream

¾ cup sifted confectioners' sugar

3 cups fresh red raspberries

6) Fold the gelatin mixture together with the whipped cream and the remaining Champagne-cassis mixture. Make sure that all the components are completely combined. It can be helpful at this stage to use a large balloon whisk to make sure the mousse is smooth and very well blended.

7) Rinse the mold with cold water and shake dry. Scrape the mousse into the mold, level the surface with a small offset spatula, and refrigerate for at least 6 hours, or preferably overnight.

8) Unmold right before serving. Rinse a large, flat serving platter with cold water; shake dry. Fill a larger bowl with warm water and submerge the mold for 5 to 10 seconds, taking care that water does not come up over the sides. Shake the mold back and forth gently to help release the surface tension. Place the serving platter over the open end of the mold and invert, and the mousse should slip out. If it does not, repeat the submersion step. Fill the center with fresh berries and serve.

TIP   The trick with this recipe is to allow the mixture with the gelatin to set up just enough so that it is easy to fold into the whipped cream. If it is too liquidy, it will sink to the bottom of the cream mixture and create a rubbery layer; if it is too firm, it will not incorporate smoothly. By chilling it over ice, stirring occasionally, and keeping an eye on it, you will be able to catch it at the right time. Just don't walk away and leave it over the ice.

warm chocolate velvet

SERVES 6

I asked my son Forrester to describe what he could envision as the most amazing dessert—and he simply stated, "It should be chocolate and it should be warm." With that as my directive, I came up with what is essentially a warm baked pudding. It is similar to the ubiquitous molten chocolate cakes that never seem to disappear from restaurant menus. The advantage here is that there is no flour to mute the chocolate flavor, and the batter can be prepared ahead and refrigerated, so you can bake these right before serving. Also, they are not unmolded, making them even easier. Make up to a day ahead, take out of the refrigerator while you prepare dinner, and simply bake for about 15 minutes right before serving. I like to serve these with ice cream, for a contrast of temperatures and textures, or a simple dollop of whipped cream.

for the puddings Have ready six ½-cup, deep ovenproof ceramic or glass ramekins. Put the eggs, still in the shell, in a bowl of very warm tap water. Let them sit for 5 minutes.

1) Meanwhile, melt the chocolate and butter together in the top of a double boiler or in a microwave; stir until smooth. Cool slightly.

2) Crack the eggs into the bowl of a stand mixer, add the sugar, and beat using the wire whip attachment on medium-high speed until thickened, frothy, and tripled in volume. Fold the chocolate mixture into the egg mixture until no streaks remain. Divide evenly between the ramekins. Cover each one with plastic wrap, taking care not to touch the wrap to the surface of the pudding. Refrigerate for up to 1 day.

for serving Remove the puddings from the refrigerator at least 1 hour before serving. Position a rack in the middle of the oven. Preheat the oven to 350°F. Place the ramekins in a large roasting pan and add hot water to come halfway up the outside of the ramekins.

1) Bake for 15 to 20 minutes, or until the surface of the puddings is puffed and looks dull. A toothpick inserted in the center will show moist pudding clinging when removed. Serve immediately.

PUDDINGS

4 large eggs, at room temperature

8 ounces bittersweet chocolate, finely chopped, such as Valrhona Caraïbe (66%)

3 tablespoons unsalted butter, at room temperature, cut into pieces

¼ cup sugar

Vanilla or coffee premium ice cream, such as Häagen Dazs or lightly sweetened and softly whipped heavy cream, optional

pomegranate panna cotta

with pomegranate–chocolate sauce SERVES 8

Industry food shows are a gigantic amalgam of food purveyors large and small, and it is not unusual to taste a salsa, a fruit jam, a caramel sauce, smoked fish pâté, blue cheese, chocolate, horseradish mustard, and perhaps an ice cream back to back in a 15-minute period. Your taste buds can become deadened quite quickly. During one outing my palate was quickly woken up upon tasting a pomegranate ice-cream bar covered with a crispy dark chocolate coating, made by a company called SheerBliss. If you are an ice-cream fan, you must try these. I immediately wanted to create a dessert with a similar flavor profile, and here it is: a panna cotta flavored with pomegranate juice, which gives it a delightful tart, fruity flavor as well as a seductive pink color. The sauce is a light, fluid ganache enhanced with pomegranate molasses, a Middle Eastern ingredient that truly balances between tart and sweet and adds a depth and richness to the dark chocolate. This dessert is best layered in a clear glass or goblet, so that you can enjoy the pretty colors and contrast between the layers. An added boon is that you don't have to worry about unmolding the dessert.

PANNA COTTA

1 cup 100% pomegranate juice, such as POM Wonderful

1 tablespoon unflavored powdered gelatin

6 tablespoons sugar

2 cups heavy cream

1 cup whole milk

SAUCE

⅔ cup heavy cream

6 ounces semisweet chocolate, finely chopped, such as Ghirardelli, (45%), Callebaut (52%), or Valrhona Equitoriale (55%)

for the panna cotta Have ready eight 6- to 10-ounce clear glass wine goblets or ramekins. Pour the pomegranate juice into a large saucepan. Sprinkle the gelatin over and set aside for 5 minutes to soften the gelatin. Heat over medium-low heat, stirring gently, until the gelatin dissolves. Add the sugar; stir to help dissolve. Stir in the cream and milk and heat just until warm and absolutely all the sugar is dissolved and the mixture is well combined. Strain into a large pitcher. Strain again, pouring directly into the goblets and dividing the mixture evenly. Refrigerate for at least 4 hours or until set. Refrigerate for up to 1 day, covering the tops of the goblets with plastic wrap.

for the sauce Put the cream in a medium saucepan and bring to a boil over medium heat. Remove from the heat and immediately sprinkle the chocolate into the cream. Cover and allow to sit for 5 minutes. Gently stir until smooth. Stir in the pomegranate molasses. Allow to cool; it should be as cool as possible while still being fluid.

1) Meanwhile, prep the pomegranate, working in a clean sink to contain splatter. Slice off both ends of the fruit; score through the skin and pry apart into sections. Put a clean bowl in the sink, and hold one section over the bowl, cut side down. Use a spoon to rap very firmly on the curved exterior of the fruit, and the fleshy covered seeds (called arils) will pop out. Continue doing this until you have about ½ cup of the seeds. Right before serving, spoon just enough sauce over the panna cotta to cover the surface and sprinkle with some of the seeds.

3 tablespoons pomegranate molasses, such as Al Wadi

1 pomegranate

TIP As with any dessert that contains gelatin, extended refrigeration tends to toughen the texture. Most gelatin desserts are best served as soon after they are set as possible.

measuring gelatin

Through the years I have come across some recipes calling for "1 packet of unflavored gelatin" while others might give volume and say "2 teaspoons unflavored gelatin." For the home cook, Knox gelatin is the readily available gelatin of choice, and I noticed that the company does not offer a volume equivalent for their individual packets. I called them directly, but they would only repeat what the packet was in terms of weight. This is a problem for Americans, who are used to measuring volume. What if one needs 1½ packets? Eyeballing with gelatin is not good enough. Then I came across a comparison study done by a consumer-oriented group and, lo and behold, it found that by volume measure, the packets appeared to vary from about 2¼ teaspoons to almost 1 tablespoon. In other words, even though the packets are supposed to be consistent, they are not. When you are dealing with such a lightweight item, of any kind of foodstuff, obviously a variation of even 10 percent makes a huge difference. This kind of variability with a thickener can cause problems. For this reason, these recipes are written with specific volume amounts. I have done this for two reasons: Firstly, I had learned that a packet of gelatin is not necessarily equal to every other packet, and secondly, because many scales used in the home, even digital ones, do not measure accurately with such small amounts of weight. I am trusting that you have the proper high-quality measuring spoons and will measure as carefully as possible.

mocha-cointreau
zebra éclairs MAKES 10 ÉCLAIRS

Pâte à choux is used for cream puffs and profiteroles as well as éclairs, which are defined, partly, by their elegant baton-like shape. They are typically found in bakeries and not made at home, which is curious, as they are actually fairly easy and always make an impact. These are filled with a Cointreau-flavored pastry cream, which provides an orange flavor, while the glaze is espresso flavored, accented by semisweet chocolate "zebra" stripes. Orange, espresso, and chocolate are rolled into one.

PÂTE À CHOUX

¾ cup water

4½ tablespoons unsalted butter, cut into pieces

Scant ¼ teaspoon salt

¾ cup bread flour

3 large eggs, at room temperature

Pastry bag

½-inch plain round decorating tip, such as Ateco #806 or Wilton #1A

GLAZE

1 tablespoon very hot water

1 teaspoon instant espresso powder, such as Medaglia d'Oro

¾ cup sifted confectioners' sugar

2 tablespoons semisweet chocolate, melted, such as Valrhona Equitoriale (55%), Ghirardelli, (45%) or Callebaut (52%)

1 recipe Rich Pastry Cream (page 10), liqueur variation using 2 tablespoons Cointreau

for the pâte à choux Position a rack in the middle of the oven. Preheat the oven to 400°F. Line a jelly-roll pan with parchment paper; set aside.

1) Combine the water, butter, and salt in a medium saucepan. Bring to a rolling boil over medium-high heat and immediately remove from the heat.

2) Quickly stir in the flour all at once. Keep stirring with a wooden spoon until the dough comes together. Place over very low heat and keep stirring. You want the dough to dry out. This will take 1 minute or less; the pâte à choux should come cleanly away from the sides of the saucepan. Scrape the dough into the bowl of a stand mixer fitted with the flat paddle attachment. Turn on medium-low speed and add the eggs one at a time, allowing each egg to be absorbed before continuing. The batter should be smooth, golden yellow, and firm enough to hold a shape when mounded with a spoon.

3) Scrape the dough into the pastry bag fitted with the tip. Pipe out 10 strips of pâte à choux, about 1¼ inches wide and 4 inches long, evenly spaced on the baking pan. Dip your fingertip in water and lightly press down any peak or "tail" that has formed, usually where you end piping. You want them to have a smooth appearance.

(234) UNFORGETTABLE DESSERTS

4) Bake at 400°F for about 25 minutes; they should be a light golden color. Turn down the oven to 350°F and continue to bake for 5 more minutes. Insert a sharp knife into the side of each éclair to allow steam to escape, and continue baking for 5 more minutes. They should be puffed and risen, light golden brown and dry.

5) Cool completely on the pan set on a rack. The éclairs are ready to assemble. Alternatively, place in zipper-top freezer bags and freeze for up to 1 month. Take care not to let them get crushed during storage. Defrost at room temperature. Wash and dry the pastry bag and tip.

for the glaze Make the glaze right before assembling the éclairs. Put the hot water in a small bowl, sprinkle the espresso powder over, and stir to combine and dissolve the espresso. Gradually whisk in the confectioners' sugar until smooth. Scrape the melted chocolate into a parchment cone; set aside.

for the assembly Split each éclair, slicing in half along one long side, and gently open each éclair like a book. Scrape the pastry cream into the clean pastry bag fitted with the tip and pipe into each éclair, filling the "bottom" half of each. Fold the "top" half over to "close" the éclair. Use a spoon to scoop glaze onto each éclair, and use the back of the spoon to spread it so that it covers about three-quarters of the top. While the glaze is still soft, cut off the tip of the parchment cone to make a small opening and pipe the chocolate back and forth crosswise across each éclair, making about 5 looping passes back and forth. While the chocolate is still soft, take a toothpick or bamboo skewer and gently draw it through the chocolate and glaze lengthwise, first going one way, then the other. You will be able to make maybe 4 passes back and forth. This technique creates the desired striped effect. The éclairs may be served immediately or refrigerated for up to 8 hours.

concord grape gelée
panna cotta parfait serves 6

> I cannot get enough of the incomparable, musky, aromatic flavor of Concord grapes. Unfortunately, they have a very short season and are often hard to find. They also have a tough skin and are full of large seeds. Concord grape juice, however, is available in most supermarkets, and I have put it to good use here in two forms: It makes a generous portion of dark purple gelée, layered beneath a creamy panna cotta, and it is reduced into a sauce for a seedless red grape compote, which crowns the parfait. The result is a dessert that is filled with Concord grape flavor, without the fuss. See page 233 for a sidebar on measuring gelatin.

for the gelée Have ready six 10- to 12-ounce clear wineglasses. Pour about ¼ cup of the grape juice in a saucepan and sprinkle the gelatin over; allow to sit for 5 minutes to soften. Begin to melt the mixture over very low heat, add the remaining juice, and whisk gently until the gelatin is completely dissolved. Strain through a fine-mesh strainer into a large measuring cup or pitcher with a spout. Divide the mixture between the glasses. Refrigerate for at least 4 hours, or until set.

for the panna cotta Pour the milk into a large saucepan. Sprinkle the gelatin over and set aside for 5 minutes to soften the gelatin. Heat over very low heat, stirring gently, until the gelatin dissolves. Add the sugar; stir to help dissolve. Stir in the cream and heat just until warm and absolutely all the sugar is dissolved and the mixture is well combined. Strain into a large pitcher and cool to barely warm. Divide the panna cotta mixture between the goblets, pouring very slowly and gently over the gelée. Refrigerate for at least 4 hours, or until set. Or refrigerate for up to 1 day, covering the tops of the goblets with plastic wrap.

for the compote Put the sliced grapes in a heatproof bowl; set aside. Pour the juice and sugar into a medium saucepan and whisk to

CONCORD GRAPE GELÉE

2 cups 100% grape juice, such as Welch's

2 teaspoons unflavored powdered gelatin

PANNA COTTA

1 cup milk

2¼ teaspoons unflavored powdered gelatin

4½ tablespoons sugar

2 cups heavy cream

GRAPE COMPOTE

12 ounces small or medium red seedless grapes (about 2 cups), sliced in half lengthwise

3 cups 100% grape juice, such as Welch's

½ cup sugar

custards, gelées, mousses, and puddings (237)

combine. Bring to a boil over medium-high heat and simmer until reduced to about 1 cup; this will take quite a while—at least 20 minutes. Watch carefully. As it reduces, the aroma will become more pronounced, and bubbles that slowly pop open will cover the surface. The mixture will start to reduce very quickly at this point. Once it is slightly thick and syrupy, pour over the grapes and gently toss to coat. Allow to cool to room temperature. Cover with plastic wrap and store at room temperature for up to 6 hours.

for serving Simply divide the compote between the glasses and serve immediately.

TIPS As with any dessert requiring gelatin, accurate measuring is important; too much gelatin and the texture will be overly firm. When making the compote, it does take a while to reduce the juice mixture, but watch it carefully because it can overly reduce and burn quite easily, ruining your pan. Believe me; I know.

bajan crème brûlée

SERVES 8

Whenever I travel, my greatest joy is derived from sampling new ingredients and local dishes. While I have yet to write a book that might feature the absolutely mind-opening hot, vinegary, spicy pork souse I found in Barbados, I thought the flavors of Ponche Kuba, a creamy rum-based liqueur offered to me at the Mount Gay distilleries, would be perfect in a dessert. At first glance it looks like Irish cream–style liqueur, but the flavor is more sophisticated, subtler, and less sweet. It is velvety and lightly spiced and based on the island's fine rums. The term *Bajan* refers to the island locals and is fitting for this crème brûlée featuring this native liqueur as well as sugar from the region. While this recipe does require two specialty ingredients (liqueur and sugar), it makes a sophisticated ending to a meal featuring Caribbean flavors, or anytime you want something creamy, smooth, and rich.

for the topping If the sugar is moist, it must first be dried out. You can spread it out in a single layer on a plate and let it sit at room temperature overnight, or you can spread it out in a small pan and dry it out in the oven or toaster oven at 250°F until it feels crunchy and dry. Cool before proceeding. Take the dry Demerara sugar and crush into a powder using a spice grinder, coffee mill, or mortar and pestle. Store in an airtight container until needed.

for the custard Position a rack in the middle of the oven. Preheat the oven to 325°F. Arrange eight 5-ounce shallow ramekins (1 inch high) in a larger roasting pan(s); set aside.

1) Heat the cream in a medium saucepan to just below a boil. Remove from the heat and whisk in the liqueur. Meanwhile, whisk together the egg yolks and sugar in a heatproof bowl until thick and creamy. Slowly pour the warm cream mixture into the egg mixture to temper the eggs, whisking all the while. Strain through a fine-mesh strainer into a pitcher. Pour into the ramekins, dividing evenly. Fill

TOPPING

½ cup Demerara sugar, such as Billington's

CUSTARD

3½ cups heavy cream
½ cup Ponche Kuba
9 large egg yolks
⅔ cup sugar

the larger pan(s) with hot tap water to reach halfway up the outside of the ramekins.

2) Bake for 35 to 40 minutes, or just until the edges of the custard are set but the center still quivers if shaken gently. It will firm up upon cooling. Remove from the oven and remove the ramekins from the pan. Cool the ramekins directly on a rack to room temperature. Refrigerate for at least 3 hours, or up to 2 days covered with plastic wrap, taking care not to touch the wrap to the surface.

for the brûlée Sprinkle the Demerara powder in a thin, even layer over each custard. Caramelize using a propane or butane torch or under a broiler (see page 220). Serve immediately.

TIP When making any crème brûlée, I like using shallow dishes. This gives what I think is the best ratio of cream to crackly sugar. There are all sorts of sizes and shapes available, and sometimes the smaller ones are more suitable to the occasion. I have some that hold a mere 2 ounces and are quite elegant. In this case your yield will obviously be higher and the baking time will be reduced to about 25 minutes, but consider making these tiny brûlées if you are also offering other desserts.

frozen desserts and sauces

ICE CREAM, IN some form, is always offered on dessert menus, as it consistently retains a universal appeal for children and adults alike. Special occasions in the home also often feature ice cream, be they birthdays or summer gatherings in the yard. This chapter presents frozen desserts that either take advantage of purchased ice cream or that can be made without an ice-cream maker. These range from granitas, with their icy, refreshing crunch, to frozen parfaits, which have the texture of frozen velvet, to frozen semifreddo, with its lighter, fluffier texture. Not only can these all be made without an ice-cream maker, but many of them can be made ahead, making them great for entertaining. In general, all frozen deserts improve in texture if allowed to soften slightly before serving; their creamy texture will be highlighted to its fullest.

browned butter–oatmeal cookie
sandwiches with pan-roasted blueberry ice cream

MAKES 8 SANDWICHES (16 COOKIES)

Oatmeal cookies might seem plain, but when made with melted and browned-butter they take on a divinely chewy texture and sophisticated, nutty flavor. Purchased vanilla ice cream is folded together with deep purple, juicy, syrupy, caramelized blueberries and forms the filling for our ice cream sandwiches. These can be made ahead and stored in the freezer for up to 3 days, after which the brightness of the fruit flavor declines.

for the cookies Position racks in the upper third of the oven. Preheat the oven to 350°F. Line 2 jelly-roll pans with parchment.

1) In a small saucepan, melt the butter over medium heat. Once melted, continue to simmer over medium-low heat until the liquid turns a deep, rich golden color, 3 to 5 minutes. The milk solids, which sink to the bottom, will turn very dark brown; do not overcook and allow the mixture to burn. Skim away any foam on the surface.

2) Pour the browned butter into a large bowl, leaving the milk solids behind. Whisk in the brown sugar and sugar until combined. Allow to cool briefly, then whisk in the egg and vanilla. In a separate bowl, whisk together the oats, flour, baking soda, cinnamon, and salt. Add the dry mixture to the wet ingredients and stir until just combined.

3) Place scant 2-tablespoon-size scoops of cookie batter on the pans, placing them 2 inches apart (just make sure you have 16 equal-size cookies). Do not flatten. Bake for 10 to 14 minutes, or until the cookies are a light golden brown around the edges, but still a little soft, but not wet, in the center.

4) Cool on the pans set on a rack for 5 minutes, then remove the cookies to a cooling rack and cool completely. Store at room temperature for up to 1 day in an airtight container.

COOKIES

½ cup (1 stick) unsalted butter, at room temperature, cut into pieces

⅓ cup firmly packed dark brown sugar

⅓ cup sugar

1 large egg

½ teaspoon vanilla extract

1½ cups old-fashioned rolled oats (not quick or instant)

¾ cup all-purpose flour

½ teaspoon baking soda

½ teaspoon ground cinnamon

¼ teaspoon salt

ICE-CREAM FILLING

1 cup fresh blueberries

1½ tablespoons sugar

1 teaspoon water

1 pint premium vanilla ice cream

for the filling Spread the blueberries in a single layer in a nonstick skillet. Sprinkle with the sugar and water. Stir to coat. Heat over medium heat until the sugar begins to dissolve, then mash with a potato masher. Bring to a simmer and continue to cook, stirring occasionally, until the juices have begun to reduce and thicken, about 4 minutes. The mixture should be a deep, dark purple, with a syrupy consistency. It should be thick enough so that when you draw a spoon along the bottom you can see the pan for a few moments. Remove from the heat and cool completely.

1) Remove the ice cream from the freezer and allow to sit at room temperature for 5 to 10 minutes, or until softened but not melted. Fold in the cooled blueberry mixture until it is a uniform color. If you have the time, it is best to chill the ice cream at this point until it is solid again. The blueberry ice cream can be made a day ahead and frozen overnight in an airtight container.

for the assembly Have a tray in the freezer that will fit all 8 of the ice-cream sandwiches. Remove the ice cream from the freezer and let soften at room temperature for a few minutes. Place a generous 2 tablespoon-size scoop of ice cream on a bottom side of a cookie and top with another cookie, bottom side against the ice cream. Squeeze gently so that the ice cream presses out to fill the entire cookie surface. Immediately place on the tray in the freezer. Repeat with the remaining cookies and freeze until solid. Place the sandwiches in a zipper-top plastic bag and place back in the freezer until needed. Remove the sandwiches from the freezer about 5 minutes before serving. The sandwiches may be frozen for up to 3 days in zipper-top bag or an airtight container.

TIPS   Take care when browning the butter; you do want it browned, but not burnt. The dark brown sugar, as opposed to light brown, accentuates the deep, rich flavors from the browned butter and the caramelization of the berries. The choice of oats is very important as well. Old-fashioned rolled oats give the right chewy texture.

frozen milk chocolate—
peanut butter pie SERVES 10 TO 12

The word *pie* might be a misnomer, as this is actually a very tall, impressive creation made in a springform pan, taking up the entire height. It began its life as an actual pie, with shallow layers, but to take it into the realm of "unforgettable" I made it bigger, and I think, better. It is very easy to make. In fact, I have used this as an impressive dessert to teach children. The peanut butter, milk chocolate, and dark chocolate flavors appeal to young and old alike, and while the ingredients are humble, the look is fairly dramatic. The very dark, almost black chocolate wafer crust lines the bottom and the entire height of the sides. Within are two equally thick layers— one of a rich peanut butter cream, the other a satiny milk chocolate mousse. Crunchy peanuts crown the top. Make sure you have room in the freezer for the pan before beginning— it must be a flat surface so that the dessert can be level.

for the crust Coat a 9 x 3-inch springform pan with nonstick spray. Stir together the cookie crumbs and melted butter in a bowl until combined. Press the crumbs evenly along the bottom and sides of the prepared pan, stopping $1/4$ to $1/2$ inch from the top. Place in the freezer while you prepare the fillings.

for the peanut butter filling Whisk together the milk and sugar in a small saucepan. Heat over medium heat just until the sugar dissolves. Remove from the heat and whisk in the peanut butter and vanilla. Cool to room temperature. (You may hasten this by stirring over an ice bath.)

1) In the bowl of stand mixer with the wire whip attachment, whip the cream until soft peaks form. Fold about one-quarter of the cream into the peanut butter mixture to lighten, and then fold in the remaining whipped cream. Scrape the peanut butter cream over the prepared crust and smooth until level with a small offset spatula. Return to the freezer while you prepare the chocolate filling.

CRUST

One 9-ounce box Nabisco Famous Chocolate Wafers, finely ground (about 1¾ cups)

7 tablespoons unsalted butter, melted

PEANUT BUTTER FILLING

1 cup whole milk

½ cup sugar

1 cup creamy peanut butter (such as Skippy or Jif; do not use natural)

1 teaspoon vanilla extract

1 cup heavy cream

frozen milk chocolate–peanut butter pie (*continued*)

MILK CHOCOLATE FILLING

9 ounces milk chocolate, finely chopped, such as Callebaut (31%) or Ghirardelli (31%)

¼ cup water

1⅓ cups heavy cream

TOPPING

½ cup dry roasted salted peanuts, finely chopped

for the chocolate filling Melt the chocolate and water in the top of a double boiler or in a microwave. Stir until smooth. Allow to cool to room temperature, but it should still be fluid. In the bowl of a stand mixer with the wire whip attachment, whip the cream until soft peaks form. Fold about one-quarter of the cream into the chocolate mixture to lighten, and then fold in the remaining whipped cream. Gently spoon the chocolate mousse over the peanut butter cream in the pan, taking care not to upset the initial layer. Smooth the chocolate layer until level with a small offset spatula.

for the topping Sprinkle the chopped nuts in a wide band around the outer edge of the chocolate mousse.

1) Freeze until solid, for at least 4 hours. To unmold, wrap a hot, damp towel around the outside of the pan for a minute or two, then run a very thin sharp knife between the pan and the crust. Unhinge the pan. If the crust seems to be sticking to the pan, repeat the towel and knife technique. The dessert is ready to serve. It may be frozen for up to 4 days; cover the top with plastic wrap. (If I only serve a few pieces, I snap the sides back on to store the remainder in the protective pan.)

peach melba
profiteroles MAKES 8 PROFITEROLES

This is a summer dessert to make when peaches and raspberries are at their peak. This incarnation nestles vanilla ice cream in pâte à choux pastry and is served with a fresh, uncooked raspberry sauce and barely cooked peaches. By placing peeled sliced peaches in a heatproof bowl and pouring a hot sugar syrup over them, they are just barely cooked. This technique retains their bright color and flavor, but softens them slightly, resulting in a texture that melds with the pastry and ice cream. The bread flour used in the pâte à choux gives a great dry, crisp texture. You can usually find small bags of this flour in the supermarket, and it is inexpensive. You can substitute all-purpose if necessary.

for the raspberry sauce Defrost the berries completely overnight in the refrigerator or at room temperature for a few hours. Do not defrost in the microwave, as the heat will cook the fruit and you will lose some of the fresh color and flavor. Pour off any liquid and reserve.

1) Puree the berries in a blender or food processor fitted with the metal blade attachment. Pour the puree into a strainer set over a large bowl. Press the puree through the strainer. Discard the seeds. Stir 2 tablespoons of the sugar and the lemon juice into the resulting puree. Allow to sit for 5 minutes to dissolve the sugar. Taste and adjust the sweetness if desired. If the puree is too thick, add some of the reserved berry juice. You do want it to have some body, so be careful not to overly thin it out. Refrigerate for up to 1 week in an airtight container.

for the pâte à choux Position a rack in the middle of the oven. Preheat the oven to 400°F. Line a jelly-roll pan with parchment paper; set aside.

1) Combine the water, butter, and salt in a medium saucepan. Bring to a rolling boil over medium-high heat and immediately remove from the heat.

RASPBERRY SAUCE

Two 12-ounce bags unsweetened frozen (IQF) raspberries

2 to 4 tablespoons superfine sugar

1 teaspoon freshly squeezed lemon juice

PÂTE À CHOUX

½ cup water

3 tablespoons unsalted butter, cut into pieces

⅛ teaspoon salt

½ cup bread flour

2 large eggs, at room temperature

Pastry bag

½-inch plain round decorating tip, such as Ateco #806 or Wilton #1A

PEACHES

6 medium, fresh, firm but ripe peaches

frozen desserts and sauces (247)

2 teaspoons freshly squeezed lemon juice

1 cup water

½ cup sugar

1 pint premium vanilla ice cream, such as Häagen-Dazs

2) Quickly stir in the flour all at once. Keep stirring with a wooden spoon until the dough comes together. Place over very low heat and keep stirring. You want the dough to dry out. This will take 1 minute or less; the pâte à choux should come cleanly away from the sides of the saucepan. Scrape the dough into the bowl of a stand mixer fitted with the flat paddle attachment.

3) Turn on medium-low speed and add the eggs one at a time, allowing each egg to be absorbed before continuing. The batter should be smooth, golden yellow, and firm enough to hold a shape when mounded with a spoon.

4) Scrape the dough into the pastry bag fitted with the tip. Pipe out 8 puffs, about 2½ inches across and 2 inches tall, evenly spaced on the baking pan. Dip your fingertip in water and lightly press down any peak that has formed on the puffs; you want them to have a rounded appearance.

5) Bake for 20 to 30 minutes or until light golden in color. Turn down the oven to 350°F and continue to bake for 5 more minutes. Insert a sharp knife into the side of each puff to allow steam to escape, and continue baking for 5 more minutes. They should be high, round, light golden brown, and dry.

6) Cool completely on the pan set on a rack. The puffs are ready to use. Alternatively, place in zipper-top freezer bags and freeze for up to 1 month. Take care not to let them get crushed during storage. Defrost at room temperature.

for the peaches Peel the peaches with a sharp vegetable peeler. Remove the pit and cut into ½-inch slices. Put the peaches in a heat-proof bowl and toss with the lemon juice; set aside.

1) Combine the water and sugar in a medium, wide saucepan. Stir over medium heat until the sugar dissolves. Increase the heat and boil without stirring for 8 minutes, or until the syrup has reduced and thickened. Immediately pour the hot syrup over the peaches and

toss to coat. Cool to room temperature. The peaches are ready to use; or refrigerate for up to 2 days in an airtight container.

for the assembly Have the sauce ready and the ice cream at hand. Pry open each puff horizontally, creating equal bottom and top halves. Fill with rounded scoops of vanilla ice cream, about ¼ cup of ice cream per puff. The puffs are ready to serve; or freeze for up to 2 days in an airtight container.

1) Pour some sauce on the bottom of each serving dish; a shallow bowl is best. Use a slotted spoon to arrange the peaches on top of the sauce. Place an ice-cream-filled puff on top and serve immediately.

TIPS   The fresh crispness of the cream puffs, the smoothness of the ice cream, the not-too-sweet raspberry sauce, and the fresh peaches are the components in this dish. It is a balancing act. If any of these are subpar, the whole will suffer. I prefer to bake cream puffs the day they are made, although they can be made ahead. If you have frozen them, consider re-crisping them in a 350°F oven for a few minutes, then cool completely. The peaches must be ripe, but firm. If the nectarines at the market taste better, then feel free to substitute them.

Peaches are often peeled by blanching in boiling water until the peel loosens. Do not do that for this recipe, as it "cooks" them a bit, and we want their raw, fresh quality for this dessert.

frozen peanut butter–honey cheesecake
with warm chocolate–honey sauce SERVES 14 TO 16

When my very good friend Pam Rys was turning 50, I asked her husband what flavors she might like in a cake. His answer was, "She likes chocolate, peanut butter, and sweeter is better!" I also happened to know she likes cheesecake, and as they are beekeepers, I thought honey should make an appearance. This cake features all those favorites. A dark chocolate cookie crust is topped with a creamy, very peanut buttery filling—with a hint of honey. Serving it frozen adds to the sensory interest, especially when it is topped with the warm semisweet chocolate sauce sweetened with a touch of honey. Chopped honey-roasted peanuts are sprinkled on top of each slice right before serving. As with most cheesecakes, this keeps very well and can even be made several days ahead. If you are a peanut butter lover, this should not be missed. Make sure you have room in the freezer for the 9-inch springform pan to be stored on a level surface.

for the sauce Put the cream in a large saucepan and bring to a boil over medium heat. Remove from the heat and immediately sprinkle the chocolate into the cream. Cover and allow to sit for 5 minutes. The heat of the cream should melt the chocolate. Gently stir in the honey until smooth. If the chocolate is not melting, place over very low heat, stirring often, until melted, taking care not to scorch the chocolate. Refrigerate for up to 1 week in an airtight container or freeze for up to 1 month. Rewarm in a microwave or over very low heat in a saucepan before using.

for the crust Position a rack in the middle of the oven. Preheat the oven to 350°F. Coat a 9-inch round loose-bottomed or springform pan with nonstick spray. Put the cookie crumbs and melted butter in a bowl and stir to combine. Press the crust evenly over the bottom of the prepared pan. Bake the crust for 12 to 15 minutes, or until dry to the touch. Cool the pan directly on a rack while preparing the cheesecake. Turn the oven down to 325°F. Once the pan is cool

SAUCE

½ cup plus 2 tablespoons heavy cream

6 ounces semisweet chocolate, finely chopped, such as Ghirardelli (45%) or Callebaut (52%)

1 tablespoon honey, such as orange blossom or clover

CRUST

1 cup finely ground chocolate cookie crumbs, such as Nabisco Famous Chocolate Wafers (about half a 9-ounce box)

¼ cup (½ stick) unsalted butter, melted

CHEESECAKE

2 pounds cream cheese
(not low fat), at room temperature,
cut into pieces

1⅔ cups smooth peanut butter
(such as Skippy or Jif; do not use
natural)

1 cup sugar

¾ cup firmly packed light brown
sugar

2 teaspoons vanilla extract

2 large egg yolks, at room
temperature

⅓ cup heavy cream, at room
temperature

TOPPING

½ cup honey-roasted peanuts,
roughly chopped

enough to handle, thoroughly wrap the bottom in foil to prepare it for the water bath. (Use extra-wide foil if you have it).

for the cheesecake In the bowl of a stand mixer, beat the cream cheese with the flat paddle attachment on medium-high speed until creamy, about 3 minutes. Add the peanut butter and beat until smooth. Add the sugars gradually and beat until creamy, about 3 minutes, scraping down the bowl once or twice. Beat in the vanilla. Beat in the egg yolks one at a time, scraping down after each addition and allowing each yolk to be absorbed before continuing. Beat in the cream until smooth. Scrape the cheesecake batter on top of the prepared crust and smooth into an even layer. Place the foil-wrapped pan in a larger pan and add 1 inch of hot water to the pan.

1) Bake for 1 hour to 1 hour and 5 minutes; the top will look and feel dry, the edges should just be starting to come away from the sides of the pan, and the entire cake will jiggle slightly when you gently shake the pan. Remove the pan from the water, unwrap the foil, and cool completely in the pan set on a rack. Wrap the cake well in plastic wrap—still in the pan to protect it—and freeze at least overnight before serving. The cake may be frozen for up to 1 month.

for serving Have all the components ready to go; the sauce should be warm. Serve the cake frozen. Place the cheesecake slices on plates, top with sauce and a sprinkling of chopped peanuts, and serve immediately.

raspberry-peach parfait cake
with peach schnapps compote SERVES 12 TO 14

This ultra-creamy parfait takes advantage of summer peaches and raspberries, making it a perfect do-ahead August dessert—as an added boon, you do not need to turn on the oven, not even for the crust. The crust is largely made from purchased soft macaroons. I use the Archway brand, which is available nationwide. You will need a candy thermometer for this recipe— and make sure you have room in the freezer to store the springform pan on a flat surface. This dessert is best prepared at least 1 day before serving.

for the crust Coat a 9-inch springform pan with nonstick spray; set aside. Put the macaroons and almonds in the bowl of a food processor fitted with the metal blade attachment and process until very finely and evenly ground. Pulse in the lemon zest. Pat half of the crumbs into the pan in an even layer, covering the bottom of the pan. Wipe out the bowl of the food processor.

for the parfait Puree the peaches in the food processor just until smooth. Do not overprocess or air will be incorporated and the color will lighten. Scrape into a nonreactive saucepan and cook over medium heat, stirring frequently, until the mixture is reduced to 1 cup, about 10 minutes. Cool to room temperature, stirring occasionally to release the heat, and then scrape into a bowl, stir in the almond extract, and refrigerate until needed. Rinse out the processor bowl and puree the raspberries just until smooth; strain, discarding the seeds. You should have 1 cup puree; scrape into a nonreactive bowl and refrigerate until needed.

1) Whisk together the egg yolks, sugar, corn syrup, and butter in the top of a double boiler set over simmering water; do not allow the top of the double boiler to touch the simmering water. Whisk almost constantly until thick and creamy, 5 to 8 minutes. A candy thermometer should read 160°F. Transfer the mixture to the bowl

CRUST

One 13-ounce package soft vanilla-coconut macaroons, such as Archway

½ cup sliced almonds, toasted (see page 23)

2 teaspoons finely grated lemon zest

PARFAIT

3 large, ripe peaches, peeled, pitted, and diced

¼ teaspoon almond extract

2 cups fresh red raspberries

9 large egg yolks

¾ cup sugar

¼ cup light corn syrup

2 tablespoons unsalted butter, at room temperature

2½ cups heavy cream

COMPOTE

6 large, ripe peaches, peeled, pitted, and sliced into very thin wedges

½ cup sugar

½ cup peach schnapps

2 teaspoons freshly squeezed lemon juice

DECORATION

5 ounces white chocolate, finely chopped, such as Valrhona or Ghirardelli

2 cups firm, fresh red raspberries

of a stand mixer and beat with the wire whip attachment on high speed. The mixture will increase in volume, become lighter in color, light and fluffy in texture, and cool to room temperature in about 5 minutes. The mixture should form a ribbon. Divide the mixture in half into two separate bowls; clean the mixer bowl and wire whip. Fold the chilled peach puree into one and the raspberry puree into other. Whip the cream until soft peaks form in the cleaned bowl; fold half the cream into the peach mixture and half into the berry mixture.

2) Immediately spread the peach mixture into the pan over the crust and smooth with an offset spatula into an even layer. Sprinkle the reserved cookie crumbs evenly over the peach parfait, pressing down gently with your fingers. Immediately spread the raspberry parfait over the cookie crumbs again, smoothing the layer with an offset spatula. The parfait will come all the way to the top of the pan. Freeze the parfait for at least 8 hours or, preferably, overnight. Store frozen for up to 2 days. Cover with plastic wrap once frozen.

for the compote Mix all the ingredients together in a bowl and allow to stand for at least 15 minutes and up to 1 hour, tossing occasionally; set aside.

for the decoration and assembly About 30 minutes before serving, measure out a piece of aluminum foil 35 inches long; do not use heavy-duty aluminum foil. In fact, the cheaper, thinner brands are better here, as they are more flexible. Fold it in half lengthwise. Trim the long open edge so that the strip is $3^{1}/_{2}$ inches wide. Place flat on a work surface and smooth out the wrinkles. Make a mark with a pen at the 32-inch point. Melt the chocolate in the top of a double boiler or in a microwave and scrape into a parchment cone; snip a small opening. Pipe a thick, lacy design all over the foil within your marked area. Go up and down and side to side to make the lace very intercon-nected, which will give it strength and structure. Let the chocolate set for about 5 minutes.

1) Meanwhile, remove the cake from the freezer and unmold. Place on a flat serving platter in front of you. Pick up the aluminum strip from both short ends and place the center of the strip, chocolate side in, at the center rear of the cake (the side that's away from you). Make sure the bottom of the strip is aligned with the base of the cake. Bring the two ends of the foil around the cake and toward you. The still-moist chocolate will adhere the strip to the cake; keep the strip as even as possible, aligning the bottom of the strip with the bottom of the cake. Position the short end that has the chocolate on it so that it lies flat against the cake. The other short end, with the extra clean foil, should be left sticking out by about 1 inch. Freeze until the chocolate is set, about 8 minutes.

2) Remove the cake from the freezer; carefully peel the foil away from the chocolate band, starting with the end that is firmly against the cake. Take care as you reach the other end, where the chocolate lace will not be supported by cake. After all the foil is removed, place the palm of your hand against the lace that is still sticking out. The heat from your hand will soften the chocolate slightly. This could take 10 seconds or up to a minute. Once the chocolate softens slightly, use your palm to coax it gently into place against the cake; the band will slightly overlap. The cake is ready to serve, or may be frozen for a few hours; take care to protect the chocolate lace band.

for serving Arrange the raspberries all over the cake top. Serve after allowing the parfait cake to soften slightly, with the compote alongside.

TIPS To create a completely flat, even crust, use a flat-bottomed glass to press the cookie crumbs into place. If you do use your fingers, dip them into cold water first to keep the macaroons from sticking. The white chocolate band is optional, but fancy and fun, and certainly adds a visual "wow" factor to the dessert, but the dessert tastes just as good without it. To make the chocolate band easy to "apply," I like to replace the bottom of the springform pan with an aluminum foil—covered 9-inch cardboard round. The actual pan bottom has a raised, rounded lip, which makes applying the chocolate band—and serving the slices of cake—more difficult, although not impossible. A cardboard is perfectly flat and therefore a better option.

espresso-stracciatella semifreddo
with kahlúa-caramel sauce SERVES 8

There are several steps to this dessert, but they are all easy, and the semifreddo and sauce can both be made a couple of days ahead, which is great for entertaining. This is a rich, smooth, deeply coffee-flavored frozen dessert, formed in a loaf pan. Shavings of 70 percent chocolate are speckled throughout, and each serving gets a dose of coffee liqueur–spiked caramel sauce. For the chocolate, start with a chunk and grate on the largest holes of a box grater. The sauce is easy but requires you to make a very dark caramel. This is simply a matter of timing; do not walk away from the stove, as the caramel can go from medium dark to burnt all too quickly. Start this recipe at least 1 day ahead.

KAHLÚA-CARAMEL SAUCE

1 cup sugar

¼ cup water

½ cup heavy cream, at room temperature

2 tablespoons Kahlúa

SEMIFREDDO

5 large eggs, separated, 2 whites reserved

½ cup plus ⅓ cup sugar

½ cup very strong brewed espresso or coffee, warm or at room temperature

2 tablespoons Kahlúa

¼ teaspoon cream of tartar

1 cup chilled heavy cream

½ teaspoon vanilla extract

1 ounce bittersweet chocolate, grated on largest holes of a box grater, such as Valrhona Guanaja (70%)

for the sauce Put the sugar and water in a large, heavy-bottomed saucepan. Stir to moisten the sugar and cook over medium-high heat, without stirring, until the syrup begins to color. Wash down the sides of the pot once or twice with a damp pastry brush if necessary. When the syrup is a medium amber color, watch closely, as the color will deepen quickly. Within the next minute or so, the caramel will turn a very dark mahogany brown, the bubbles will turn tan in color, and wisps of smoke might appear. Immediately remove from the heat and swirl the pot to dissipate the heat. Place on a cool burner and slowly pour in the cream. The mixture may bubble up furiously. Just let the bubbling subside and whisk until smooth. If the cream is too cool, it will cause the caramel to seize. Just place the pot back over low heat and stir until the sauce liquefies. Cool to room temperature; stir in the Kahlúa. Refrigerate for up to 1 month in an airtight container. Reheat in a double boiler or microwave before using.

for the semifreddo Line a straight-sided loaf pan that measures $8\frac{1}{2}$ × $4\frac{1}{4}$ × 3 inches with plastic wrap. (You may use a standard 6-cup loaf pan, if desired.) Press and smooth out the plastic wrap so that it hugs the contours of the pan with as few wrinkles as possible.

1) Whisk together the egg yolks, ½ cup of the sugar, the espresso, and Kahlúa in the top of a double boiler set over simmering water; do not allow the top of the double boiler to touch the simmering water. Attach a candy thermometer. Whisk almost constantly, until very thick and tripled in volume and it reaches 160°F, in about 5 to 8 minutes. Remove from the heat and cool completely, whisking occasionally to hasten the process.

2) In the clean, grease-free bowl of a stand mixer, whip the egg whites on low speed using the wire whip attachment until frothy. Add the cream of tartar and turn the speed to medium-high. When soft peaks form, add the remaining ⅓ cup sugar gradually. Continue whipping until stiff, glossy peaks form. Set this bowl over simmering water and whisk until it reaches 160°F. Remove from the heat and cool completely, whisking occasionally to hasten the process.

3) In the bowl of a stand mixer, whip the cream and vanilla on medium-high speed using the wire whip attachment until soft peaks form. Fold the egg white mixture into the espresso mixture. Scrape the whipped cream over the semifreddo mixture and sprinkle the grated chocolate over all. Gently fold everything together just until combined. Scrape into the prepared pan, smooth the top with a small offset spatula, and cover with plastic wrap. Freeze overnight. The semifreddo may be made 3 days ahead. Keep frozen until serving.

to serve Have the sauce warmed and fluid. Unmold the semifreddo. Remove the plastic wrap from the top, invert on a cutting board, lift the pan away, and peel off the remaining plastic wrap. Slice with a very sharp, thin-bladed knife into 1-inch-thick slices. Lay the slices flat on plates and spoon the warmed sauce over and around. Serve immediately.

TIPS If you would like to eliminate the alcohol, increase the brewed espresso to 10 tablespoons for the semifreddo and simply leave it out of the caramel sauce. Also, to alter the serving presentation, simply scoop the semifreddo into glass goblets or dishes and top with sauce.

frozen caramel soufflé

with bittersweet chocolate whisky sauce SERVES 8

No need to worry about this soufflé rising (and then falling) because this one is frozen, and its "high-rise" look is created by securing a collar of parchment paper around the soufflé dish, which allows the soufflé to ascend above the rim. Indeed, it is a soufflé in looks only; no eggs used here, just lots of cream and deep, dark caramel. The flavor of the caramel base depends on its depth of color. You might think you are burning the sugar at that stage, and you are, but don't worry; it will give you the flavor you crave. This is like a soft, spoonable ice cream that you do not need to churn in an ice-cream maker. Purchased soft ladyfingers are brushed with liquor and layered within the dessert. The warm bittersweet chocolate sauce both accents the caramel flavors perfectly and offers a temperature contrast.

SYRUP

3 tablespoons sugar

1½ tablespoons water

1½ tablespoons Scotch whisky

SOUFFLÉ

1½ cups plus 1 tablespoon sugar

Scant 1 cup water

3⅓ cups plus 2 tablespoons heavy cream

One 3-ounce package soft 3-inch ladyfingers (found in bakery section of supermarket)

1 recipe Dark Chocolate Ganache (page 7), made with bittersweet chocolate such as Valrhona Caraïbe (66%); stir in 2 tablespoons Scotch whisky until smooth

for the syrup Put the sugar and water in a small saucepan and stir to combine. Bring to a boil over high heat, swirling the pan to help the sugar dissolve. Cool to room temperature and stir in the whisky; set aside.

for the soufflé Put the sugar and water in a large, heavy-bottomed saucepan. Stir to moisten the sugar and cook over medium-high heat, without stirring, until the syrup begins to color; wash down the sides of the pot once or twice with a damp pastry brush if necessary. When the syrup is a medium amber color, watch closely, as the color will deepen quickly. Within the next minute or so, the caramel will turn a very dark mahogany brown, the bubbles will turn tan in color, and wisps of smoke might appear. Immediately remove from the heat and swirl the pot to dissipate the heat. Place on a cool burner and slowly pour in 1¼ cups of the cream. The mixture may bubble up furiously; just let the bubbling subside and whisk until smooth. Scrape into a large bowl and cool to room temperature.

1) Meanwhile, wrap a parchment paper collar around the lip of an 8-cup soufflé dish (8 x 3½ inches). Tape the pieces of parchment

together. Have the collar extend about 2 inches above the rim and make sure it is snug against the dish. Make sure you have a flat area in the freezer large enough for the dish.

for the assembly Once the caramel is at room temperature, whip the remaining cream just until soft peaks form. Fold a scant quarter of the whipped cream into the caramel to lighten it, and then fold in the remaining cream until thoroughly combined. Scoop about one-third of the caramel-cream mixture into the bottom of the soufflé dish and spread evenly with a small offset spatula. Arrange a single layer of ladyfingers over the surface and brush thoroughly with the whisky syrup mixture. Top with another third of the caramel cream and another layer of ladyfingers brushed with syrup, and finish with a layer of the remaining caramel cream. Freeze overnight. Once it is frozen, cover the top with plastic wrap. Freeze for up to 3 days.

for serving Have the chocolate sauce warm and fluid. Unwrap the collar from the soufflé dish and discard. Present the soufflé at the table so everyone can admire its towering, impressive silhouette. Simply scoop the soufflé out onto plates and serve with the sauce over and around. Serve immediately.

frozen apricot parfait

with amaretto-poached apricots SERVES 8

I like to make this dessert in early spring, when I am a bit tired of the winter fruits and am hankering for something with a bright flavor. This dish uses dried apricots, which I enjoy using year round, in addition to juice-packed canned apricots. The canned apricots are one of the select canned fruits whose quality I enjoy (canned pumpkin and tart cherries being others). The combination of the two brings a depth of flavor to the dish; the dried offer a concentration of flavor and slight chewiness, while the canned offer additional flavor and a tender texture. Both are accented beautifully by the amaretti cookies in the crust. While they have an almond flavor, they are actually made from apricot kernels. The poached apricot compote is further emboldened by a splash of amaretto liqueur. This is a pretty, elegant dessert on the plate, and perfect for entertaining, as all the components can be made ahead. The Blenheim apricots are a California-grown apricot that are incredibly vibrant in color and flavor, and other apricots will not do this dish justice.

POACHED APRICOTS

1 cup water

¼ cup sugar

¾ cup dried Blenheim apricots (whole or halves)

¼ cup Disaronno Amaretto

CRUST

1¼ cups finely ground Lazzaroni Amaretti di Saronno cookies (about 38 cookies)

¼ cup melted unsalted butter

FILLING

¾ cup dried Blenheim apricots, chopped

1 cup water, divided

for the poached apricots Put the water and sugar in a medium saucepan and stir to combine. Add the apricots and bring to a simmer over medium heat, cooking until tender, 6 to 8 minutes. Cool and add the liqueur. Refrigerate for up to 4 days in an airtight container.

for the crust Position a rack in the middle of the oven. Preheat the oven to 350°F. Coat a 9 X 3-inch springform pan with nonstick spray; set aside.

1) Stir together the cookie crumbs and melted butter until the crumbs are evenly moistened. Scrape into the prepared pan and press in a thin, even layer along the bottom of the pan and up the sides about 1½ inches. Bake for 10 to 12 minutes, or until the crust is dry to the touch and just beginning to color. Cool in the pan on a rack.

for the filling Combine the chopped dried apricots and ½ cup of the water in a small saucepan and bring to a simmer over medium-high heat. Cook until tender, about 5 minutes. Cool to room temperature. Scrape into a food processor fitted with the metal blade attachment, add the drained canned apricot halves, and puree until as smooth as possible. Scrape the mixture into a large bowl; set aside.

3⁄4 cup juice-packed canned apricot halves, drained

1 cup sugar

6 large egg whites, at room temperature

1½ cups chilled heavy cream

½ teaspoon almond extract

1) Meanwhile, stir the sugar and the remaining ½ cup water together in a small saucepan. Bring to a boil over medium-high heat and cook to 238°F. While the sugar syrup is cooking, in the clean, grease-free bowl of stand mixer, whip the egg whites using the wire whip attachment on medium speed until frothy. Increase the speed to high and beat until stiff, but not dry, peaks form. When the sugar syrup is ready, slowly drizzle the hot sugar syrup onto the egg whites with the machine running on low speed, taking care not to allow any to drip on the sides of the bowl or the whip attachment. Increase the speed to high and whip until the meringue is thick, glossy, and cool to the touch. Fold about one-quarter of the meringue into the apricot puree to lighten it, and then fold in the remaining meringue in two batches.

2) Whip the cream and almond extract in a separate bowl just until soft peaks form. Fold into the apricot mixture until thoroughly blended, and then scrape into the prepared crust, smoothing the top with a small offset spatula. Freeze for at least 8 hours or overnight, until very firm. Cover with plastic wrap once frozen, for up to 2 days. Allow to soften for about 5 minutes before cutting into wedges. Serve with the poached apricots alongside.

TIP The Lazzaroni Amaretti di Saronno cookies come in their iconic red tin, which is reusable and quite decorative. I have seen miniature versions of these cookies, but for this recipe I am calling for the standard size, which are about 1⅓ inches across. They are wrapped in pairs, so count accordingly. While pricey, they have an incomparable flavor that cannot be duplicated.

frozen chocolate–mint parfait

with crystallized mint SERVES 8

The exceedingly smooth texture of this frozen chocolate dessert is achieved without an ice-cream maker—and it thrills me every time because you almost can't believe it's that good. The mint flavor is provided by crème de menthe liqueur; the alcohol content also helps achieve the velvety texture. I like to use green crème de menthe, as it adds a subtle hue to the whipped cream, but the clear liqueur version may be used as well. This recipe is scaled for a standard 9 x 5 x 3-inch loaf pan; however, I find the look of straight-sided loaf pans to be much more elegant. They are also typically a tad smaller, so if you go this route, you might have some extra parfait to scrape into an extra container and nibble on the side. In terms of choosing fresh mint, if you have a farmers' market, you might have choices including peppermint, black mint, spearmint, and others. I like a strong peppermint for this dish. The look of this parfait, with its chocolate polka dots and stripes, was inspired by a creation of Lauren Chattman's in her *Icebox Desserts* (The Harvard Common Press, 2005).

CRYSTALLIZED MINT

1 bunch fresh mint leaves

1 cup superfine sugar

1 large egg white

Small, soft artist's brush

PARFAIT

8 ounces semisweet chocolate, finely chopped, such as Ghirardelli or Valrhona Equitoriale (45%)

½ cup plus 1 tablespoon water, divided

¼ cup crème de menthe liqueur, divided

4 large eggs

¾ cup sugar

for the crystallized mint Line a jelly-roll pan with parchment paper and top the paper with a cooling rack; set aside. Swish the head of the bunch of mint around in a bowl of water to loosen and remove any dirt. Dry thoroughly; this step is very important, as mint is often dirty and it must be completely dry before proceeding. Break off small sprigs of mint with 3 to 5 mint leaves per sprig. Put the sugar in a small bowl. Whisk the egg white until frothy in another small bowl. Hold the sprigs of mint one at a time with your fingertips. Use the brush to apply a thin, even coat of egg whites to all of the mint leaf surfaces, top and bottom. Immediately hold the sprig over the bowl of sugar and, using a teaspoon, scoop and sprinkle sugar evenly over the mint so it sticks. Gently shake the mint to remove excess sugar. Place the sprig on the rack to dry. Repeat with the remaining sprigs.

1) Put the pan and rack in a warm, dry location (inside a turned-off oven with a pilot light is perfect). Let the mint dry thoroughly, at least

overnight, or until completely dry and crisp. Store for up to 4 days in an airtight container in a single layer.

for the parfait Line a 9 x 5 x 3-inch loaf pan with plastic wrap so that there is overhang on all sides. Smooth out the wrinkles as thoroughly as possible.

1) Melt the chocolate with ½ cup of the water and 2 tablespoons of the crème de menthe in the top of a double boiler or in a microwave. Stir until smooth, and cool slightly until warm.

2) Put the eggs and sugar in the bowl of a stand mixer and create a double boiler by setting it in a large pot so that the bottom of the bowl is submerged a few inches in simmering water. Attach a candy thermometer. Whisk the eggs and sugar frequently and cook until the mixture reaches 160°F. Remove from the heat and beat with the wire whip attachment on high speed until light and thick and the mixture forms a ribbon.

3) Meanwhile, soften the gelatin in the remaining 1 tablespoon of water, allowing it to sit for 5 minutes. Heat this mixture until melted, either in the microwave or in a small saucepan on top of the stove. Whisk into the warm chocolate mixture. Fold the chocolate and egg mixtures together.

4) Whip 1½ cups of the cream just until soft peaks form, fold thoroughly into the chocolate mixture. Place 3 cookies, top side down, evenly along the center bottom of the prepared pan. Scrape about half of the parfait mixture into the pan. Arrange the remaining cookies vertically in 3 rows (lengthwise) of 4; they will stand up in the thick parfait mixture. Scrape the remaining parfait into the pan and smooth the top. Fold the excess plastic wrap over the top; add an extra piece if necessary to cover completely. Freeze overnight or for up to 2 days.

5) Right before serving, whip the remaining 1½ cups cream with the confectioners' sugar and remaining 2 tablespoons liqueur until soft peaks form. Serve slices of the parfait with dollops of cream and sprigs of crystallized mint.

1 teaspoon unflavored powdered gelatin

3 cups chilled heavy cream, divided

15 Nabisco Famous Chocolate Wafers

3 tablespoons confectioners' sugar

TIP if you do not want to use raw egg white for the crystallized mint, use pasteurized egg white or reconstituted egg white.

poached nectarines

with rosé granité and frozen sabayon SERVES 6 TO 8

This recipe was inspired by the red wine–poached peaches that my mom made every summer. While I loved her rendition, I decided to use nectarines, because I like the contrast of the slightly chewy intact skin and the tender poached flesh, and I use a rosé wine, to allow a little more delicacy in flavor and to let the natural colors of the fruit shine though. In this assembled dessert, the poached fruit is chopped and layered in a glass with a granité made from the same rosé wine and a rosé sabayon that is still frozen. The colors are spectacular and range from pale yellow to orange to peachy red. All three components can be made up to 3 days ahead. Take advantage of that fact and you will be able to assemble and present these right before serving quite easily.

for the poached nectarines Stir together the wine, water, and sugar in a narrow, deep saucepan and bring to a simmer over medium heat, stirring occasionally, until the sugar dissolves. Add the fruit; the liquid should cover the fruit. Simmer just until the fruit is tender when pierced with a knife tip, 8 to 10 minutes. Remove the poached fruit from the liquid with a slotted spoon and set aside on a cutting board. Measure out 1 cup of the poaching liquid and set aside. Boil any remaining poaching liquid until it reduces and becomes thick and syrupy. Cool, and then pour into an airtight container. Once the fruit is cool, chop into ½-inch dice, discarding the pits. Scrape the fruit into the container with the syrup. Refrigerate until chilled or for up to 3 days.

for the granité Stir together the wine and the 1 cup reserved poaching liquid in an 8-inch metal baking pan. Cover the pan tightly with plastic wrap. Freeze until solid or for up to 3 days.

for the sabayon Whisk the egg yolks and wine together in the top of a double boiler (or deep bowl for a makeshift double boiler). Whisk in the sugar. Set over boiling water that just touches the bottom of the bowl and whisk constantly until very thick and almost tripled in

POACHED NECTARINES
1½ cups slightly fruity rosé wine, such as French syrah

1½ cups water

¾ cup sugar

6 ripe nectarines

GRANITÉ
1 cup slightly fruity rosé wine

1 cup poaching liquid

SABAYON
4 large egg yolks

⅓ cup slightly fruity rosé wine

¼ cup sugar

½ cup chilled heavy cream

volume. The mixture should form a ribbon when you lift the whisk; this will take 5 to 8 minutes. Remove from the heat and immediately set over a bowl of ice water. Whisk the mixture until it is completely cool. Whip the cream in a separate, clean bowl until soft peaks form, and then fold into the egg mixture. Scrape into an airtight container and freeze until solid or for up to 3 days.

for the assembly Have 6 to 8 clear wine goblets available. Right before serving, scoop a layer of fruit into the bottom of the glasses. Top with a scoop of sabayon. Use a fork to make coarse, icy flakes of granité and scoop them onto the sabayon. Repeat the layers, ending with the granité, and serve immediately.

TIP The sabayon will freeze pretty solid. In theory, it is best after it has softened at room temperature for about 5 minutes. The reason I don't suggest taking it out ahead of time is that because by the time you have all the desserts assembled, it will have come to the proper temperature and consistency.

boozy raisin-pecan
butterscotch sauce MAKES ABOUT 2¼ CUPS

This sauce puts the "Scotch" back in butterscotch and also includes toasted pecans and two kinds of raisins. It adds a warm contrast to ice creams, as well as texture. It keeps very well and makes a great host/hostess gift during the holidays. If they are really good friends, give them a jar of this and a jar of the hot fudge sauce on page 7. It is also put to good use in the ButterScotch-Pecan Brownies with Boozy Raisins (page 85).

1) Put the sugar and water in a large, heavy-bottomed saucepan. Stir to moisten the sugar and cook over medium-high heat, without stirring, until the syrup begins to color. Wash down the sides of the pot once or twice with a damp pastry brush if necessary. When the syrup is a medium amber color, watch closely, as the color will deepen quickly. Within the next minute or so, the caramel will turn a very dark mahogany brown, the bubbles will turn tan in color, and wisps of smoke might appear. Immediately remove from the heat and swirl the pot to dissipate the heat. Place on a cool burner and slowly pour in the cream. The mixture may bubble up furiously. Just let the bubbling subside and whisk until smooth.

2) Whisk in the lemon juice, salt, whiskey, and butter until combined. Stir in the nuts and raisins. Cool to room temperature. Refrigerate for up to 1 month in an airtight container. Reheat in a double boiler or a microwave before using.

2 cups sugar

½ cup water

1 cup heavy cream

½ teaspoon freshly squeezed lemon juice

⅛ teaspoon salt

¼ cup Scotch whisky

2 tablespoons unsalted butter, at room temperature

½ cup pecan halves, toasted (see page 23)

¼ cup raisins

¼ cup golden raisins

candies, confections, truffles, and tidbits

THIS CHAPTER IS filled with the diminutive somethings that might be offered alongside a more substantial dessert, after dessert, or on their own as a sweet treat. They might not be full-fledged desserts unto themselves per se, but they have a cachet all their own and deserve a spotlight. Many of these focus on chocolate, and as I have said many times before, your choice of chocolate is paramount. With several of these recipes, where there are so few ingredients, the specific chocolate becomes even more important. If you are out to impress, consider making three or four of these treats and presenting them on a platter at the end of an elegant meal.

chocolate raspberry
bliss bites MAKES 60 TRUFFLES

These are raspberry truffles like no other. Each blissful bite-size truffle features a whole, perfect raspberry enveloped in a soft, silky bittersweet chocolate ganache, the whole encased in a thin, crisp chocolate shell. Consider serving these instead of a traditional dessert with coffee, tea, or an after-dinner drink—when raspberries are in season, of course. Valrhona Manjari and Scharffen Berger Bittersweet both have a very fruity, acidic profile, which complements the raspberries beautifully. The chocolate shell is made with tempered chocolate (see the sidebar on page 272).

for the ganache Put the cream in a medium saucepan over medium heat just until it comes to a simmer. Remove from the heat and immediately sprinkle 8 ounces of the chocolate into the cream. Cover and let sit for 5 minutes; the heat will melt the chocolate. Stir gently until smooth. Pour the ganache into a small bowl.

1) Line a jelly-roll pan with aluminum foil. Gently pat the raspberries dry, if necessary. Drop one raspberry onto the surface of the ganache. Use two spoons to carefully toss the berry back and forth until it is completely covered with ganache. You want just enough ganache to adhere to the berries to cover them completely without having any extra; this will give you the right proportion of fruit to chocolate. They will not be neat and round; they will look like odd-shaped lumps of chocolate, which is fine. Place the chocolate-covered berry on the prepared pan, repeat with the remaining berries, and then refrigerate the pan until the ganache is completely firm, for about 2 hours, or overnight.

for the chocolate shell Line a jelly-roll pan with aluminum foil, shiny side up, smoothing out any wrinkles. Temper the remaining 12 ounces of chocolate (see instructions on page 272).

1) Drop the chilled raspberry centers one at a time into the tempered chocolate and use two forks to help submerge and remove

¾ cup heavy cream

20 ounces bittersweet chocolate, very finely chopped, such as Valrhona Manjari (64%) or Scharffen Berger (70%), divided

2 cups firm, dry fresh raspberries

60 small fluted paper cups

them; you are aiming to make as thin and even a coating as possible. When you remove a center from the tempered chocolate, have it balanced on the flat part of the fork and rap the base of the fork on the side of the pot to help any excess chocolate drip back into the pot. Place the dipped center on the prepared pan. Repeat with the remaining berries and refrigerate until firm, then place in the fluted paper cups. Refrigerate in an airtight container in a single layer for up to 2 days. Remove from the refrigerator about 30 minutes before serving.

TIP   The raspberries for this recipe must be very firm and dry. You cannot substitute frozen, and even if they are fresh, but the least bit wet or mushy, the recipe will not work. If you follow the directions carefully you will be rewarded with the ultimate truffle experience; these are truly impressive.

tempering chocolate

~~~~~~

Tempering is the process of carefully heating and cooling chocolate so that after cooling it will display a crisp texture, shiny appearance, and stability at room temperature. Most chocolate is "in temper" when purchased and will display these hallmarks. If your chocolate has grayish streaks, is tacky to the touch, or has a crumbly texture, it is "out of temper." When you melt chocolate, it can lose its temper unless careful attention is paid to temperature fluctuations at certain stages. You need a thermometer with a range from 40° to 130°F that shows 1° increments for this technique.

tempering instructions

* Start with the desired amount of chocolate as stated in the recipe and chop it very finely.

* Place about two-thirds of it in the top of a double boiler with gently simmering water in the lower half of the double boiler. Place a thermometer in the chocolate.

* Occasionally stir very gently to encourage melting, but do not stir vigorously, which will add air.

* Do not allow chocolate to heat above 115°F for bittersweet and semisweet chocolate and 110°F for milk or white chocolate. As soon as the chocolate is almost completely melted, remove from the heat and wipe the bottom of the pot to eliminate any chances of water droplets reaching the chocolate, which would cause it to seize.

* Add about one-third of the remaining chopped chocolate and stir gently. The residual heat will melt it. You want to cool the chocolate down to 79°F. Adding the reserved chopped chocolate will bring down the temperature gently and gradually; do not just let the chocolate sit and cool, as it will not cool quickly or evenly, and the tempering process will be thrown off. Add the remaining chocolate in two more stages, if necessary, to cool the chocolate further, continuing to stir gently until 79°F is reached.

* Place the pot back over hot, not simmering, water and rewarm gently. Bittersweet and semisweet chocolates should be brought back up to 88°

to 90°F, milk chocolate to 85° to 88°F, and white chocolate to 84° to 87°F. Do not allow any chocolate to rise above 90° or you will have to begin entire process again. Sometimes chocolate labels will tell you what their specific tempering temperatures are, so heed that advice.

* The chocolate is now ready to use for dipping truffles, making chocolate decorations, etc.

* To test the temper, thinly spread a teaspoon amount on a piece of aluminum foil and allow it to cool. If your room temperature is warm, refrigerate it for about 2 minutes. The chocolate should look shiny and smooth and break with a crisp snap. Any dull spots or streaks or a soft texture indicate that the chocolate is not in good temper.

* Now you must retain the chocolate's temperature while you are working with it. Try setting a heating pad on low and placing your bowl of tempered chocolate on top of it. Always keep checking the temperature, keeping it fluid but not over 90°F. Stir it occasionally to keep the entire amount evenly heated, as it will cool around the edges.

* It is easiest to temper at least 8 ounces of chocolate at a time, and it is not that much more difficult to temper two to three times that amount. Take advantage and plan your approach, so that if you need tempered chocolate for more than one recipe, you can do them all at once. Any leftover chocolate can be scraped out onto a piece of aluminum foil and allowed to harden; then you can chop it up and fold it into your favorite cookie batter, or save it to melt for brownies or other recipes.

how to choose, and use, chocolate

When we reach for a piece of chocolate just to eat, it can be as easy as grabbing what's around, or simply purchasing what we feel like eating at the moment—very dark bittersweet, a velvety milk chocolate, or what have you. When we incorporate chocolate into a recipe, however, we need to think about how that chocolate harmonizes with the other ingredients, in terms of both flavor and texture. This wasn't always the case. When I was growing up, we typically had semisweet chocolate morsels in the pantry as well as some squares of unsweetened chocolate, both purchased at the supermarket. There was never a choice of brands; I would venture a guess that many of you know what the brands were and probably had them in your household, too, if your formative baking years were the 1960s and 1970s. They worked; our chocolate chip cookies were fine, as were our batches of fudge brownies. Well, the world has changed—big-time! The choice of chocolate has never been greater, and this is a boon to the baker, as we can pick and choose chocolates best suited to the recipe at hand. But how do we choose?

High-end brands, as well as easily found commercial brands, have begun to give us cacao mass percentages right on the label. These will be represented by something that says "50% cacao" or "65% cacao" or "55% cacao." That's a start. But the flavor profile of each individual chocolate is unique and also carries with it certain textural components. An understanding of all of these factors should be taken into account when choosing a chocolate to incorporate into a recipe.

If you are making a recipe with fruity, acidic flavors, perhaps one that includes berries or citrus, you should consider using a chocolate with the same assertive flavor notes, perhaps Scharffen Berger Bittersweet or Valrhona Manjari. On the other hand, if you are making a recipe where the chocolate is meant to be soft and round and full on the palate, without any readily discernable flavors other than "chocolate," then Callebaut Semisweet or Valrhona Equitoriale would be better choices. The recipes will be greatly affected by your choice. This was most dramatically revealed to me years ago when I was making a chocolate–peanut butter tart. At the time I was quite fond of the Manjari, and I used it for the recipe; the results were not worth repeating! The very sharp, acidic flavors in this chocolate clashed horribly with the creamy, nutty peanut butter flavors. Particularly since we are so used to that flavor combo in classic peanut butter cup candies, my combination was especially jarring. I re-made the recipe using Callebaut Semisweet, and it was like night and day; this was the correct chocolate choice. The best-case scenario is to taste chocolates and take notes. That way, when you are ready to approach a recipe, you will have an idea which chocolate will work best. This can be a work in progress—a chocolate notebook for your own reference points. If you want to substitute a different chocolate for one that is suggested, try to stay as close as possible to the percentage of cacao mass of the chocolate listed.

Another aspect to consider is texture. All of the chocolates I suggest are delectable to eat on their own and also work as chunks or pieces incorporated into recipes. However, when melted and blended into a recipe, chocolates "act" in very different ways. Some seem to be drier and thicker, others are fluid and smooth. In a recipe such as a ganache, where you have only one other ingredient (cream), this can be especially important.

The long story short is that I urge you to use the specific chocolates suggested, where they are notated. Using different chocolates will give you variable results, and I cannot vouch for the outcome.

hot chocolate
truffle bombs MAKES 36 SERVINGS

When my twins were young and wanted hot chocolate, one day I just scooped some ganache into a mug, topped with milk and microwaved until hot, stirred until blended, and voilà, truly delicious hot chocolate prepared in record time. These are essentially truffles, sized so that you use two of these chocolate "bombs" per 6 ounces of liquid per serving. Half-and-half will give you a rich drink, milk will make a more typical hot chocolate, and water will make a thinner but very chocolaty drink. By not adding extra dairy, the chocolate flavors shine through when you use water; try it. The choice of chocolate is very important, so make sure to use one that you really like to eat out of hand.

1) Put the cream in a large saucepan and bring to a boil over medium heat. Remove from the heat and immediately sprinkle the chocolate into the cream. Cover and allow to sit for 5 minutes. The heat of the cream should melt the chocolate. Gently stir the ganache until smooth. If the chocolate is not melting, place over very low heat, stirring often, until melted, taking care not to scorch the chocolate. Scrape into an airtight container and refrigerate until firm enough to roll, for at least 6 hours or preferably overnight.

2) Put the cocoa in a shallow dish, such as a pie plate. Have a clean shallow dish on the side. Use a 1-inch ice-cream scoop (such as a Zeroll #100) or cereal teaspoon, and make about 4 "bombs" at a time and deposit them on top of the cocoa. You are aiming to make "bombs" that are about 1¼ inches across and as round as possible. Coat your palms with cocoa and roll the "bombs" into round balls. Place them in the clean plate, and repeat with the remaining ganache. You should end up with about 72 "bombs." Refrigerate in an airtight container for up to 1 month, or freeze for up to 2 months.

3) To make hot chocolate, use 2 "bombs" and 6 ounces of cream, milk, or water per serving. Heat in a saucepan on the stove top or in the microwave, stir until smooth, and serve immediately.

1½ cups heavy cream

19 ounces semisweet or bittersweet chocolate, such as Valrhona Equitoriale (55%) or Scharffen Berger (62%)

½ cup sifted Dutch-processed cocoa

TIP This recipe makes many "bombs," but they can be refrigerated for up to 1 month and frozen for up to 2 months, and they make great winter gifts. Package in a decorative clear glass container with an instruction card included for storage and hot chocolate preparation.

chocolate-covered caramelized
macadamias MAKES ABOUT 30 SERVINGS (ABOUT 6 NUTS PER SERVING)

These are very elegant, perfect for gift giving during the winter holidays, Valentine's Day, even Mother's or Father's Day. Buttery macadamias are first covered with a thin coating of glassy, crisp caramel, then coated in dark chocolate, and finally given a veneer of cocoa powder. These look like simple chocolate- and-cocoa covered nuts, but when you bite through the outer coatings to the crunch of caramel beneath, a confection of refinement is revealed. They are not difficult to make, but do pay attention to the caramelization technique; I have taken pains to describe the process as carefully as possible. You may substitute whole almonds (either blanched or natural), if you like. You will have to temper the chocolate, so familiarize yourself with that process (see page 272).

1¾ cups sugar

¾ cup water

3¼ cups whole unsalted raw macadamia nuts

12 ounces bittersweet chocolate, finely chopped, such as Valrhona Caraïbe (66%) or Guanaja (70%)

1½ cups sifted Dutch-processed cocoa

1) Line a jelly-roll pan with aluminum foil, smooth out any wrinkles, and coat with nonstick spray; set aside.

2) Put the sugar and water in a large saucepan and stir to combine. Bring to a boil over high heat and cook until the sugar dissolves. Add the macadamias and continue to cook over high heat, at first stirring occasionally. Carefully watch the sugar syrup. At first it will be fluid with small bubbles as it boils. Gradually the bubbles will get larger and the syrup might begin to darken in color and caramelize. At this point the syrup begins to thicken; start stirring constantly with a large wooden spoon, tossing the nuts within the syrup. Keep stirring; the mixture will eventually turn foamy. At this point about 10 minutes will have elapsed from the beginning. Continue stirring; the syrup will crystallize and become sugary. Keep stirring the nuts within the mixture so that they become evenly coated with a sugary coating.

3) Turn the heat down to medium-high; watch very carefully at this point. The grainy, sugary mixture will begin to reliquefy within a few

minutes and become fluid and amber in color. Keep stirring the nuts until they are coated with a mostly shiny, fluid caramel. There might still be a few sugary crystals here and there—that's okay. Immediately scrape the nuts out onto the prepared pan and quickly separate as many individual nuts as possible. The mixture will harden quickly. Allow the nuts to sit at room temperature for about 30 minutes, until the caramel is hard and cool.

4) Temper the chocolate as directed on page 272. Use your fingers to separate any nuts that are clumped together; it is fine if a few stick together in small clumps. Put the nuts in a large bowl. Pour about one-quarter of the tempered chocolate over the nuts and stir to evenly coat; keep stirring until it begins to harden around the nuts, which will happen quickly. Add another quarter of the chocolate and stir some more, again allowing the chocolate to coat the nuts. Add more chocolate only if necessary; they should be evenly coated. Now, quickly while the chocolate is still a little soft and tacky, add the cocoa powder and stir some more. Keep stirring until the cocoa coats each nut or each small nut cluster. Shake the bowl frontward and back with a vertical circular motion so that the nuts tumble over one another. This action will help them take on a bit more cocoa. Each nut should be covered in crisp caramel, then a shell of chocolate, and finally a layer of cocoa. Store at room temperature for up to 1 month in an airtight container.

TIP This recipe is about having a feel for the cooking process. The caramel mixture will turn sandy in the beginning quite easily with your stirring. The tricky part comes next; you must adjust the heat so that it is high enough to reliquefy the caramel, but not so high that it burns. Then, the moment the nuts are pretty much covered with that reliquefied caramel, you must stop and scrape them out onto the prepared pan. As I said in the headnote, this is not hard, but it does require you to pay attention to the visual cues and act accordingly. Even 30 seconds too short or too long at that point and the nuts will not take on their crisp caramel covering.

matcha chocolate-covered
almonds MAKES ABOUT 15 SERVINGS (ABOUT 6 NUTS PER SERVING)

I first encountered these at Ito En, my favorite store for anything and everything related to green tea. The first thing you notice is the brilliant mossy green color of the matcha (powdered green tea) on the outside. What is hiding is the dark chocolate coating between the nuts and the tea coating—Heaven! The matcha, which is the powdered green tea used in the traditional Japanese tea ceremony, is expensive. This would be a candy to make and offer at special occasions. You will need to follow the chocolate tempering instructions on page 272.

1) Line a jelly-roll pan with aluminum foil, smooth out any wrinkles, and coat with nonstick spray; set aside.

2) Temper the chocolate as directed on page 272. Put the nuts in a large bowl. Pour about one-quarter of the tempered chocolate over the nuts and stir to evenly coat; keep stirring until it begins to harden around the nuts, which will happen quickly. Add another quarter of the chocolate and stir some more, again allowing the chocolate to coat the nuts. Add more chocolate only if necessary; they should be evenly coated. Now, quickly while the chocolate is still a little soft and tacky, add the matcha and stir some more. Keep stirring until the matcha coats each nut. Shake the bowl frontward and back with a vertical circular motion so that the nuts tumble over one another. This action will help them take on a bit more matcha. Store at room temperature for up to 1 month in an airtight container.

6 ounces bittersweet chocolate, finely chopped, such as Valrhona Caraïbe (66%) or Guanaja (70%)

1⅔ cups blanched whole almonds, toasted (see page 23)

½ cup matcha (powdered green tea)

fleur de sel
caramels MAKES 64 CARAMELS

Here dark caramel is enhanced with fleur de sel, a large-flake crunchy salt, and made into chewy candies. Make sure to use a very deep pot for this recipe so that you don't have a boilover problem.

1) Line an 8-inch square pan with aluminum foil. Smooth out the wrinkles and generously butter the bottom and sides; set aside.

2) Stir the sugar, corn syrup, and water together in a deep, heavy-bottomed 5-quart pot. Bring to a boil over medium-high heat, swirling the pot once or twice to combine the ingredients, but do not stir. Boil until the mixture turns a medium amber color; watch closely, as the color will deepen quickly. Within the next minute or so the caramel will turn a very dark mahogany brown, the bubbles will turn tan in color, and wisps of smoke might appear. Immediately remove from the heat and add the cream, butter, and salt. The mixture may bubble up furiously; just let it sit for a moment to subside. Place back over medium-high to high heat, and swirl the pot around a few times to combine the ingredients. Clip on a candy thermometer and boil until the mixture reaches 250°F. Immediately pour the mixture into the prepared pan without scraping the bottom of the pot.

3) Allow to sit overnight or until firm enough to cut. Cut into 64 squares (8 × 8). Place each one in a small fluted paper candy cup, sprinkle a few more grains of fleur de sel on top, and offer as part of a petits fours array. They may also be wrapped individually in cellophane.

2 cups sugar

⅔ cup light corn syrup

½ cup water

2 cups heavy cream

½ cup (1 stick) unsalted butter, at room temperature, cut into pieces

½ teaspoon fleur de sel, plus extra

64 small fluted paper cups

TIP Occasionally when I used to make these, the candies did not firm up enough to cut, even though I used a thermometer. I realized that what happened was that the thermometer was only testing the temperature in one small area of the mixture. It is important to swirl the mixture several times during boiling to make sure that the temperature is consistent throughout.

mango pâte de fruit

I admit to having a fascination with these French jellies. In most Parisian pâtisseries and specialty food emporiums, you can view row upon row of these sparkly gems—mango, berry, passion fruit, citrus flavors, and others exotic and otherwise. Not only are they bursting with fruit flavor, but they also offer an alternative to chocolate candies—and, last but not least, they seem to have a mystique. They are not commonly made in the home kitchen, and finding and developing a recipe for the home cook was a challenge I couldn't resist. You can double the recipe and form the jellies in an 8-inch square pan. Note that the sugar will be divided into 3 parts: ½ cup for the initial step, 7 tablespoons for the second step, and ¾ cup left over for coating the jellies at the end of the recipe. If using fresh mango, you will need either 2 large or 3 small mangoes; either will give you a generous amount of chunks. Any extra can be eaten as is, or freeze it for smoothies, as I do. That said, I love the frozen mango chunks from the supermarket freezer section.

8 ounces fresh or defrosted frozen mango chunks

1½ cups plus 3 tablespoons sugar, divided

3 tablespoons liquid pectin, such as Certo

⅛ teaspoon cream of tartar

1) Line an 8½ x 4¼-inch straight-sided loaf pan with plastic wrap, allowing the wrap to overhang on two sides. Smooth out any wrinkles, making sure to press the plastic into the corners of the pan. Coat lightly with nonstick spray.

2) Process the mango in a food processor fitted with the metal blade attachment until completely pureed. Press through a medium-mesh strainer.

3) Put the puree and ½ cup of the sugar in a small heavy-bottomed saucepan and whisk to combine. Attach a candy thermometer. Cook over medium-high heat until it comes to a boil. Use a silicone spatula to constantly stir the mixture and push it toward the thermometer as it cooks. Cook until the mixture reaches 215°F. Remove from the heat and quickly whisk in 7 tablespoons of the sugar and the pectin. Place back over the heat and boil until the mixture reaches between 225° and 230°F, again using a spatula to stir it and push it toward the

thermometer to register the temperature effectively. Whisk in the cream of tartar to thoroughly combine, and then immediately scrape the mixture into the prepared pan, quickly smoothing the top with a small offset spatula. The mixture might be fluid enough to settle and smooth out on its own with a few firm raps of the pan on the counter. Allow to cool and firm up at room temperature. Refrigerate until firm enough to cut, for about 2 hours.

4) Pull up on the overhanging edges of plastic wrap, releasing the jellies from the pan. Place on a work surface and peel the sides of the plastic down. Use a very sharp, thin-bladed knife to trim the edges. Cut into small squares (5 × 4), wiping the knife with a damp cloth between cuts. Put the remaining ¾ cup sugar in a small bowl. One at a time, gently toss the jellies in the sugar to coat thoroughly. Store in airtight containers in single layers separated by parchment paper for up to 1 week.

TIPS   It can be hard to find a straight-sided loaf pan. Mine is a Wear-Ever loaf pan #5433, and it can be found at Kerekes at www.bakedeco .com (see Resources, page 287). Also when making pâte de fruit, depending on the water content of the fruit, it can be hard to get the temperature up to 215°F during the initial cooking stage. If this happens, don't fret; just get it as close as possible, but do make sure to get the final temperature at least up to 225°F. I have had success with this approach.

ganache squares
with blueberry pâte de fruit   MAKES ABOUT 20 SQUARES

> This is a two-layered truffle-esque confection—a creamy dark ganache layer just firm enough to hold its shape, topped with a glistening blueberry pâte de fruit that verges on purple-black. I have suggested a generous quantity of blueberries to start with so that once you have pureed and strained the fruit, you will have the amount of puree needed. The two-layered confection can be presented, as suggested, with one or the other side facing up; in this way you get two looks in one, each being quite elegant.

BLUEBERRY LAYER

1⅔ cups fresh or frozen defrosted blueberries (to yield 4 ounces puree)

7½ tablespoons sugar, divided

1½ tablespoons liquid pectin, such as Certo

GANACHE LAYER

7 tablespoons heavy cream

4 ounces bittersweet chocolate, finely chopped, such as Valrhona Caraïbe (66%)

COATING

20 small fluted paper cups, optional
Dutch-processed cocoa

for the blueberry layer Line an 8½ x 4¼-inch straight-sided loaf pan with plastic wrap, allowing the wrap to overhang on two sides. Smooth out any wrinkles, making sure to press the plastic into the corners of the pan. Coat lightly with nonstick spray.

1) Process the blueberries in a food processor fitted with the metal blade attachment until completely pureed. Press through a medium-mesh strainer and weigh out 4 ounces of puree.

2) Put the puree and ¼ cup of the sugar in a small heavy-bottomed saucepan and whisk to combine. Attach a candy thermometer. Cook over medium-high heat until it comes to a boil. Use a silicone spatula to constantly stir the mixture and push it toward the thermometer as it cooks. Cook until the mixture reaches 215°F. Remove from the heat and quickly whisk in the remaining 3½ tablespoons sugar and the pectin. Place back over the heat and boil until the mixture reaches between 225° and 230°F, again using a spatula to stir it and push it toward the thermometer to register the temperature effectively. Immediately scrape the mixture into the prepared pan, quickly smoothing the top with a small offset spatula. Allow to cool and firm up at room temperature.

for the ganache layer Put the cream in a wide 2-quart saucepan and heat over medium heat just until it comes to a simmer. Remove from the heat and immediately sprinkle the chocolate into the cream. Cover and allow to sit for 5 minutes; the heat should melt the chocolate. Stir very gently until smooth. If the chocolate isn't melting, place the saucepan over very low heat and stir until smooth, but take care not to let it get too hot or burn.

1) Pour the ganache over the fruit layer and tap the pan on the work surface to release any air bubbles and even out the top surface. Cool to room temperature, and then refrigerate until firm enough to cut, for at least 4 hours or preferably overnight.

for the coating Pull up on the overhanging edges of plastic wrap, releasing the layered truffle from the pan. Place on a work surface and peel the sides of the plastic down. Use a very sharp, thin-bladed knife to trim the edges. Cut into small squares (5 × 4), wiping the knife with a damp cloth between cuts. Place half of them blueberry side up in fluted paper cups. Place other half ganache side up on a parchment lined jelly-roll pan. Use a fine-mesh strainer to thoroughly dust the tops with cocoa, then carefully place these in fluted paper cups. Refrigerate in airtight containers in single layers for up to 1 week. Serve at slightly cool room temperature.

marcona almond—cacao nib
praline bark MAKES ABOUT 20 SERVINGS (ABOUT 10 OUNCES OF CANDY)

Classic southeastern U.S. pralines (pronounced PRAH-leens) are buttery and sweet and straddle an interesting line between creamy and sandy. This recipe is sugary, creamy, and sandy all at once, with the sweetness tempered by the lightly salted, roasted Spanish Marcona almonds and the bitter cacao nibs (both of these can be found at specialty stores or online.

1 cup firmly packed light brown sugar

½ cup heavy cream

2 tablespoons unsalted butter, at room temperature, cut into pieces

⅔ cup whole Marcona almonds

¼ cup cacao nibs, such as Scharffen Berger

1 teaspoon vanilla extract

20 small fluted paper cups, optional

1) Line a jelly-roll pan with aluminum foil, smooth out the wrinkles, and coat with nonstick spray; set aside.

2) Combine the brown sugar, cream, and butter in a deep sauce-pan; clip a candy thermometer onto the side with the bulb immersed. Cook over medium heat and bring to a boil; swirl the pan to combine the ingredients but do not stir. Cook to 240°F.

3) Remove from the heat and immediately add the almonds, cacao nibs, and vanilla. Stir gently until the mixture just begins to look creamy and more opaque; this will happen within a minute or two. Immediately scrape onto the prepared pan and spread out so that the almonds are in single layer. Allow to sit at room temperature until firm enough to pick up and break apart into pieces. Store at room temperature for up to 1 week in an airtight container. Serve as part of a candy or cookie array, placing in small fluted paper cups if desired.

TIPS This recipe will not be the same with your more common blanched almond. You can often find Marcona almonds at Whole Foods, Trader Joe's, and even Costco. Cacao nibs can be found at some specialty stores, Whole Foods, or through stores featured in the Resources section (page 287). The most important technique in this recipe is the stirring after the mixture is removed from the heat. If you stir too much, it will turn very grainy and sugary. Stop stirring the moment it becomes creamy and opaque. Even two or three more stirs of the spoon will bring you into "sandy" territory.

resources

Al Wadi al Akhdar
www.alwadi-alakhdar.com
This pomegranate molasses has
the best flavor of any I have tried.
Go to the Web site, or go to local
stores specializing in Middle Eastern
ingredients.

**American Almond Products
Company, Inc.**
103 Walworth Street
Brooklyn, NY 11205
(800) 825-6663
www.americanalmond.com
www.lovenbake.com
I use the almond paste, premade
marzipan, and hazelnut paste from
this company. Their products can
also be ordered from The Baker's
Catalogue.

Apricot King Orchards
55 Henry Street
Hollister, CA 95023
(831) 637-1938
www.apricotking.com
For the most flavorful, sunset-colored
dried apricots, look to this online seller.

**Beryl's Cake Decorating & Pastry
Supplies**
P.O. Box 1584
North Springfield, VA 22151
(800) 488-2749
www.beryls.com
Beryl provides highly personal and
professional customer service and her
company supplies pans of all shapes
and sizes, food colors, pastry bags and
decorating tips, cardboard rounds,
cake turntables, decorative sugars,
edible gold and silver products, many
decorative paper liners, books, and
more.

Chocosphere
(877) 99-CHOCO
www.chocosphere.com
If you are looking for high-quality chocolate, this company has the best. Owners Joanne and Jerry Kryszek offer excellent personal service, and they ship nationwide. Either order through the Web site or call to place your order.

Kerekes
6013 15th Avenue
Brooklyn, NY 11219
(800) 525-5556
www.bakedeco.com
You can visit the store in Brooklyn, New York, or order online or over the phone. They carry a very complete line of products such as cake pans in all shapes and sizes, cookie cutters, pastry bags and tips, food colors, cookbooks, and my favorite straight-sided loaf pan.

Ito En
822 Madison Avenue
New York, NY 10021
(888) 697-8003
www.itoen.com
This company specializes in green tea of all sorts. They have a large online catalog, and if you are in New York, be sure to visit their flagship store. I use their matcha for the Matcha Tea Leaf Shortbreads on page 61 and

the Matcha Chocolate-Covered Almonds on page 279 .

Kaiser Bakeware, Inc.
3512 Faith Church Road
Indian Trail, NC 28079
(800) 966-3009
www.kaiserbakeware.com
Kaiser makes very high-quality baking pans. I especially like their decorative pans, such as ring-type pans with interesting patterns. Their nonstick surface is so good, your cakes will unmold beautifully every time.

King Arthur Flour The Baker's Catalogue
P.O. Box 876
Norwich, VT 05055
(800) 827-6836
www.kingarthurflour.com
This company offers high-quality flours, extracts, chocolates, almond and hazelnut pastes, marzipan, scales, high-quality measuring cups (including ones in odd sizes), decorative sugars, and more. A print catalog is also available.

KitchenAid
PO Box 218
St. Joseph, MI 49085
(800) 541-6390 (small appliance information)
(800) 422-1230 (major appliance information)
www.kitchenaid.com

Go directly to this Web site for a complete listing of their high-quality products. All of my recipes were tested in a KitchenAid oven and made with a KitchenAid mixer.

L'Epicerie
(866) 350-7575
www.lepicerie.com
Fruit purees; gold leaf; vanilla extract, including Tahitian; high-quality chocolates from Valrhona, Guittard, and Cacao Barry; cacao nibs; hazelnut paste (100% and lightly sweetened); matcha; marzipan; and more. Order online or use the toll-free number.

Luce Corporation
P.O. Box 4124
Hamden, CT 06514
(203) 787-0281
This company manufactures Blue Magic, a wonderful product that removes moisture from closed containers: Use it for crystallized flowers, cookies, or anytime you need a very dry container.

New York Cake and Baking Distributors
56 West 22nd Street
New York, NY 10010
(800) 942-2539
www.nycake.com
This New York institution offers a variety of high-quality

chocolates, food colors, gold and silver powders, pastry bags and decorating tips, cake pans, tart pans, parchment paper, cardboard rounds, cake turntables, chocolate chipper tools, decorative sugars, decorative muffin and cupcake paper liners, and more.

Parrish's Cake Decorating Supplies, Inc.
225 West 146th Street
Gardena, CA 90248
(800) 736-8443
www.parrishsmagicline.com
Here is where you can find the Magic Line brand of cake pans. They offer cake pans of all sorts, decorating equipment, heavy-duty turntables, my favorite loose-bottomed pans, and more.

Penzeys Spices
(see Web site for retail locations)
(800) 741-7787
www.penzeys.com
I turn to this company for its comprehensive selection of herbs and spices and excellent customer service. For poppy seeds, try the Holland blue poppy seeds.

Sur La Table
Pike Place Market
84 Pine Street
Seattle, WA 98101
(206) 448-2244
(800) 243-0852
www.surlatable.com
Here you will find high-quality bakeware, high-heat-resistant spatulas, great measuring cups, and fabulous display plates and pedestals. See the Web site for retail locations. A print catalog is available.

Sweet Celebrations/Maid of Scandinavia
7009 Washington Avenue South
Edina, MN 55439
(800) 328-6722
www.sweetc.com
This company offers a huge array of equipment, including pans of all sizes, pastry bags and decorating tips, chocolates, cardboard rounds, cake turntables, many decorative muffin and cupcake paper liners, books, etc. A print catalog is available.

Williams-Sonoma
P.O. Box 7456
San Francisco, CA 94120
(800) 541-2233
www.williams-sonoma.com

Famous for their mail-order catalog, they also have stores nationwide. You will find well-made accurate measuring tools, KitchenAid mixers, vanilla extract, some chocolate and cocoa, and other baking equipment including pans and spatulas of all sorts.

Wilton Industries, Inc.
2240 West 75th Street
Woodbridge, IL 60517
(800) 794-5866
www.wilton.com
They have a great catalog, with heavy-duty pans, pastry bags and decorating tips, food colors, cookie cutters, parchment paper, and much more.

Zeroll
P.O. Box 999
Fort Pierce, FL 34954
(800) 872-5000
www.zeroll.com
Be sure to check out their Universal EZ Disher, which is an ice-cream-style scoop with a spring-like action (although there are no springs to break). They are perfect for making uniform truffles and cookies and for getting muffin and cupcake batter into pans.

index